Contents

3

Nelson Thornes and AQA

Nelson Thornes has worked in partnership with your awarding body to make sure that this book offers you the best possible support for your GCSE course. All the content has been approved by the senior examining team at AQA, so you can be sure that it is closely matched to the specification for your subject, and gives you just what you need when you are preparing for your exams.

How to use this book

This book covers everything you need for your course.

Learning Objectives

At the beginning of each section or topic you'll find a list of Learning Objectives based on the requirements of the specification, so you can make sure you are covering everything you need to know for the exam.

Objectives

Objectives

Objectives

Objectives

First objective.

Second objective.

AQA Examiner's Tips

Don't forget to look at the AQA Examiner's Tips throughout the book to help you with your study and prepare for your exam.

AQA Examiner's tip

Don't forget to look at the AQA Examiner's Tips throughout the book to help you with your study and prepare for your exam.

AQA Examination-style questions

These offer opportunities to practise doing questions in the style that you can expect in your exam so that you can be fully prepared on the day. Examination-style Questions are reproduced with permission of the Assessment and Qualifications Alliance.

Controlled Assessment

The Controlled Assessment tasks in this book are designed to help you prepare for the tasks your teacher will give you. The tasks in this book are not designed to test you formally and you cannot use them as your own Controlled Assessment tasks for AQA. Your teacher will not be able to give you as much help with your tasks for AQA as we have given with the tasks in this book.

Visit **www.nelsonthornes.com/aqagcse** for more information.

What is this book for?

This student book has been written to help you with your AQA course in leisure and tourism – whether you are taking the GCSE or the double award option. It is in two parts:

- Units one and four: Leisure and tourism destinations – the places that people visit
- Units two and three: The nature and business of leisure and tourism – different types of leisure and tourism facilities.

What can you expect from Leisure and Tourism?

You can expect to learn about the different sorts of places that people visit in the UK and abroad – beach (or seaside) resorts, cities, ski resorts and national parks. You will find out about how people travel to these places and about the effects that they have on the environment and on local people.

You will also learn about the different types of leisure and tourism facilities ranging from leisure centres to multiscreen cinemas and from theme parks to airports. There will be the chance to discover why people use these facilities, how they are changing, how they are run as businesses and the range of employment opportunities that they provide.

Why should you study Leisure and Tourism?

- Leisure and Tourism is real.

It is a practical subject about the real leisure activities that people do and about the fun places that they visit. It is a subject where you can have lessons on exciting destinations around the world and about how real facilities like health and fitness clubs, restaurants and concert arenas are run.

- Leisure and Tourism is interesting.

Leisure and tourism is about real world places and real people. You will have the chance to investigate leisure facilities and tourism destinations for yourself. You will use the computer and internet, as well as travel brochures, leaflets, maps and guides to support your learning.

Leisure and tourism affects the environment and the lives of people. You will learn how this happens and how leisure and tourism can be positive for the future of the places we visit and of the people who live in them.

- Leisure and Tourism is useful.

Studying Leisure and Tourism will develop your knowledge and understanding of the world and one of its most important modern industries. It will help you grow into an effective and independent learner with an enquiring mind who can make a real future contribution.

Where can studying Leisure and Tourism take you?

AQA Leisure and Tourism is a GCSE. Like all GCSEs it contributes to your progression:

- educationally to GCE A Level and other Level 3 courses perhaps on the way to higher education and university
- towards the world of work.

Leisure and tourism is one of this country's most rapidly growing industries. It offers many career opportunities. In 2009 more than 3 million people were working in leisure and tourism in the UK – more than 1 in 8 of the country's workforce.

GCSE Leisure and Tourism is a really useful educational and career step to make.

How will your work be assessed?

Of your marks, 60% will be from the controlled assessment of coursework. This is explained in more detail later in this book but basically you undertake investigative project work into leisure and tourism organisations and destinations. Then you score marks for the quality of your research and what you learn from it.

Of your marks, 40% will come from external examination. For GCSE that means a 1-hour test and for the double award 2 1-hour tests.

Controlled Assessment overview

Most of the marks for GCSE Leisure and Tourism come from the Controlled Assessment. Controlled Assessment accounts for 60% of the overall marks whether you are following the GCSE or the GCSE (double award) course.

For GCSE Leisure and Tourism you have to plan and carry out an investigation for Unit 2: The nature of leisure and tourism. If you are following the GCSE (double award) course you will have two pieces of Controlled Assessment work to do: for Unit 2 (as above) and for Unit 4: Investigating tourism destinations and impacts.

■ What is Controlled Assessment?

Controlled Assessment is the internal assessment of tasks under controlled conditions to see how good you are at:

- analysing problems
- identifying, gathering and recording relevant information
- communicating knowledge and understanding
- analysing and evaluating evidence
- making reasoned judgements and conclusions.

There are controls to make sure that everyone does coursework properly and that marks scored are fair. Three phases of your assessment are controlled. They are:

- task setting
- task taking
- task marking.

Task setting

You pick (or your teacher picks) a coursework task from a menu of three options set by AQA. There is one menu for Unit 2 and another menu for Unit 4. Every two years these menus are reviewed. Someone following the same course as you in a later year may be choosing from a menu that has been changed.

Task taking

This is the phase when you actually do your work. It should take about 45 hours for you to complete a GCSE Leisure and Tourism coursework task. That includes time for you to plan your work and for you to collect information but it does not include the time that it takes for you to learn about the unit. Coursework projects assess what you have learned: you still need to have lesson and homework time to learn about the subject in the first place.

During the task taking phase you are under the informal supervision of your teacher who has to check that:

- you complete the task you have been set
- your work is your own
- you do not copy, for example from another student or from a source of information such as a book or a website
- you clearly record the sources of information that you choose and use.

Task marking

Your teacher marks your work using a marking grid. There is a marking grid for Unit 2 and a different marking grid for Unit 4. These grids are published in the AQA specification. The mark your teacher gives is sent to AQA in May.

AQA moderates the assessments made by teachers in different schools and colleges across the country. This is to make sure that every student is treated the same. It may mean that the mark your teacher gives is different from your final mark.

Advice

- Split each task into sections. It will be marked in five sections that are called strands. It is a good idea to complete one strand at a time.
- When you do your research you should not have to be under the direct supervision of your teacher all the time. You can collect information on your own or as part of a small group.
- If you collect information as part of a small group you must make sure that everything you write is your own and that you make clear exactly what was collected as a group effort.
- Keep a record of your research while you are doing it. There are marks for how well you describe and explain what you did. You do not want to forget!
- You can either word process your work or handwrite it.

Finally . . .

Your Controlled Assessment is your chance to really show what you can do in Leisure and Tourism. Make the most of it!

1 Destination types

Objectives

Outline different types of destinations.

Describe examples of each type of destination.

Describe the difference between long and short-haul destinations.

Introduction

Leisure and tourism destinations are the places where people go to have fun in their spare time, on a business trip or to visit friends and relatives.

What is this chapter about?

This chapter is about the different types of leisure and tourism destinations. Beach (or seaside) resorts, city destinations, ski and snowsports resorts and national parks are different sorts of places that people visit. These different types of destinations are located in the UK and overseas. You will learn about each type in Chapter 1.

Starter activity

Talk about places you and your friends/family have visited:

- Where are these destinations?
- Why did you/your friends/your family go there?
- How did you travel?
- What did you see and do there?
- Did you enjoy your trips? Why (or why not)?
- Where would you like to visit? Why?

1.1   Destinations

Tourists visit **leisure** and **tourism** destinations. This is often to have a holiday or to spend a fun day in a resort or a city destination. Tourists also visit destinations to see friends or relatives or on a business trip.

Different types of leisure and tourism destinations are:

- beach (or seaside) resorts
- city destinations
- ski/snowsports resorts
- **national parks**.

Beach resorts are popular for sun, sea and sand holidays. However, there is more to seaside resorts than just the beach. Many have harbours or marinas, often lined by bars, cafés and restaurants. In the UK, seaside resorts often have amusement arcades and sometimes piers as well. City destinations are usually large or historic towns with famous monuments and art galleries. They usually offer exciting nightlife and designer shopping too.

Ski/snowsports resorts are found in mountainous areas. While people do ski in the UK (at Aviemore in Scotland, for example), the major ski/snowsports resorts that UK people visit are abroad. They are located in mountain ranges such as the Alps. France, Switzerland, Italy and Austria are countries that have Alpine ski/snowsports resorts. Snowsports other than skiing include snowboarding and tobogganing.

National parks are found in many countries. They are large areas of countryside, which usually have wild and attractive landscapes. Tourists visit national parks to admire the natural beauty of the scenery or to take part in leisure activities such as hiking, climbing and canoeing.

A   *Some examples of UK and overseas tourism destinations*

Destination type	UK examples	Examples abroad
Beach (or seaside) resorts	Blackpool, Scarborough, Brighton	Benidorm, Bodrum, Phuket
City destinations	London, Edinburgh, Bath	Paris, Rome, New York
Ski/snowsports resorts	Glencoe, Glenshee	St Moritz, Klosters, Aspen
National parks	Lake District, Broads, South Downs	

B   *Dbrovnik – a seaside resort and historic city destination in Croatia*

C   *Ullswater – in the Lake District National Park*

▉ Sources

Sources of information about leisure and tourism destinations include:

- ▓ holiday brochures
- ▓ travel guidebooks
- ▓ the internet.

Holiday brochures are available from travel agents or online from tour operators such as Kuoni, Thomson and Shearings. Rough Guide and Lonely Planet are two publishers of travel guidebook series. Their books are stocked by public libraries, as well as by bookshops. Holidays to destinations all over the world can be researched using internet search engines like Google.

Amari Palm Reef Resort - Koh Samui - family offer

Renowned for genuine Thai hospitality, excellent cuisine and very high standards of accommodation, this fresh, modern superior first class hotel also boasts an excellent location in Chaweng.

Koh Samui holiday highlights:

Glorious soft white sand beaches and clear waters are ideal for swimming, snorkelling and Scuba diving

A wide choice of superb bars and local restaurants

The sensational sights of protected Ang Thong Marine National Park

View *Amari Palm Resort*, *Koh Samui hotels* or *Koh Samui information*

One child stays from £639 (departing Manchester)*

D   *An extract from a brochure*

AQA *Examiner's tip*

For your exam you only need to learn about the destination types that have examples named in Diagram **A**. This means you do not have to learn about a UK ski/snowsports resort or an overseas national park.

Think about it

Nice (in southern France) is a beach resort that is also a city destination. The same idea applies to the US's Miami in Florida. So, thinking about it, some destinations belong to more than one type. Can you think of any others?

Summary questions

1. What is meant by a leisure and tourism destination?

2. Give examples of beach (or seaside) resorts and city destinations in the UK and abroad.

3. Give one example of a ski/snowsports resort overseas and one example of a national park in the UK.

4. Why do tourists visit leisure and tourism destinations?

5. What is the name of a large area of countryside that is legally protected for people to enjoy?

Summary

Leisure and tourism destinations are places that people visit for recreation, holidays, business or visiting friends or relatives.

There are different types of destinations in the UK and abroad: beach (or seaside) or ski/snowsports resorts, city destinations and national parks.

Case study

Scarborough is a seaside resort with two beaches. It is located on the North Yorkshire coast at the end of the railway line from the historic city destination of York. York is about 50km south-west of Scarborough. The map gives more information about Scarborough's location and how tourists can travel to it.

The South Bay is the more developed, busier part of the resort of Scarborough. As well as the sandy beach, there is a harbour and the historic **spa**. Originally the spa was where tourists came to drink natural mineral water for their health. Nowadays it is used for concerts and to host conferences.

Pleasure cruises operate out of the harbour. Tourists can enjoy trips along the coast on vessels, including the *Coronia* and the *Regal Lady*. The foreshore is the seafront area that stretches from the harbour south to the spa. Along here there are amusement arcades, fish and chip restaurants, ice cream parlours and some pubs. It is the busiest part of the resort.

The ruined castle on the headland that separates Scarborough's two bays is a visitor attraction. North of it the North Bay offers generally quieter attractions, including another sandy beach. There are two parks here: Peasholm Park, which includes a boating lake, and Northstead Manor Gardens, with its miniature railway on which tourists can ride to Scalby at the far end of the bay.

The Stephen Joseph Theatre includes the nationally famous theatre-in-the-round auditorium. Another cultural attraction in Scarborough is the Rotunda Museum in Valley Gardens on the South Bay.

Accommodation in the resort itself is a mix of larger hotels and smaller guest houses, some of which have been converted into self-catering apartments. Hotels include the Grand and the St Nicholas. Such establishments cater for coach parties and for business people, as well as for leisure tourists. Columbus Ravine, near Peasholm Park, is one street that has many guest houses.

Objectives

Describe one UK example of a beach (or seaside) resort.

Key terms

Spa: a leisure facility that people visit for health or beauty reasons. In the past, and still sometimes today, this was 'to take the waters'. Modern spas offer a range of health and beauty treatments.

A   *Example of a hotel in Scarborough*

▮ Sources

Sources of information about UK beach (or seaside) resorts' locations, attractions and transport links include:

- destinations' own websites (see links for Scarborough's own)
- travel guidebooks, including seaside town guides and brochures
- travel and general atlases
- coach and train operator brochures
- individual attraction leaflets.

While the internet is very useful for finding out about leisure and tourism, it is better to get into the habit of using other types of sources as well, to back up and check your internet research.

▮ Background knowledge

UK seaside resorts developed largely in the 19th century when the development of railways allowed tourists from industrial towns to visit

AQA *Examiner's tip*

When you are asked to describe a destination such as a UK beach (or seaside) resort, make sure you include information that is specifically about that place. Include the names of places and facilities. Write a 'somewhere' answer not a 'nowhere' answer!

∞ links

www.discoveryorkshirecoast. com is the official website for short breaks, holidays and days out in Scarborough.

them. For example tourists from Leeds could travel by train to Scarborough. Since the mid 20th century less people have spent their annual holidays in UK seaside towns partly because they have been able to afford to travel to sunnier beach resorts abroad.

B   South Bay, Scarborough

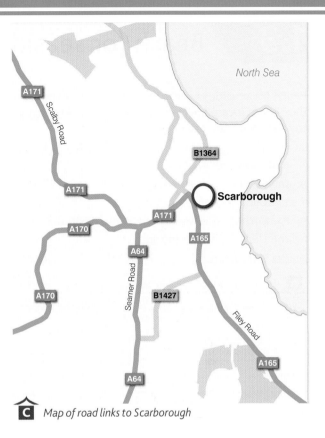

C   Map of road links to Scarborough

Activity

Choose a UK beach (or seaside) resort other than Scarborough. Research and describe:

a   where it is located

b   what it is about the resort that attracts tourists

c   how tourists can travel to it.

Extension activities

1   Make a map of ten of the UK's main beach (or seaside) resorts from different parts of the country.

2   Write a newspaper article to review how well one UK beach (or seaside) resort's facilities and attractions meet the needs of teenage visitors.

3   In a group, discuss UK beach (or seaside) resorts you know about. Where are they? What do they have that attracts visitors? How can tourists travel to them? What do people like and dislike about them?

Summary questions

1   Describe the location of one UK beach (or seaside) resort.

2   Compare the attractions of Scarborough with those of another UK beach (or seaside) resort.

3   Compile a table to illustrate different ways tourists can travel to one UK beach (or seaside) resort.

Coursework activity

Describe how far one UK beach (or seaside) destination is from your home area. Include distance and time in your description. Different ways of travelling to your destination will involve different lengths of journey.

Summary

Scarborough is one good example of a UK beach (or seaside) resort.

1.3 Beach (or seaside) resorts overseas

Beach (or seaside) resorts that are visited by many tourists from the UK are located around the Mediterranean Sea and in other **tourist-receiving areas** such as:

- northern and western France (for example Normandy, Brittany and the Vendee)
- the Algarve in Portugal
- the Canary Islands
- Asia, where Goa and Thailand are destinations popular with UK visitors
- the USA, especially Florida
- the Caribbean.

A Some examples of beach (or seaside) resorts in tourist-receiving areas

Tourist-receiving area	Beach (or seaside) resort
Mediterranean	Chania, Crete
Northern and western France	La Baule, southern Brittany
Algarve	Praia da Luz
Canary Islands	Playa de las Americas
Thailand	Phuket
Florida	St Petersburg
Caribbean	Negril, Jamaica

Beach (or seaside) resorts are towns, so, for example in the Caribbean, Negril is a resort whereas Jamaica is a tourist-receiving area.

Many tourists from the UK buy package holidays to overseas beach (or seaside) destinations. Others opt for independent travel, for example travelling by car to nearby destinations in France or flying by budget airline to European destinations.

Praia da Luz

The beach

Even though the the Algarve is only some 90 miles long and 30 miles at the widest point, there are still more than 100 miles of beaches. About 150 of them have names, thirty of which are European Union 'BLUE FLAG' beaches which I guess makes them the 'real' beaches. They are among the best and cleanest in Europe with most of the main beaches having Lifeguards on safety patrol at least during the peak season.

Many of the beaches, in or near to the holiday resorts, offer most water sports facilities as well as bars, restaurant food

and snacks.

Just follow any signs that indicate "Praia" (which means "beach" in Portuguese) and I'm pretty sure you won't be disappointed with what you find.

B Praia da Luz

C Phuket, Thailand

Sources

Sources of information about overseas beach (or seaside) resorts' locations, attractions and transport links include:

- tour operator brochures and websites
- travel guidebooks
- travel and general atlases
- individual attraction and resort websites
- airline websites.

Background knowledge

Mass tourism to overseas beach (or seaside) resorts has grown since the mid 20th century. UK tourists have had more money to spend on holidays. They have had greater disposable income since then, as well as the opportunity to buy package holidays and, more recently, to fly on budget airlines, especially to European destinations.

D *Windsurfing from an overseas beach*

Activities

1. Make a map to show the locations of 10 overseas beach (or seaside) resorts in different parts of the world.

2. Choose one overseas beach (or seaside) resort. Research and describe:
   a where it is located
   b what it is about the resort that attracts UK tourists
   c how tourists can travel to it from the UK.

3. Compare the attractions of one UK and one overseas beach (or seaside) destination.

4. Use Diagram **B** to help you outline the health and safety features of the beach at Praia da Luz.

Coursework activity

Evaluate how well the attractions and activities available at one overseas beach (or seaside) resort are likely to appeal to couples belonging to these three age groups:

- young adults
- mature adults
- retired people.

Extension activity

Produce a short video about the suitability of one overseas beach (or seaside) destination for a family with young children.

Summary questions

1. Name and locate two overseas beach (or seaside) resorts that are popular with UK tourists in the:
   a Mediterranean
   b Caribbean.

2. Describe how far away one overseas beach (or seaside) resort is from the UK. Include distance and time in your answer.

3. Describe what it is about one overseas beach (or seaside) resort that attracts UK tourists.

4. Describe two different ways that UK tourists can travel to one overseas beach (or seaside) resort.

Summary

Overseas beach (or seaside) resorts that are popular with UK tourists are found in different parts of the world.

Praia da Luz is an example of a resort in the Algarve, and Phuket of one that is located in the Far East.

1.4 City destinations in the UK

Many city destinations in the UK promote themselves as historic destinations. Destinations such as Durham, Exeter and York are cathedral cities. Bath has its Roman Baths and the world-famous Georgian architecture of streets such as the Royal Crescent. In recent years, many industrial cities have marketed their more recent historical and cultural attractions, for example the Piece Hall art gallery in Halifax where the Eureka interactive museum for children adds to the town's tourist appeal.

Newcastle-upon-Tyne has acquired an image as a 'party city'. It attracts tourists who want to enjoy its nightlife, as well as more cultural attractions such as the Baltic art gallery and the Sage music venue in neighbouring Gateshead. In 2008 Liverpool was the European Capital of Culture.

Edinburgh, the historic capital of Scotland, has the additional appeal of its annual arts festival.

Visit London is the official organisation promoting London as a city destination.

Objectives

Describe one UK example of a city destination.

∞ links

www.enjoyengland.com
www.visitlondon.com
www.visitbath.com
www.visitcardiff.com

A Some of London's major sights

Case study

As the UK's capital city, London has a broader appeal and is the country's major destination for inbound tourists. Leisure visitors, including many domestic tourists, are drawn to London because of:

- historic attractions like the Tower of London
- royal connections such as Buckingham Palace
- famous sights such as Tower Bridge
- leisure activities such as a visit to London Zoo or a flight on the London Eye
- cultural attractions like the British Museum and the Tate gallery
- nightlife and shopping such as in the West End.

London is also a major destination for purposes of tourism other than leisure, notably business tourism. The city's hotels and conference centres host many business meetings daily, and its major exhibitions and trade fairs attract business tourists from around the world.

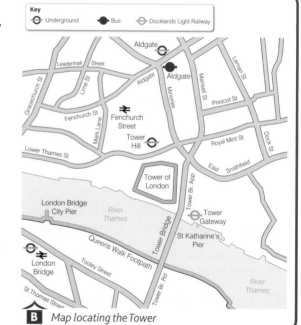

B Map locating the Tower

Sources

Sources of information about UK city destinations' locations, attractions and transport links include:

- destinations' own websites
- travel guidebooks, including city destinations' own town guides
- travel, motoring and general atlases
- coach and train operator brochures
- domestic (including budget) airline websites and in-flight magazines
- individual visitor attraction leaflets and other promotional materials.

C The top five **countries of origin** *of inbound tourists to the UK (2007)*

Country	Visits (millions)	£ spent (billions)
US	3.6	2.6
Germany	3.4	1.2
France	3.3	1.0
Republic of Ireland	3.0	0.9
Spain	2.2	0.8

Activities

1 Use the map to help you describe the location of the Tower of London visitor attraction and to outline some of the ways a visitor to London can travel to the tower.

2 Show ways tourists can travel to one UK city destination.

Extension activity

Recommend a programme for a weekend break to one UK city destination for two student visitors. Include your recommendations for attractions they can visit, and for their accommodation.

Coursework activity

Locate two UK city destinations on a map or maps. Compare how far they are from your home area in distance and time.

Summary questions

1 Describe what it is about one UK city destination that attracts tourists.

2 Describe two different ways inbound tourists can travel from their home country to one UK city destination.

3 Make a map to show where 10 UK city destinations are located.

AQA *Examiner's tip*

Research a city destination that means something to you – perhaps one that is local or that you yourself have visited as a tourist.

Key terms

Countries of origin: countries where inbound tourists come from.

Group activity

Discuss the top five countries of origin for inbound tourists to the UK in 2007. Why do you think these are the top five countries? How do the numbers of visits and money spent relate to each other?

Summary

UK city destinations include, but are not confined to, the country's many historical cities. City councils are keen to promote towns as leisure and tourism destinations because of the economic benefits that visitors bring.

City destinations overseas

Overseas city destinations that are especially popular among outbound tourists from the UK include New York, Paris, Amsterdam, Rome and Barcelona. However, most major cities in the world attract some tourism from the UK for leisure or business purposes, or for visiting friends and relatives.

In recent years, short-break holidays to city destinations have grown in popularity, especially to cities in Europe such as Prague and Madrid, but also across the Atlantic Ocean to cities such as New York.

Objectives

Describe one overseas example of a city destination.

Case study

New York City is a major overseas city destination for tourists from the UK. The city's location in the north-east of the US makes it closer to the UK than some other US cities such as Chicago and Los Angeles.

The appeal of New York for UK tourists lies in the excitement of a city whose people seem constantly on the move. It has been called 'the city that never sleeps'. Attractions that are popular with tourists to New York include:

- the Statue of Liberty
- skyscrapers, including the Empire State Building and the Rockefeller Centre
- Central Park
- Brooklyn Bridge
- Times Square
- art galleries such as MOMA (Metropolitan Museum of Modern Art) and the Guggenheim
- theatres and nightlife on and around Broadway
- famous stores like Bloomingdales, Macy's and Tiffany's.

Although New York City has five boroughs, most tourism activities are concentrated on the central island borough of Manhattan. New York is described as cosmopolitan because people of many different ethnic and cultural backgrounds live there. The cultural life, heritage and food of ethnic neighbourhoods such as Chinatown, Little Italy and Harlem are part of the city's appeal for many tourists.

Themed tours and excursions are a popular tourist activity in New York. Examples include gospel tours to Harlem, harbour cruises, helicopter flights over the major sights, and walking tours of locations used in television shows and movies. These are often offered as optional extra excursions by tour operators, including **online travel providers** such as Expedia.

A *The Empire State Building at night (seen from the top of the Rockefeller Centre)*

B *Helicopter tour – an optional excursion*

▉ Sources

Sources of information about overseas city destinations' locations, attractions and transport links include:

- tour operator brochures and the websites of online travel providers
- travel guidebooks
- travel and general atlases
- airline websites

C   *Tourists view the Manhattan skyline*

- destinations' own websites
- television travel programmes
- individual visitor attraction websites and leaflets.

Key terms

Online travel providers: internet-based businesses that supply travel services, often acting as tour operators. Expedia, Travelocity and Opodo are examples.

⬭links

www.expedia.co.uk is the internet address of one online travel provider.

www.nycgo.com is a New York City destination website.

Activity

Investigate one overseas city destination. Produce a display that shows:

a   on a map where it is located in relation to the UK

b   what it is about the destination that attracts tourists

c   how UK tourists can travel there.

AQA   Examiner's tip

Many tourists travel to overseas city destinations (especially those outside western Europe) by air, through different ways, for example different routes.

For city destinations in western Europe, ferry, car and train are transport modes other than air.

Extension activity

Discuss why New York City is more popular with UK tourists than other city destinations in eastern North America.

Group activity

Discuss how the growth of budget airlines and increased popularity of short city breaks have supported each other.

Coursework activity

Evaluate how well two ways of travelling to one overseas city destination meet the needs of a young couple who want to travel cheaply.

Summary questions

1   Make a map to show the locations of a range of overseas city destinations that are popular with UK tourists.

2   How is the growth of budget airlines and UK tourist visits to overseas city destinations linked?

3   Why are holidays to city destinations often short breaks?

Summary

Overseas city destinations visited by UK tourists are found worldwide.

More budget airline flights have led to more short city break holidays to destinations.

Online travel providers have made it easier for customers to organise their own city breaks.

1.6   A ski resort

Ski and snowsports resorts abroad that are used by UK tourists are mainly in Europe and North America, although there are some further afield still, for example in Australia and New Zealand. The Alps is a mountain range in Europe where there are many ski resorts.

Objectives

Describe one overseas example of a ski/snowsports resort.

Case study

Cervinia is one of the highest resorts in the Alps, with an altitude of over 2,000 m above sea level. It is 2 hours' drive away from the Italian gateway city of Turin, with its international airport.

As well as skiing, tourists take part in other snowsports such as snowboarding. There is cross-country, as well as downhill skiing available, and motorised vehicles called skidoos are available for hire.

Facilities that are provided for skiers and snowboarders at Cervinia (see Diagram **A**) include 30 ski lifts.

Après-ski activities are an important part of skiing and snowsports holidays. In Cervinia there are numerous restaurants, cafés, bars and nightclubs to cater for demand. The jobs provided in these facilities are a positive economic impact of tourism for ski resorts, at least in season. Other leisure facilities that are provided include a bowling alley, a natural ice rink for skating, swimming pool and cinema.

The seasonality of **tourism flow** is an issue for ski resorts. It is more difficult to encourage tourism in the summer when much of the snow melts. Climate change is likely to mean that summers will become longer. Tourists do still visit then, to admire the scenery and take part in leisure activities such as hiking, but there are fewer of them.

B Cervinia

A Cervinia ski resort	
Level of difficulty:	
beginner	16%
intermediate	65%
advanced	19%
Total Kms of Piste	350
Longest run	22km
Off-Piste	good
Cross-country	8km
Glaciers	1
Mountain restaurants	18
Lift Capacity	75,030/hr
Number of lifts	30 (2 cable-cars, 3 gondolas, 13 chairlifts, 12 drag-lifts

■ Sources

Sources of information about ski and snowsports resorts' locations, attractions and transport links include the brochures and websites of general tour operators (such as Thomson), as well as specialist providers (such as Crystal Ski).

∞ links

www.skiclub.co.uk is the website of the Ski Club of Great Britain, which publishes an annual Snowsports Analysis.

AQA *Examiner's tip*

The Ski Club of Great Britain is a valuable source of information about skiing as a leisure and tourism activity.

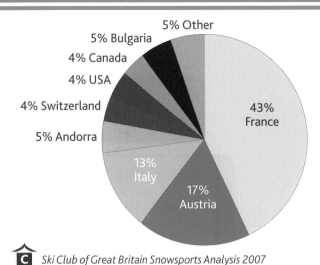

C   *Ski Club of Great Britain Snowsports Analysis 2007*

D   *The location of Cervinia*

Activities

1. Outline the range of leisure facilities provided by a ski resort such as Cervinia.

2. The pie chart shows how the UK tourism market is shared between different countries. Describe and comment on the pattern shown.

3. Describe two different ways tourists from the UK can travel to Cervinia.

4. Investigate an overseas ski/snowsports resort other than Cervinia. Write a report on:

   a its location

   b what it is about the resort that attracts UK tourists

   c how tourists from the UK can travel there.

Extension activities

1. Make a Powerpoint presentation about an overseas ski/snowsports resort. Your presentation should be suitable to show to an audience of parents whose children are to visit the resort on a school skiing trip.

2. Investigate the range of ski/snowsports resorts in regions other than the Alps.

Coursework activity

Evaluate the suitability of one overseas ski/snowsports resort for short skiing breaks for family tourists from the UK.

Summary questions

1. What is meant by:

   a piste

   b après-ski?

2. Outline and account for the range of activities that leisure and tourism organisations provide in one ski/snowsports resort overseas.

Key terms

Après-ski: evening leisure activities provided in ski and snowsports resorts.

Tourism flow: the volume of tourists visiting a destination. This often varies according to season.

Pistes: snow slopes in ski resorts that have been prepared for skiing and/or snowboarding.

Group activity

Discuss the extent to which you think seasonality is likely to be an issue in:

- ski/snowsports resorts
- city destinations
- beach (or seaside) resorts.

Summary

Ski/snowsports resorts are located in mountainous areas.

Ski resorts provide specialist leisure facilities for skiing and snowsports, including **pistes** and ski lifts.

Ski tourism brings economic benefits to ski resorts, but the seasonality of **tourism flow** can be an issue.

1.7 A UK national park

National parks are large areas of attractive countryside that are legally protected for the enjoyment of the public. Many leisure activities, often with an outdoor aspect, are provided for by leisure and tourism organisations in the UK's national parks. This is a small selection:

* walking
* angling
* windsurfing
* canoeing
* climbing
* mountain biking
* horse riding and pony trekking
* painting and photography
* bird watching.

Because of the natural beauty of their landscapes, their wildlife and the wide range of leisure activities they offer, national parks are major tourist destinations in the UK. The map shows the locations of the UK's national parks.

Each national park is the responsibility of its own **National Park authority**. The first to be designated by the government were the Peak District, Lake District, Snowdonia and Dartmoor. The most recent designation was given to the South Downs National Park in 2009 and there are now 15 national parks in the UK.

▉ Sources

Sources of information about UK national parks' locations, attractions and transport links include:

* national park websites (see links), educational and promotional materials
* travel guidebooks
* travel, motoring and general atlases
* coach and train operator brochures
* individual visitor attraction leaflets and promotional materials.

A Map showing the location of national parks in the UK

Objectives

Describe one example of a UK national park.

Case study

The Pembrokeshire Coast National Park is in south-west Wales. Uniquely among the UK's national parks it is entirely coastal. The Pembrokeshire Coast Path, which passes through the national park, is one of the UK's 15 national trails (the Pennine Way is another) and is a major tourist attraction. Coastal scenery in the Pembrokeshire Coast National Park includes rugged cliffs, sandy beaches and attractive and wooded river estuaries.

Historic attractions include Castell Henllys Iron Age Fort, between the towns of Fishguard and Cardigan, and the medieval Carew Castle, which is further south, between Tenby and Pembroke.

Pembrokeshire Coast National Park profile:

* total park area – 620km²
* length of coastline – 416km
* employment – economically active people: 8,817; unemployed people: 569.

⚭ links

www.nationalparks.gov.uk is the website for information about the UK's national parks.

www.pcnpa.org.uk is the Pembrokeshire Coast's site.

AQA *Examiner's tip*

Do not confuse national parks with other types of countryside protection such as **areas of outstanding natural beauty (AONBs)**, or with other types of parks such as those found in towns.

B   *Newgale*

N

Cardigan

Fishguard

St Davids

WALES

Haverfordwest

Narbeth

Milford
Haven

Pembroke Dock

Pembroke

Tenby

Key

National Park

C   *Pembrokeshire Coast National Park*

Activities

1   What is meant by a national park?

2   Investigate and make a table to outline the characteristics of two national parks in the UK other than the Pembrokeshire Coast National Park.

3   Research and give detailed travel instructions to the Pembrokeshire Coast National Park for a motorist wishing to drive there from either your home area or a major city in the UK.

4   Design a poster to advertise 'the UK's national parks' to inbound tourists.

Extension activity

Recommend a programme for a weekend break to one UK national park for two adult visitors from abroad who are in their 40s. Include your recommendations for attractions they can visit, and for their accommodation.

Summary questions

1   Describe:
  a   what a national park is
  b   the attractions of one UK national park.

2   Make a map to show the location and main transport routes leading to one UK national park.

Key terms

National Park authority: a management organisation responsible for one UK national park.

Areas of outstanding natural beauty (AONBs): scenic areas of countryside, legally protected but distinct from a national park. In 2008 there were 49 AONBs in the UK.

Group activity

Make a poster to show the range of leisure activities provided by leisure and tourism organisations in one UK national park.

Summary

The UK has 15 national parks. They are large areas of countryside conserved for the public's enjoyment. The Pembrokeshire Coast National Park is one. It has scenic and historic attractions and is located on the south-west Wales coast.

1.8 Short-haul and long-haul destinations

Leisure and tourism destinations overseas can be classified as short haul and long haul depending on where they are located. **Short-haul destinations** are within Europe and the Mediterranean basin (usually 3 hours or less flight time from the UK), while **long-haul destinations** lie beyond Europe and the Mediterranean in the wider world – a longer flight away.

All European destinations that are outside the UK are short-haul destinations. This means that the Republic of Ireland and Iceland, for instance, are short-haul destinations. Islands like the Canary Islands (which include Gran Canaria, Tenerife and Lanzarote) and Madeira are short-haul destinations, and so are destinations in non-European countries that have Mediterranean coastlines. Such countries include Morocco, Lebanon and Turkey.

Long-haul destinations are found further afield than Europe and the Mediterranean basin. Destinations in North and South America, the Caribbean, Africa south of the Sahara, the Indian Ocean, south and south-east Asia, the Far East, Australasia and the Pacific Ocean are all long-haul destinations.

Map **A** and Table **B** show short and long-haul destinations referred to in this chapter.

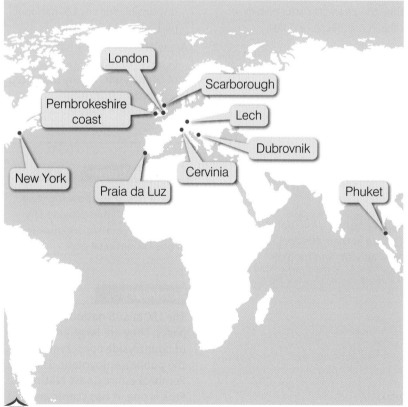

A *The locations of Chapter 1's destinations*

B   *Chapter 1 destinations*

	Short haul	Long haul
Beach (or seaside) resorts	Benidorm, Bodrum, Nice, Dubrovnik, Chania, La Baule, Praia da Luz, Playa de las Americas	Miami, Phuket, St Petersburg (Florida), Negril
City destinations	Paris, Rome, New York, Nice, Dubrovnik, Amsterdam, Barcelona, Prague, Madrid, Turin	Miami, New York, Chicago, Los Angeles, Boston, Sydney
Ski/snowsports resorts	St Moritz, Klosters, Lech, Cervinia, Sauze d'Oulx, Courmayeur, Livigno, Passo Tonale	Aspen

Schedule	Flight No.	Departing To	Status	Terminal
10:45	VS043	LAS VEGAS	GATE OPEN	S
11.10	8U913	TRIPOLI	TAXIED 1401	S
12:40	BA2906	MANCHESTER	AIRBORNE 1310	N

C   *Departures from Gatwick Airport, 9 August 2008*

Activity

1   Draw a spidergram to classify examples of leisure and tourism destinations such as those referred to in this chapter, by type.

Activities

2   Beach resorts are one type of destination. Name two others.

3   What type of destination is Scarborough?

4   Name one city destination and one ski/snowsports resort in Italy.

5   What is a piste?

6   Name a national park in Scotland.

7   True or false? Marrakesh is a short-haul destination.

Coursework activity

Compare the travel distances and times to a range of short and long-haul destinations from your home area.

Summary questions

1   Make a map to show the:

a   difference in meaning between short and long-haul destinations

b   locations of examples of each.

2   Classify the flights from Gatwick Airport that are shown in Diagram **C** into short and long-haul flights.

Summary

Leisure and tourism destinations are places that people visit for recreation, holidays, business, or to see friends or relatives.

There are different types of destinations in the UK and abroad.

Sources can be used to investigate leisure and tourism destinations.

Destinations overseas are classified as short haul or long haul.

1

In this chapter you have learnt:

✔ Leisure and tourism destinations are places that people visit for recreation, for holidays, on business, or to see friends or relatives.

✔ There are different types of destinations in the UK and abroad: beach (or seaside) resorts, city destinations, ski/snowsports resorts and national parks.

✔ Sources, including the internet, guidebooks, brochures, leaflets and atlases, can be used to investigate leisure and tourism destinations.

✔ Destinations overseas are classified as short haul or long haul.

Revision quiz

1 What is a leisure and tourism destination?

2 Name three types of destinations.

3 Why do people visit leisure and tourism destinations?

4 Give two examples of UK beach (or seaside) resorts.

5 What is meant by a national park?

6 Name three overseas city destinations.

7 What is the difference between short-haul and long-haul destinations?

AQA Examination-style questions

1 The map on the right shows the locations of some leisure and tourism destinations overseas.

Name one of the destinations shown on the map which is a short-haul city destination. *(1 mark)*

2 Name an overseas beach (or seaside) resort you have studied and describe one of its attractions. *(3 marks)*

3 Evaluate how well one ski/snowsports resort you have studied meets the needs of people of different ages. *(6 marks)*

Read every question carefully and answer it exactly. Evaluate, in examination-style question 3, means you need to decide whether the resort meets the needs of people of different ages well, very well or not well at all, justifying your answer.

2 How people choose which destinations to visit

Objectives

Explain the following factors that can affect people's destination choices:

- range of products and services on offer
- weather and climate
- personal interests and taste
- cost
- accessibility
- promotion of destinations
- events.

Introduction

People choose which destinations they want to visit. These destinations can be in the UK or overseas (short or long haul). They may be:

- beach (or seaside) resorts
- city destinations
- ski/snowsports resorts
- national parks.

What is this chapter about?

This chapter is about the factors that influence people when they choose leisure and tourism destinations. It also considers the appeal of different destinations to different customer types.

Starter activity

Discuss leisure and tourism destinations you have visited. Why did you visit them? What were your reasons for choosing them? How important were these reasons compared to each other?

People choose leisure and tourism destinations to visit. There are various considerations involved. These are the factors in the decision a person makes about which leisure and tourism destination to visit. They are:

- range of products and services on offer
- weather and climate
- personal interests and taste
- cost
- accessibility
- **promotion** of destinations, including by organisations such as transport and accommodation providers, tour operators and travel agents
- events.

Objectives

Understand the factors that affect people's choices of destinations.

Key terms

Promotion: how leisure and tourism organisations bring the products/services they provide to the attention of their customers.

Case study

Matthew is a 17-year-old student who chose to go to the Ring of Kerry, in the Republic of Ireland, on a walking and cycling holiday.

The Ring of Kerry is in south-west Ireland. Matthew chose to stay in the town of Killarney, and he and his friends enjoyed walking and cycling in the Killarney National Park.

The spidergram shows the factors that affected Matthew's choice of destination.

Weather/climate: While it can rain, temperatures should be warm enough for walking and cycling without being too hot.

Products/services: Matthew has found budget airline flights to Kerry International Airport. He can stay with relatives in Killarney.

Interests/tastes: Matthew enjoys activities like walking and cycling, especially in scenic areas. He likes all sorts of music.

Matthew's choice

Cost: As a student, he is on a budget and looking for a cheap price.

Promotion: Matthew saw promotional materials about the Ring of Kerry and low-cost flights on the internet.

Events: Summerfest is a musical festival in Killarney in July.

Accessibility: Matthew lives near enough to Stansted Airport for his parents to drive him there.

A *Spidergram showing Matthew's choices*

What you should already know about destinations:

- Destinations are places people visit for leisure, on business or to see friends or relatives.
- Types of leisure and tourism destinations include:
  - beach (or seaside) resorts
  - city destinations
  - ski resorts
  - national parks.

- Locations of destinations can be in the UK or overseas:
  - Short-haul destinations are in Europe or the Mediterranean basin (generally within a 3-hour flight of the UK).
  - Long-haul destinations are places to which UK tourists travel that are beyond Europe and the Mediterranean, for example in North America or the Far East. These are more than a 3-hour flight away.

Let's all go on holiday together this summer!

Yeah, somewhere hot.

Where?

My sister went to Ibiza last year. She said it was really good.

OK. How do we get there?

Where do we stay?
...and how much will it cost?

B   *Holiday Chat*

Think about it

A holiday is a major expense for many people. This makes them careful about choosing where to go.

People do not often make a checklist of factors in their head, consciously ticking off each as they browse the websites of travel and tourism organisations. Nevertheless their decisions are, whether they realise it or not, influenced by various considerations.

AQA Examiner's tip

Think about the importance of each factor. How much difference does it make? Weighing up how much difference each factor makes is putting a value on it. This is evaluating, which you may be asked to do in the exam.

Remember

Overseas leisure and tourism destinations can be either short haul (within Europe and the Mediterranean) or long haul (further afield).

Summary questions

1   Assess which factor was most important in Matthew's choice of holiday destination.

2   a   Identify four different factors that affect destination choice from the young people's discussion about Ibiza.

   b   Outline two other factors that are likely to affect their choice of destination.

   c   Evaluate the extent to which these factors would make a difference to you if you were one of them.

Summary

People choose the destinations they visit because they are influenced by what travel and accommodation (products/services) is available, by the weather and climate of the destination and by their personal interests and tastes, as well as other factors.

The range of leisure and tourism products and services on offer is one factor that affects people when they are deciding which destination to visit. Products and services provided by leisure and tourism organisations include:

- transport
- accommodation
- attractions
- activities.

This range includes travel products and services that customers may choose to use to reach destinations, as well as those that are available in destinations themselves. A person's choice of destination is likely to be influenced by how easy (and cheap) it will be to travel, as well as by what there is on offer in the destination.

Questions people consider are:

- What accommodation is available in the destination?
- What attractions and activities are there?
- What are the travel options?

Extract from a travel guidebook about the West End of Negril – a strip of cafés, restaurants and bars to the west of the resort's centre:

Sources

There are many sources of information on the range of destination-specific products and services on offer. Taking the long-haul destination of Negril in Jamaica as an example, sources include:

- tour operator brochures and websites
- travel guidebooks such as the Lonely Planet and the Rough Guide series
- travel advice blogs such as tripadvisor, which publishes reviews that past visitors have posted on the internet.

Background knowledge

All-inclusive hotels

All-inclusive hotels are most frequently found in long-haul beach (or seaside) resorts. The customer pays a single bill, normally in advance. This one-off charge covers accommodation, meals, drinks and leisure activities at the hotel. Sometimes however,

Objectives

Explain how the range of products and services on offer can affect people's destination choices.

Case study

Dev and Sue were attracted by the idea of a holiday in the Caribbean. They chose to visit Negril in Jamaica. Dev and Sue explain how the range of products and services on offer influenced their choice below.

Why Negril? Well, there were the hotels to start with – we really wanted something just for couples if possible and definitely right on a sandy beach. We checked out a travel guide and the tripadvisor site too.

Watching a Caribbean sunset would really be idyllic. We think Negril's going to be just right for us.

An all-inclusive hotel deal suits us too. There are lots of watersports available – snorkelling, diving, windsurfing, sailing – all you could want. There's paragliding from the beach as well.

People who'd been before really seemed to rate Negril. The bars and restaurants of the West End sound like great fun.

 A *Holiday Chat*

B *Negril Beach, Jamaica*

more expensive optional activities like diving, gourmet restaurant meals and branded drinks do attract an additional charge.

Many all-inclusive hotel guests have bought a package holiday, including the hotel, airline flight and airport transfer. For such people, the principal advantage of an all-inclusive arrangement is that the whole of their holiday is paid for in advance. They can relax without having to worry about money at all.

However, all-inclusive hotels are a leisure and tourism issue. They have advantages and disadvantages for destinations' environments and for local people. All-inclusive holidays have attracted some controversy as a result. This is explained later in the book (see Chapter 5).

Types of accommodation

Two types of accommodation are provided by leisure and tourism organisations:

- serviced accommodation
- non-serviced accommodation.

The difference is that in serviced accommodation (like a hotel, for example) customers' bedrooms are cleaned and tidied for them, while in non-serviced accommodation (like many, but not all, self-catering apartments) this is not the case.

Activities

1. What is meant by an all-inclusive hotel?

2. Explain how the range of products and services on offer affected Dev and Sue's choice of Negril as a destination to visit.

3. Evaluate the extent to which Dev and Sue's destination choice is likely to meet their expectations.

Extension activity

Find out why all-inclusive hotels are a controversial issue.

Coursework activity

Evaluate how well the range of products and services on offer at one destination meets the needs of young couples.

Summary questions

1. What are leisure and tourism products and services?

2. Identify two sets of products and services that can affect people's choice of leisure and tourism destination.

3. Explain, using an example, how the range of products and services on offer can affect people's destination choices.

4. Outline two other factors that can affect how people view the range of products and service on offer when they pick a destination to visit.

Key terms

All-inclusive hotels: hotels where customers pay for products and services by a one-off payment, in advance.

Issue: a debate in which different people hold different views.

Think about it

The range of products and services on offer is one factor affecting people's destination choices. There are others. Each factor is a part of the eventual decision. It cannot entirely be separated from others.

links

www.tripadvisor.com is an internet site on which people post their own reviews of destinations they have visited.

AQA   Examiner's tip

Do not worry about what is a product and what is a service. You are not expected to be able to describe the difference between them.

Group activity ●●●●

Discuss the extent to which the range of products and services on offer has affected the destination choices of people you know.

Summary

The range of products and services on offer is one factor that can affect people's destination choice.

Products and services offered include accommodation, attractions and activities, as well as the travel options customers can use to reach them.

2.3 Cost, interests and tastes

The cost of a trip, and personal interests and tastes are factors that can affect people's decisions about which destination to visit. While the range of products and services on offer may appeal to a customer, he or she will only choose to visit a destination if the cost of doing so is sufficiently low. Equally, the range of products and services on offer is only likely to appeal to a particular customer if it matches his or her interests or personal tastes. Customers will decide not to visit destinations they do not find appealing.

Objectives

Explain how personal interests and tastes can affect people's destination choices.

Case study

Budget airlines have affected the cost of visiting many short-haul city destinations. Venice, in Italy, is a popular destination of this type. Budget airline flights have made it possible to travel to the city from the UK more cheaply than previously.

Table **A** shows some airline routes to Venice from the UK in 2008.

British Airways and Alitalia are **flag-carrier** airlines. The others shown in the table are budget airlines. Normally customers expect budget airlines to offer cheaper fares because of their **no-frills** policy.

The cost of flights from the UK to a destination such as Venice varies with:

- departure airport
- date and day of the week of the flight
- time of day
- demand from customers
- events in the destination, for example trade fairs and major sports events
- special promotions
- how far in advance the flight is booked.

The flight from the UK to a destination airport is not the only cost incurred by customers, as Diagram **C** shows.

> 66 *Venice radiates beauty, attracting visitors like moths to a flame. Alternating between the street cafés and diving indoors to explore the stunning palazzos, museums and galleries, you'll be overloaded by scenic wonders.* 99
>
> www.easyjet.com Destination Guide

A *Airline routes to Venice*

Airline	UK departure airports
easyjet	Belfast, Bristol, East Midlands, London Gatwick
Ryanair	Liverpool, London Stansted
Jet2	Leeds Bradford
British Airways	London Gatwick
Alitalia	London Heathrow

B Venice

Sources

www.expedia.co.uk is the website of an online travel company. Others include www.lastminute.com, www.travelsupermarket.com and www.holidayhypermarket.co.uk.

People you know are a valuable source of information. Survey their interests and tastes.

■ Background knowledge

Until the growth of budget airlines (since the 1990s) city break holidays were largely package holidays booked through travel agents from tour operator brochures. Now, tourists often make their own arrangements. Better internet access has made it possible to surf websites such as those of airlines and online travel companies to look for low-cost deals.

C   *Flowchart showing costs an independent traveller may pay on the outward part of a journey to a destination overseas*

Activities

1   **a**   Find out three different costs of travelling to Venice by air next week.

    b   Explain why the cost of flights from the UK to a destination such as Venice varies.

2   Read the easyJet Destination Guide extract. Suggest the probable personal interests/tastes of customers who are likely to find Venice appealing.

Coursework activity

Analyse the appeal of a city destination such as Venice to three different types of visitors. Visitor types you may choose to consider are:

- single people
- couples
- families with children
- groups travelling together
- different age groups: children, teenagers, young adults, mature adults, retired people
- different ethnic and cultural groups
- people with special needs.

Summary question

Explain, using examples, how the factors of cost, and personal interests and tastes can affect someone's choice of leisure and tourism destination.

○○ links

www.easyjet.com, **www.ryanair.com** and **www.jet2.com** are budget airline websites.

www.ba.com and **www.alitalia.com** are two flag-carrier websites.

AQA   *Examiner's tip*

Cost, and personal interests and tastes are two of a range of factors that can affect people's choice of destination. The cheapest options will not always be chosen. The cheapest flights may be at inconvenient times, for instance.

Key terms

Flag carrier: a traditional (as opposed to budget) airline that is regarded as its country's national airline.

No-frills: the policy of budget airlines, which is to keep costs low by eliminating or charging for 'extras' such as in-flight catering.

Group activity

Why do customers not always choose the cheapest destination option?

Summary

Cost, and personal interests and tastes are two factors that can affect people's destination choices.

Budget airlines have brought down the cost of travelling to city destinations abroad.

The internet has made it easier for people to compare costs of travelling.

2.4 Special interests and events

People's special interests and the events that are held in destinations can also affect their choices of where to visit. Leisure and tourism organisations provide special-interest holidays and day-trips. Special-interest holidays are based on a leisure activity that customers particularly enjoy and want to spend a large part of their holiday pursuing.

Examples of special-interest holidays include:

- skiing and snowsports (see 1.6)
- climbing, trekking or walking
- angling
- sailing or other water sports holidays
- diving
- golfing
- painting, cookery and wine tours
- birdwatching.

Special-interest day trips are often organised to allow customers to attend events. Coach or train operators, for example, often organise excursions to sporting occasions such as race meetings, or events like Clothes Show Live at the National Exhibition Centre (NEC) in Birmingham.

Objectives

Explain how events and special interests can affect people's destination choices.

A The location of the NEC

Case study

The NEC is a major venue for leisure events held in the UK. As its name suggests, it is a venue that seeks to attract visitors from all over the UK. Such visitors are domestic tourists. The extract shows events at the NEC (including Clothes Show Live) in December 2008. In the run up to Christmas these are all open to the public – to attract as many leisure visitors as possible.

At other times of the year, trade fairs are often staged at the NEC. Such events are intended to attract business tourists rather than members of the general public.

What's on at the NEC (December 2008)

The International Motorcycle & Scooter Show (Public)
28 Nov–7 Dec

Clothes Show Live 2008 (Public)
5–10 Dec

LKA Championship Dog Show (Public)
12–13 Dec

Toy Collectors Fair (Public)
14 Dec

B What's on at the NEC

Sources

- Tour operator brochures and websites provide information on special-interest holidays.
- Websites and other promotional materials are produced by **event** organisers (for example the Clothes Show Live website (see links)).
- Coach and other transport provider leaflets and websites publicise organised tours to events.

Background knowledge

Special-interest holidays are provided by specialist companies, as well as by larger general tour operators like Thomson, First Choice and Kuoni. Golfing holidays to Portugal, for instance, are offered by specialist operators, including Algarve Golf (UK) and Golfbreaks.com.

Fact

As a major visitor attraction, the NEC group of venues in Birmingham includes the NEC itself, NEC Arena, ICC (International Convention Centre) and NIA (National Indoor Arena) and brings money to the region (an estimated £1.3bn per year), as well as supporting up to 22,000 jobs.

C   *Specialist events are held at the NEC*

⊂⊃links

www.clothesshowlive.com is the website for Clothes Show Live.

www.necgroup.co.uk is the internet portal for the NEC group.

Think about it

Visitors attending an event such as Clothes Show Live will include people who have a strong special interest in fashion or dressmaking and those for whom it is an occasion for a fun day out. Leisure event organisers need to cater for both groups to make the event successful by attracting sufficient visitors to be profitable.

Activities

1   Research and describe two examples of special-interest holidays.

2   a   Find out what events are organised at the NEC in Birmingham next month.

   b   What special interests do these events cater for?

3   Describe the location of the NEC in Birmingham.

4   Outline the range of special-interest holidays available to a skiing and snowsports resort such as Cervinia in Italy (see 1.6).

AQA   Examiner's tip

An event will attract visitors to a destination because of their special interests, but event organisers need to provide for the needs of general visitors too.

Key terms

Event: a single, specially organised leisure occasion that acts as a temporary visitor attraction. Sports matches and competitions, concerts, festivals and fêtes are examples.

Flyer: a piece of promotional material that consists of a single, unfolded sheet of paper.

Group activity   ▪▪▪▪

Discuss your special interests, and events that you have attended or would like to attend. How much have these affected (or might they affect) the destination choices of the members of your group?

Coursework activity

Evaluate how well a leisure event caters for the special needs of visitors.

Extension activity

Choose one event that is to be held in a destination. Design a **flyer** to promote a trip to attend this event.

Summary questions

1   a   What is meant by a special-interest holiday?

   b   Give three examples of a special-interest holiday.

2   Explain how people's choice of destination can be influenced by:

a   events

b   special interests.

Summary

The special leisure interests that people have, and events that are organised in destinations, are factors that can affect destination choices.

Weather and climate can affect people's choice of destination. Outdoor activities are especially affected, in particular when the destinations are beach (or seaside) or ski/snowsports resorts. Windsurfing depends on wind, and skiing on snowfall. Most leisure and tourism customers prefer sunny weather.

Beach (or seaside) resort holidays overseas are sometimes referred to as **sun, sea and sand** holidays. During the 1960s there was a boom in the UK in package holidays to Mediterranean destinations. Many UK tourists visited beach (or seaside) resorts in countries such as Spain and Greece for the first time. Weather and climate were an important factor and remain so today. Millions of holidaymakers from the UK continue to travel to Mediterranean destinations such as Praia da Luz (Algarve, Portugal), Benidorm (Costa Blanca, Spain) and Ayia Napa (Cyprus) in search of summer sunshine.

The climate of Mediterranean areas is characterised by hot, dry summers and mild, wet winters. A dry climate tends to mean a sunny one and, at least initially, it was the hotter, sunnier climate of the Mediterranean in summer that was appealing to people from the UK. On a typical summer's day in a destination with a Mediterranean climate, visitors can expect hot, sunny weather. As resorts in the Mediterranean developed, the mildness of the winters proved attractive to **out-of-season** visitors as well.

The growth of mass tourism to Mediterranean resorts from the 1960s was due to a number of factors:

- sunny, hot summers
- sandy beaches
- relatively easy and cheap to reach from the UK
- greater availability of affordable package holidays by jet aircraft
- rapid development of resorts (hotels and attractions) along the coasts of the Mediterranean Sea.

Objectives

Explain how weather and climate can affect people's destination choices.

Case study

Palma Nova is a large beach (or seaside) resort on the southern coast of the Spanish Mediterranean island of Mallorca. It is one of Mallorca's original mass tourism resorts. Situated 15km west of Palma the resort has developed alongside three white sand beaches on the edge of the clear blue sea. Platja de Carregador beach lies just next to Palma Nova's marina. The Passeig Marítim (marine promenade) is a flat, pedestrianised walkway that overlooks the sea and which stretches the whole length of the resort's three beaches. 'Golf Fantasia' is a popular mini-golf park in the gardens that lie to the rear of the Bahia Palma Nova Hotel. The Restaurante Bahia Palma Nova there specialises in genuine Spanish cuisine. The Blau Mas café has an attractive terrace where customers can sit beneath the stars and gaze looking over the bay.

A *Palma Nova*

Sources

Sources of information about destinations' weather and climate include:

- tour operator brochures and websites
- travel guidebooks and destination information websites
- atlases, including travel atlases
- weather websites (such as bbc.co.uk/weather).

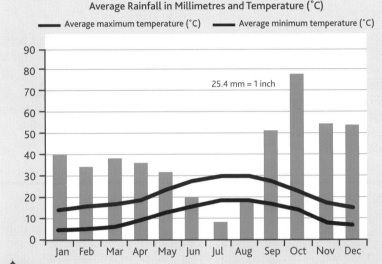

B   *Climate graph*

Activities

1   Explain how two leisure activities other than windsurfing and skiing are dependent on the weather.

2   Using the graph provided, write a short paragraph for a travel brochure outlining Mallorca's Mediterranean climate.

3   Why did mass tourism to the Mediterranean boom in the 1960s?

4   Using Photo A and Diagram B, analyse Palma Nova's appeal to UK tourists.

Group activity

Make a poster to show the effect that weather and climate can have on people's destination choices. Include examples of different types of destinations in the UK and overseas.

Summary questions

1   a   What is meant by a sun, sea and sand holiday?

b   Give two examples of other types of holidays affected by weather and climate.

2   Explain, using examples, how people's choice of destination can be influenced by weather and climate.

∞links

www.spanish-fiestas.com is a website that gives information about Spanish destinations.

www.bbc.co.uk/weather is the BBC's weather and climate website.

AQA *Examiner's tip*

Different people have different views about weather and climate. Some enjoy hot, sunny weather, but sightseeing in a city destination can be tiring for a UK tourist in the heat of a Mediterranean summer or a tropical day.

Key terms

Sun, sea and sand: a description of a summer beach holiday, particularly to an overseas destination.

Out of season: a time of year when a destination or facility has a quiet period. Some facilities may close out of season.

Extension activity

Investigate the extent to which weather and climate vary between the western and eastern Mediterranean. Assess the extent to which such variations affect people's destination choices within the Mediterranean region.

Coursework activity

Compile a questionnaire to assess how much different people's destination choices are affected by factors such as weather and climate.

Summary

Weather and climate affect people's choices of destinations.

Accessibility and promotions

The accessibility of destinations and how they are promoted can affect people's decisions about which destinations to visit.

Accessibility is the ease of reaching a destination.

Factors affecting accessibility include:

- location
- transport types
- measures taken to meet the special needs of visitors.

Promotion is concerned with bringing leisure and tourism products and services to the attention of potential customers. Leisure and tourism organisations, including **regional tourist boards**, promote destinations using promotional materials that contain advertisements, brochures and websites. The Northumbria Tourist Board is the regional tourist board for the north-east of England, including Durham.

Objectives

Explain how accessibility and promotion can affect people's destination choices.

⬯links

www.ukworldheritage.org.uk is the portal for the UK's World Heritage Site.

AQA *Examiner's tip*

Accessibility means how easy it is to reach a destination, as well as how easy it is to move around it and its facilities.

Case study

Durham is a UK city destination. The heart of Durham's appeal to tourists, especially inbound tourists, is the **World Heritage Site** of Durham Cathedral and Castle. Durham Castle is part of Durham University. Durham Cathedral, while still an active church building, attracts more visitors.

The cathedral contains the shrine of St Cuthbert and the tomb of St Bede. It is widely considered to be the finest example of Norman architecture in England and houses the Treasures of St Cuthbert exhibition. Visitors can climb the stairs of the tallest of the cathedral's three towers to admire the view from the top across the city, the river Wear and the surrounding wooded countryside.

A *Durham*

Access to the cathedral is an issue for some visitors. It is located at the top of a steep medieval street (North Bailey) leading up from Market Place. Some visitors find it a difficult walk, and vehicle access is limited. The cathedral bus service operates from the city centre and railway station. The buses themselves are minibuses. A feature of their design is that the driver can lower the front doorway to pavement level. This enables wheelchair users and parents with children in buggies to board more easily. There is a ramp available as well. This can be used to make access easier still. Inside, each bus has a level floor, and space to accommodate a wheelchair or child's buggy. The cathedral bus makes Durham's main visitor attraction more accessible and therefore the destination as a whole more appealing to visitors. People are more likely to choose Durham as a destination as a result.

Sources

Sources of information about the accessibility of destinations include promotional materials produced by regional tourist boards.

B   *Durham Cathedral bus*

C   *Transport links to Durham*

Mode	Provision
Rail	main-line services: • north to Newcastle-upon-Tyne and Scotland • south to York and London • cross-country to Birmingham and the south-west
Road	A1(M) motorway, north and south
Air	Durham Tees Valley Airport, 40km south
Ferry	nearest passenger ferry port: Newcastle-upon-Tyne, with links to Scandinavia and the Netherlands

Activities

1 Describe:
   a the appeal of Durham as a leisure and tourism destination
   b ways tourists can travel to Durham.

2 a Why is accessibility for visitors a particular issue in Durham?
   b How has it been tackled?

3 a What is meant by a World Heritage Site?
   b Describe the visitor appeal of a World Heritage Site other than Durham Cathedral and Castle.

Summary question

Explain, using an example or examples, how accessibility and promotion can affect people's choice of destination to visit.

2.7 How appealing are destinations?

How well do the attractions and activities at destinations **appeal** to different people? Not everyone's tastes are the same. Some people may find a UK seaside resort more appealing than an overseas city (or one UK seaside resort more appealing than another). Other people may prefer a holiday in an overseas ski resort to one in a UK national park.

The likely appeal of different destinations for different types of visitors can be assessed. Different types of visitors are:

- single people
- couples
- families with children
- other groups of people who are travelling together
- different age groups: children, teenagers, young adults, mature adults, retired people
- different ethnic and cultural groups
- people with special needs.

People's decisions about which destination to visit are based on a range of factors:

- range of products and services on offer
- weather and climate
- personal interests and tastes
- cost
- accessibility
- promotion of destinations, including by organisations such as transport and accommodation providers, tour operators and travel agents
- events.

These factors are also factors in the appeal of the destination's attractions and activities. For example the range of attractions and activities at a destination is part of the range of products and services that is on offer. The cost of a destination's attractions and activities helps people to decide whether they are sufficiently appealing to persuade them to visit.

Objectives

Describe the appeal of leisure and tourism destinations to different types of people.

∞links

www.roughguides.com is the homepage of the Rough Guide website.

AQA Examiner's tip

If you are asked about the appeal of a destination, then the question is about why people like that place. You must link this to different types of people and explain why they would like it.

Key terms

Appeal: what it is about a destination that attracts people to visit.

Assess: decide how well something is done or how important it is.

■ Background knowledge

Ibiza is one of Spain's Balearic Islands. Others include Mallorca, Menorca and Formentera.

Ibiza's nightlife (bars, restaurants and clubs) is a major part of its appeal to some visitors. These include:

- younger adults and teenagers
- single people
- people travelling in groups.

However, like most destinations, Ibiza actually appeals to a wide variety of people. There is much more to the island than just its nightlife, as this extract from a travel guidebook shows:

A *Clubbing in Ibiza – everyone's cup of tea?*

> *Ibiza in the autumn, winter and spring is a completely different, much more peaceful place. Only one club (Pacha) and a handful of other nightspots stay open all winter. Ibiza town is close to the beaches of Ses Salines and Es Cavallet. It's full of bars, restaurants and has plenty of shopping available. Around the island's shore there are dozens of lovely little coves, each with its own tiny beach (calas). Inland, Ibiza's landscape is hilly and wooded with tiny picturesque villages, with whitewashed churches and atmospheric local bars and cafes.* 99

B *The likely appeal of a UK beach (or seaside) resort to different types of visitors*

Attractions and activities	Visitor types
Amusement arcades and funfair	• families with children • teenagers
Boating lake	• couples • families with children
Harbour pleasure cruises	• retired people • single people • families with children
Beach activities	• families with children • groups travelling together • children
Leisure pool	• children • teenagers
Afternoon band concerts in the park	• retired people • single people • couples • mature adults

What we look for is somewhere:

- hot and sunny
- with a nice beach and plenty to do for the kids
- that doesn't cost too much
- where there's a local festival or some other event happening too
- not too hot
- that's easy to get to from our local airport
- that we're happy to pay a bit more for a decent hotel.

C   *Deciding where to go on holiday*

Activities

1 Outline the likely visitor-type appeal of the destination activity shown in the photograph.

2 a Recommend, with reasons, a destination to satisfy the needs of the family shown in the cartoon.

   b Suggest what other factors the family could consider when choosing a destination to visit.

Extension activity

Assess the likely appeal of the attractions and activities of one destination type other than a UK beach (or seaside) resort to a range of different visitor types.

Coursework activity

Analyse and evaluate the appeal of one destination to different types of visitors.

Summary question

Evaluate the appeal of one UK and one overseas leisure and tourism destination to two different types of customers.

Group activity

Discuss the extent to which the table is correct in linking a UK seaside resort's appeal to the visitor types shown. Are there any amendments you would suggest?

Summary

The appeal of a destination to different people depends on how they view these factors:

range of products and services on offer

weather and climate

personal interests and tastes

cost

accessibility

promotion of destinations

events.

2

In this chapter you have learnt:

People's decisions about which destinations to visit are affected by a range of factors. These factors are:

✔ range of products and services on offer

✔ weather and climate

✔ personal interests and tastes

✔ cost

✔ accessibility

✔ promotion of destinations, including by organisations such as transport and accommodation providers, tour operators and travel agents

✔ events.

Destinations are likely to appeal differently to different groups of people.

Revision quiz

1 Give three factors that can affect people's decisions about which destination to visit.

2 What is a World Heritage Site? Give an example.

3 What and where is the NEC?

4 Where are:
  a Negril
  b Palma Nova
  c Cervinia?

AQA Examination-style questions

1 Many factors affect people's choices of destinations. Analyse and evaluate the factors that may affect either a group of young people deciding on a destination for a first holiday abroad on their own, without adults, or a single retired person visiting a UK destination. *(6 marks)*

AQA Examiner's tip Make sure your answer is clearly about the type of visitor given in the question: a better-quality answer is one that answers the question head on because it:
(a) analyses
(b) is about the group of young people.

Objectives

Describe the range of leisure activities available at UK and overseas attractions.

Describe how and explain why attractions try to meet the needs of different customers.

Apply your knowledge and understanding to an attraction you have not so far studied.

Introduction

Visitor attractions draw tourists to leisure and tourism destinations. They vary a lot. A natural feature such as a waterfall – Niagara Falls, for example – is a visitor attraction. So are historic monuments such as Stonehenge and the Great Pyramid at Giza in Egypt. Equally, theme parks like Alton Towers and Disneyland Paris are visitor attractions, as are museums, art galleries, and major sports and entertainment venues like London's O2 arena.

What is this chapter about?

Chapter 3 is about the different types of visitor attractions and about examples of each type, in the UK and overseas. It is about how these attractions try to attract and meet the needs of different types of customers.

Starter activity

Make a display or poster to illustrate the variety of visitor attractions that you and others have enjoyed.

Types of visitor attractions

Visitor attractions are leisure facilities. Their customers are mostly tourists. Visitors to an attraction are likely to have travelled to it from where they normally live. Alternatively they may be staying in or near the destination where the attraction is located.

Types of visitor attractions are:

- natural attractions – physical features such as waterfalls, mountains and valleys that attract visitors
- historic sites – places such as ancient monuments and old buildings that have become attractions for visitors
- theme parks – large attractions, including rides that are spread over a large site
- major sports/entertainment venues – nationally important sports or entertainment facilities such as stadia, arenas and theatres
- built attractions – facilities such as museums and galleries, and other than theme parks and sports/entertainment venues, that have been specifically built to attract visitors.

Objectives

Understand the range of visitor attraction types.

Key terms

Visitor attractions: leisure facilities that customers visit and which are a natural, historic or built site, a theme park or a major sports/entertainment venue.

National Trust: a charity that conserves historic and scenic sites.

A *Some examples of UK and overseas visitor attractions*

Type of visitor attraction	UK examples	Overseas examples
Natural attractions	High Force (waterfall, Teesdale) Giant's Causeway (rock formation, Antrim Coast – see Photo **B**)	Grand Canyon (valley, US) Mount Vesuvius (volcano, Italy)
Historic sites	Stonehenge (prehistoric stone circle, Salisbury Plain) Tower of London (fortress, beside Tower Bridge)	Notre-Dame (cathedral, Paris) Machu Picchu (ruined Inca city, Peru, Photo **C**)
Theme parks	Legoland (Windsor)	Disneyland Paris Seaworld (Florida)
Major sports/ entertainment venues	Wembley Stadium (London) Odyssey Centre (Belfast)	San Siro (stadium, Milan, Italy) Madison Square Garden (indoor venue, New York)
Built attractions	Life Centre (Newcastle-upon-Tyne) Lowry (Salford Quays, Greater Manchester)	Eiffel Tower (Paris) Kennedy Space Centre Visitor Complex (Florida)

∞**links**

www.andeantravelweb.com/peru/destinations/machupicchu gives information about the Machu Picchu visitor attraction and about independent travel to it.

Remember

Destinations you have studied include visitor attractions, which are part of their appeal, for example the UK seaside resort of Brighton includes the Brighton Pavilion visitor attraction.

The Giant's Causeway is located on the County Antrim coast in Northern Ireland and is famous for its remarkable geometric columns of igneous rock, which are said to make it look like a road laid by a giant (see Photo **B**). This part of the Giant's Causeway attraction is the Grand Causeway. There is a legend that the mythical Irish giant

B   *The Giant's Causeway – a natural attraction*

Finn MacCool built the causeway to allow him to cross the sea to Scotland. However, it was actually formed by the natural cooling and solidification of hot, molten rock from deep within the earth. The Giant's Causeway is the only World Heritage Site in Northern Ireland and is managed by the **National Trust** – although the local council runs the tourist information centre and car park on the cliff above.

Machu Picchu is another World Heritage Site. It is an overseas historic-site attraction and is located in the Andes mountains in Peru, 80 km north-west of the city of Cusco. It is a ruined city of the Inca civilisation that existed here before the Spanish conquered the Inca Empire in the 16th century.

Sources

Sources of information about types of visitor attractions include:

- attractions' own websites and leaflets
- travel guidebooks
- destination websites
- tour operator brochures and the websites of online travel companies.

Summary questions

1   Outline the five different types of visitor attractions.

2   Choose one overseas leisure and tourism destination you have studied. Make a table to give examples of the different types of visitor attractions that are provided there.

AQA **Examiner's tip**

Visitor attractions vary a lot. Be clear about the type of attraction you are writing about in an answer.

Activity

Choose one UK leisure and tourism destination you have studied. Describe the range of visitor attractions provided there.

C   *Machu Picchu – an overseas historic site*

Summary

Visitor attractions are found in leisure and tourism destinations. There are different types of visitor attractions:

natural attractions

historic sites

theme parks

sports/entertainment venues

built attractions.

Natural attractions appeal to visitors because of their physical beauty. Waterfalls, mountains, valleys and canyons, volcanoes and unusual rock formations like the Giant's Causeway (see 3.1) are examples of visitor attractions of this type.

Objectives

Describe the range of leisure activities available at one UK and one overseas example of a natural attraction.

Case study

High Force – a waterfall in the UK

A   *High Force*

High Force is a spectacular waterfall on the river Tees in County Durham. The water falls some 21 m – the highest unbroken fall in England. The High Force visitor attraction is run as a **commercial** facility. An attractive woodland walk links the falls to a car park 500 m away on the B6277 road, 7 km west of Middleton in Teesdale. Visitors can view the astonishing sight from both top and bottom vantage points. Charges are made for car parking and for admission. There are toilets and a gift shop. Bed and breakfast accommodation is provided by the nearby High Force and Langdon Beck hotels.

Visitors can also view the falls free of charge by public right of way along the south bank of the Tees. Durham County Council operate a car park and picnic area at Bowlees. A waymarked footpath, part of the Pennine Way long-distance footpath, links these **public sector** facilities to High Force (an hour's walk away), passing Low Falls – a series of lesser waterfalls along the way. Durham Wildlife Trust, a **voluntary** organisation, runs a visitor centre at Bowlees. The centre provides information and presents displays about the landscape and life of Upper Teesdale. There are refreshments available and a small shop.

Key terms

Commercial: attractions that are operated usually by a private sector organisation, to try to make a profit.

Public sector: attractions that are operated by a public body.

Voluntary: attractions that are run on a not-for-profit basis, usually by a charity.

⚭ **links**

www.rabycastle.com/high_force is the High Force page website of the Raby Estate's website.

B *Leisure activities available at High Force*

Leisure activity	Place-specific detail
Walking	Hill walkers can enjoy the stretch of the Pennine Way that passes High Force on the south bank of the Tees.
Sightseeing	High Force can be viewed from either bank. The short woodland walk to the falls on the north bank is the gentler option.
Photography	The 21-m fall at High Force is much photographed.
Birdwatching	Sandpipers, oystercatchers and redshanks are among the birds for ornithologists to spot.
Observing plants	Local outcrops of sugar limestone rock support rare flowers, including bird's-eye primrose and orchids.
Angling	Anglers can fish on the stretch of the Tees that is upstream of the falls.

AQA *Examiner's tip*

You need to know about one UK natural attraction and one overseas one.

When describing the leisure activities available at an attraction, use place-specific detail (see Table **B**).

Leisure activities available at natural attractions vary, but typically include sightseeing, active physical activities such as walking, climbing and cycling, and more passive ones such as birdwatching and angling. Some of these activities such as the woodland walk to the falls at High Force, are offered to visitors by leisure and tourism organisations; others are enjoyed by individuals independently, for example walking the Pennine Way. Public footpaths do however, have to be maintained (typically by the local council) to allow this type of leisure activity. Visitors also demand car parking facilities, visitor information centres and cafés.

Extension activity

Evaluate the range of leisure activities available for visitors to one UK natural attraction other than High Force.

Activities

1 Make a poster to show examples of different types of natural attractions.

2 Give examples of leisure facilities around High Force waterfall that are:

a commercial

b run by the public sector

c run by a voluntary organisation.

Coursework activity

Analyse the leisure activities and facilities that are available for different types of visitors to one overseas natural attraction.

Summary

Natural attractions appeal to visitors because of their physical beauty.

UK examples of natural attractions include waterfalls like High Force, and rock formations, including the Giant's Causeway.

Summary questions

1 What is the meaning of each of these?:

a commercial leisure attraction

b voluntary leisure and tourism organisation.

2 Compare the ranges of leisure activities available at one UK and one overseas natural attraction.

3.3 Historic sites

Historic sites are places such as ancient monuments and old buildings that have some historical significance and have become attractions for visitors.

Examples of different types of historic-site visitor attractions are:

- stately homes and palaces
- historically significant places of worship such as cathedrals, mosques and temples
- abbeys, priories and monasteries
- castles and other fortifications
- other ancient sites such as prehistoric stone circles and cities that date from previous civilisations.

A *Some examples of UK and overseas historic attractions*

Type of historic attraction	UK examples	Overseas examples
Stately homes and palaces	Beaulieu Buckingham Palace	Sans Souci, Berlin Palace of Versailles, France
Historic cathedrals, mosques, temples, etc.	Canterbury Cathedral York Minster	Dome of the Rock, Jerusalem Golden Temple, Amritsar
Abbeys, priories and monasteries	Fountains Abbey	Meteora monasteries, Greece
Castles and other fortifications	Hadrian's Wall Edinburgh Castle	Great Wall of China
Other ancient sites	Stonehenge	Machu Picchu, Peru

Objectives

Describe the range of leisure activities available at one UK and one overseas historic-site visitor attraction.

∞ links

www.nationaltrust.org.uk is the internet homepage for the National Trust.
www.unesco.org is the website of the United Nations Educational, Scientific and Cultural Organisation. UNESCO is responsible for designating World Heritage Sites.

AQA *Examiner's tip*

Historic sites include old buildings and monuments that have become visitor attractions. They were not built to be attractions. Built attractions are usually modern sites that were specifically built to attract visitors (see 3.4).

Key terms

Heritage site: a place that helps us understand how people used to live.

Case study

Fountains Abbey

Fountains Abbey is a World **Heritage Site** in North Yorkshire, close to the market town of Ripon. It was founded as an abbey in the 12th century and became one of the wealthiest in England. The Fountains Abbey community of monks, like many others, was dissolved by Henry VIII in the 16th century. Today the abbey ruins are well preserved and set in a landscaped estate along with Studeley Royal Water Garden.

The estate is owned by the National Trust, who runs leisure activities and events at Fountains Abbey that include guided walking tours, opera performances and fireworks displays. There is a visitor centre with refreshments and a gift shop. Many visitors explore the abbey, gardens and grounds from this base. Organ recitals are held in St Mary's church.

Events for Mar 2009

 Sat 14/03/09
Taster Tour
A tour of this World Heritage Site ...

 Sat 28/03/09
Bird Watching for Beginners
An illustrated talk about equipment and photography ...

 Two National Trust events at Fountains Abbey

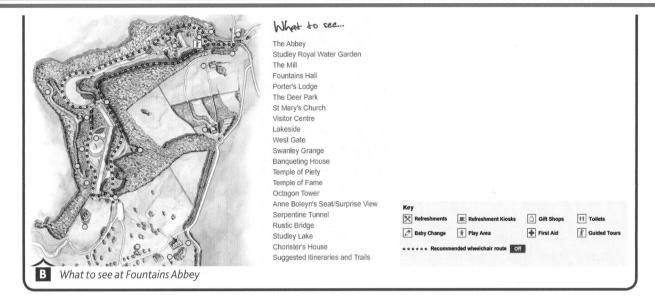

The Abbey
Studley Royal Water Garden
The Mill
Fountains Hall
Porter's Lodge
The Deer Park
St Mary's Church
Visitor Centre
Lakeside
West Gate
Swanley Grange
Banqueting House
Temple of Piety
Temple of Fame
Octagon Tower
Anne Boleyn's Seat/Surprise View
Serpentine Tunnel
Rustic Bridge
Studley Lake
Chorister's House
Suggested Itineraries and Trails

Key

Refreshments | Refreshment Kiosks | Gift Shops | Toilets
Baby Change | Play Area | First Aid | Guided Tours
••••• Recommended wheelchair route Off

B *What to see at Fountains Abbey*

Sources

- attractions' own websites and promotional materials
- websites and publicity material of leisure and tourism organisations that run attractions (such as the National Trust)
- brochures, guides and internet sites that give information about leisure and tourism destinations (see Chapter 1).

Background knowledge

Fountains Abbey is a historic-site attraction that, like the Tower of London in Chapter 1, is also a World Heritage Site.

Activities

1 Use Table **A** to help you make a display to illustrate the range of historic attractions found in the UK and overseas.

2 List a variety of leisure activities and facilities available at one historic attraction in the UK.

3 Research and describe the range of leisure activities available at one historic attraction overseas.

4 Explain what is meant by a World Heritage Site and why the Tower of London (see 1.4) is a World Heritage Site.

5 Describe in outline three examples of overseas World Heritage Sites that are found in different parts of the world.

Summary questions

1 a Identify five different types of historic-site attractions.
  b Give one UK and one overseas example of each type.

2 Describe the range of leisure activities available at one UK historic-site attraction.

3.4 Theme parks and built attractions

Theme parks are visitor attractions that include rides. They occupy large sites. Some theme parks have a clear theme. Examples include the Disneyworld and the Disneyland theme parks in Florida, California, Paris, Tokyo and Hong Kong where rides, buildings and characters are based around the common theme of Walt Disney films. Legoland Windsor in the UK, the original Legoland in Denmark and the more recently developed Legoland California and Legoland Deutschland (Germany) are all centred around the theme of Lego construction toys.

Some theme parks do not really have a clear theme as such. The UK's Alton Towers, for example, is a theme park without a theme. It is a theme park because it is a large visitor attraction with rides, but its appeal is based on rides without a central unifying theme, unlike Disneyland Paris, Legoland Windsor, or Camelot in north-west England.

Built attractions are visitor attractions that were specifically built to attract visitors. Examples include the London Eye and the Spinnaker Tower in Portsmouth. Museums and art galleries that are open to the public are types of built attractions. Part of their purpose is to conserve old objects, documents and works of art, but they have also been built or developed to display these to visitors.

Objectives

Describe the range of leisure activities available at one UK and one overseas example of each of these types of visitor attractions:

theme parks

built attractions.

∞links

The websites of the two case studies featured are:

www.legoland.co.uk

www.amnh.org for the American Museum of Natural History.

Case study 1

Legoland Windsor

There are over 50 rides at Legoland Windsor, as well as a range of restaurants, cafés and shops. Leisure activities provided for visitors are:

- enjoying the rides and features like Miniland, which is a 3-dimensional (3-D) display of large-scale Lego brick models of monuments and famous buildings, including London's Big Ben and Tower Bridge
- watching events and shows
- using the theme park's catering facilities and visiting its shops
- hands-on Lego play and construction activities.

Rides include the Jungle Coaster, Pirate Falls water chute and the Lego Driving School where children can drive small electric cars. The Lego Creation Centre features Lego set pieces, including a Wall of Fame featuring Lego brick portraits of famous people.

An event calendar is published on the Legoland website (see links). Legoland shops sell souvenirs and photographs of visitors taken on the rides. Catering outlets include carts and kiosks, the Jungle Café and the Knights Table Rotisserie restaurant. Lego construction workshops are provided for children in the Discovery Zone and at Robolab where they can build computer-controlled Lego robots.

A *Legoland Windsor*

American Museum of Natural History, New York City

The museum displays some 32 million items related to the natural world. Inside the museum are different halls, including the:

- Dinosaur Hall – the largest exhibition of dinosaur remains in the world with over 120 specimens on show
- Hall of Biodiversity – interactive and multimedia displays relating to the variety of nature
- Hall of North American Mammals – featuring stuffed creatures, including a pair of bull moose in fighting pose
- Hall of Planet Earth – a multimedia exhibition about how the earth was formed and is constantly changing.

Visitors to the Hall of Planet Earth are able to see the Dynamic Earth Globe exhibit, giving them a view of the earth as it rotates as though from a satellite or orbiting spaceship. The Haydn Planetarium is attached to the museum and shows a 3-D film called *Passport to the Universe*, inside a glass sphere more than 25m in diameter.

B *American Museum of Natural History*

Activities

1 What is meant by a:

a theme park

b built attraction?

2 Outline the range of leisure activities available to visitors at:

a Legoland Windsor

b the American Museum of Natural History.

Coursework activity

Describe the range of built attractions available for visitors to one leisure and tourism destination.

Group activity

Discuss theme parks you have visited or know about. What leisure activities did you enjoy there? What activities were there for people of different age groups? What provision did you notice for people with special needs?

Summary question

Make a poster to summarise the leisure activities available for visitors to:

a one theme park in the UK and one overseas

b one built attraction (other than a theme park) in the UK and one overseas.

Key terms

Theme parks: large visitor attractions whose appeal to visitors is primarily based on mechanical rides.

Built attractions: attractions that were specifically developed or purpose-built to be visitor attractions.

Extension activity

Research and describe the range of leisure activities available to visitors at one theme park or built attraction other than Legoland Windsor and the American Museum of Natural History.

Summary

Theme parks and built attractions are two types of visitor attractions.

Both types offer a range of leisure activities to visitors.

3.5 Major sports and entertainment venues

Major sports and entertainment **venues** attract visitors primarily to watch sports events and to attend shows. Such venues include:

- stadia
- racecourses
- arenas
- theatres, concert halls and opera houses.

Many major venues are so famous that visitors are attracted to them even when sports and entertainment events are not in progress. They are sightseeing attractions in themselves. Such venues often operate tours as a result. Tours are an important way for venues to generate extra income. A football stadium, for example, may only host a major match once every week or two – and then only during the football season. The rest of the time the ground would stand empty and no money would be coming in to maintain the facility or to help it be profitable. Secondary purposes are therefore vital to keep such facilities running.

Examples of secondary purposes for major sports and entertainment venues (as well as tours) are:

- conferences and business meetings
- exhibitions and trade fairs
- social functions such as weddings
- other leisure events such as a rock concert at a football stadium.

Objectives

Describe the range of leisure activities available at one UK and one overseas example of major sports/entertainment venues.

Key terms

Venues: leisure facilities such as a stadium or arena where events are held or shows are staged.

Stadia: the plural of stadium: a large outdoor facility where sports events such as football matches are held.

Arenas: large indoor venues.

Case study

Nou Camp stadium, Barcelona

The Nou Camp ('new ground') stadium has been the home ground for FC Barcelona football team since 1957. It is the biggest stadium in Europe, with a capacity of nearly 99,000 spectators. FC Barcelona play in the Spanish League and various European football competitions, so visitors from the rest of Spain and all over Europe come to the ground to watch football matches.

The fame of the Nou Camp has made it one of Barcelona's key visitor attractions. The Nou Camp tour allows visitors to see the stadium on the inside, when matches are not being staged. The tour includes the press facilities, president's box, changing rooms, players' tunnel and the pitch itself. There is also a visit to the Club Museum, which displays trophies the team have won and photographs and memorabilia associated with famous players of the past. Visitors have the option to use an audioguide system so they can take the tour at their own pace, listening to a recording as they go, rather than be led along by a tour guide and have to go at the same pace as the rest of the tour group. The audioguide is available in several languages, including Catalan (the local language of north-eastern Spain), Spanish, English, French, Italian, German and Dutch.

A Nou Camp stadium

Activities

1. Explain what is meant by a secondary purpose.

2. Find out about sports other than football, which are played at the Nou Camp stadium.

3. Make a chart to illustrate the range of leisure activities available at one major UK sports venue.

Extension activity

Research the leisure activities available at a major overseas entertainment venue.

Coursework activity

Describe how well a major entertainment venue meets the needs of a variety of different visitor types.

Group activity

What sports/entertainment venues are there in your region? Which could be regarded as nationally important (major)? Why (why not)? What purposes (including secondary purposes) do they have? How well do they meet the needs of different customer types? What impact do you think an event at a major stadium has on its local area?

Summary question

Describe the range of leisure activities available at one UK and one overseas example of major sports/entertainment venues.

links

www.manutd.co.uk is the website for Manchester United.

www.millenniumstadium.com is the web address for the Millennium Stadium in Cardiff.

AQA Examiner's tip

Learn about one major UK venue and one major overseas venue.

It is a good idea to prepare for the possibility of being asked to compare the UK and overseas venues you have studied.

Summary

Major sports and entertainment venues are attractions because customers go there to:

watch the sport or entertainment, which is the venue's main purpose

see or tour the venue

take advantage of a secondary purpose of the venue.

3.6 How do visitor attractions meet the needs of their customers?

Visitor attractions try to meet the needs of their customers. Attractions do so because it is important for them to appeal to **potential customers**, as well as to satisfy **actual customers**. Satisfied customers are more likely to return to the attraction on another occasion, bringing repeat business. They are also more likely to recommend it to other people and so generate new business for the attraction.

Many visitor attractions are commercial and need to make a profit. Others may be operated by the public sector or, in the case of The Deep (see below), by a charity.

Different types of leisure and tourism customers are:

- single people
- couples
- groups travelling together
- different age groups: children, teenagers, young adults, mature adults, retired people
- different ethnic and cultural groups
- people with special needs.

Different types of customers may have different needs. For example families with very young children may need baby-feeding and nappy-changing facilities, as well as easy access for pushchairs, children's menus, and activities appropriate to the children's age such as more gentle rides in a theme park. People who are visually impaired may need extra facilities such as safe walking routes, Braille signage, and audio announcements.

Objectives

Explain why visitor attractions try to meet the needs of their customers.

Assess how well they do so.

∞links

www.thedeep.co.uk is The Deep's website address.

Key terms

Potential customers: people who may decide to visit a leisure and tourism destination or attraction.

Actual customers: people who are visiting or have visited a leisure and tourism destination or attraction.

A The Deep

Case study

The Deep

The Deep is a visitor attraction in Hull. It is operated by a conservation and education charity and is a large aquarium. The Deep promotes itself as 'the world's only submarium' because visitors view its more than 3,500 fish (including 40 sharks) from under water.

This is possible because The Deep has Europe's deepest underwater viewing tunnel, from which a glass elevator lifts visitors 10m through the water of The Deep's marine-life tank.

Additional facilities at The Deep include:

- a cinema showing '4-D movies' (3-D films with added theatrical effects)
- exhibitions of other water-based life, including amphibians and reptiles
- catering facilities: three cafés and restaurants, including the Observatory Café and the Two Rivers Restaurant, which is open on Friday and Saturday evenings and for special events.

B The viewing tunnel at The Deep

"So, how was your trip to The Deep?"

"Really good, I'd recommend it. Apart from the obvious fish and sharks and stuff, there was an exhibition called The Slime about creatures like frogs and snails that depend on slime to live. The kids just loved that!"

"Anywhere to eat?"

"Three different places though the restaurant is mostly just Friday and Saturday nights. It's for adults really. But there are two cafés. The Observatory Café is open all day and the Two Rivers Café at mealtimes."

C *A friend recommends The Deep*

Deep Events 2008

February 14-22 Ocean-Art Week.

March 9-10, 15-16
National Science & Engineering Week.

March 7-8, 14-15
National Science & Engineering Week

May 7 Quiet Day - with BSL presentations

April 1 ongoing (excluding Pirate Week) Lost Oceans! Featuring 3D film Mosters of The Deep

May 30-31 Humber Environment Fair

October 8 Quiet Day - with BSL presentations

October 24 - November 1 Pirate Week

December 19 - January 4 Festive Dive Shows and Santa's Grotto

For the latest information please visit www.thedeep.co.uk or call 01482 381000

D *Event calendar*

Group activity

Discuss the customer type whose needs The Deep best meets, and why.

Extension activity

Suggest how visitor attractions such as The Deep can meet the special needs of inbound tourists.

Coursework activity

Evaluate how well the key attractions that are available at one leisure and tourism destination meet the needs of different visitor types.

Summary questions

1 What are the differences between:
  a potential and actual customers
  b repeat business and new business?

2 Explain why visitor attractions such as The Deep try to meet the needs of their customers.

3 Assess how well The Deep meets the needs of a variety of customer types.

Remember

Children visit The Deep either as a member of their family or of an organised group (on a school trip, for instance). The actual customer who decides to visit The Deep is therefore likely to be either a parent or guardian or a group organiser.

AQA Examiner's tip

Think about:

- the needs of different visitor types
- which of these the attraction meets well (and how)
- which needs are not met well (and why not)
- what the attraction could do to improve how it meets these needs.

Summary

Visitor attractions try to meet the needs of a variety of different customer types.

They are likely to meet the needs of some visitor types better than others.

You need to be able to explain how a visitor attraction you have not studied seeks to attract different customer types. This is so you would be able to answer a question in the Unit 1 exam where you might be given some information about a visitor attraction you had not learned about, and then asked to assess how it seemed to be going about attracting different sorts of visitors.

The different types of visitors you might need to consider are:

- single people
- couples
- families with children
- groups travelling together
- different age groups: children, teenagers, young adults, mature adults, retired people
- different ethnic and cultural groups
- people with special needs.

Leisure and tourism organisations that run visitor attractions wish to meet the needs of their different customers because they want to attract both new and repeat business. This is so that they will have higher visitor numbers and higher **turnover**. Commercial attractions will make more money. Those run as public services such as a local council's leisure centre for instance, will be providing better value for the **public money** spent on them.

■ Background knowledge

The Alnwick Garden is a modern garden that has been developed as a visitor attraction. It is a built attraction in the grounds of the historic site of Alnwick Castle. Customers can visit one or both attractions in a single trip.

There had been a garden on the site in the past, but by 1950 it had become neglected and was in a state of disrepair. In 1997 the Duchess of Northumberland had the idea of developing a spectacular new garden that would be open to the public. The Alnwick Garden Trust was set up to develop the garden and make it into a successful visitor attraction. The Alnwick Garden Trust is a charity, so it is an example of a voluntary leisure and tourism organisation.

Like all visitor attractions, the Alnwick Garden tries to meet the needs of different customer types. For example:

a people whose special-interest leisure activity is gardening. The Alnwick Garden contains a wide variety of plants and has the largest collection of different European plants in the UK. The gardening staff are also encouraged to answer customers' questions.

b families with children. There are mini-tractors for toddlers to ride, water features in which children can paddle, and jets of water that suddenly spout from the Grand Cascade that even teenagers enjoy dodging. The Bamboo Labyrinth maze and the rope bridges of the Treehouse are further child-friendly facilities.

Objectives

Explain how a visitor attraction you have not studied in your course seeks to attract different customer types.

Remember

Different types of visitor attractions are:

- natural attractions
- historic sites
- theme parks
- major sports/entertainment venues
- built attractions.

Key terms

Turnover: the total income of a leisure and tourism organisation. Profit is the difference between the turnover and the cost of running the organisation.

Public money: money that is collected from the population and spent on its behalf.

⬭ links

www.alnwickgarden.com is the Alnwick Garden's website address.

 http://

The Grand Cascade

The centrepiece of the Garden is the Grand Cascade, a magnificent tumbling mass of water. The largest water feature of its kind in the country, every minute 7260 gallons of water tumble down a series of 21 weirs. The Grand Cascade's water displays are not only spellbinding to watch but also an interactive experience for younger visitors who can play in the water jets.

The Ornamental Garden

Beyond the Grand Cascade lies the walled Ornamental Garden. This symmetrical, structured garden is strongly influenced by European garden design and brims with more than 16,500 plants. There are quiet places to sit and catch the sun, and inviting pathways bordered by lavender and fruit tress. At the centre of this tranquil garden lies a bubbling pool that spills onto pebbled rills which run throughout The Garden.

A *The Alnwick Garden: Grand Cascade*

Extension activity

Research the Alnwick Garden visitor attraction further to assess how well it meets the needs of visitor types other than those in the examination-style question on page 58.

Group activity

Discuss what questions you should ask yourself when evaluating how well a visitor attraction meets the needs of different visitor types.

Summary question

Research a visitor attraction other than the Alnwick Garden that you have not studied in your course so far. Explain how it seeks to attract different customer types.

Summary

Visitor attractions of all types try to meet the needs of their customers.

Promotional materials produced by visitor attractions often show how the needs of different customer types are met.

In this chapter you have learnt:

There are different types of visitor attractions: natural attractions, historic sites, theme parks, major sports/entertainment venues and built attractions.

✔ Visitor attractions provide varied leisure activities for their visitors.

✔ Some of the leisure activities provided by a visitor attraction are likely to meet the needs of some visitor types better than they meet the needs of other visitor types.

✔ Visitor attractions try to meet the needs of their customers because they want to attract both new and repeat business.

Revision quiz

1 Give two examples of each of the following:
a natural attractions
b theme parks
c historic sites.

2 What is the difference between a built attraction and a historic site?

3 'Sometimes major sports venues are also entertainment venues.' Explain.

AQA Examination-style questions

1 Choose one visitor attraction:
   (a) Describe how it provides for the needs of families with children.
   (b) Explain why it should provide for the needs of other customer types too. *(6 marks)*

2 Evaluate how well one visitor attraction meets the needs of one of these types of leisure and tourism customers:
   • single people
   • groups
   • people of different ages
   • people from different ethnic and cultural backgrounds. *(6 marks)*

AQA Examiner's tip Keep the customer type you are writing about firmly in mind throughout each answer. Clearly link products/services that the attraction provides to the specific needs of that customer type.

Travelling to destinations

◼ Introduction

People need to travel to reach leisure and tourism destinations and attractions. The trips they make range from short local hops, perhaps to visit the local leisure centre, to international journeys to and from overseas destinations, for example for a holiday in a beach (or seaside) resort abroad.

◼ What is this chapter about?

This chapter is about the methods of travel that are available to leisure and tourism destinations and why people choose them. You will learn about the different ways in which domestic and international tourists move around, enter and leave the UK. This will include how they reach the destinations you have used as case studies, as well as the advantages and disadvantages of different ways of travelling for different types of customers and journeys.

Starter activity

Think about a journey you have made. What would it have been like if you had used another form of transport? Is there a different route you could have used? How does it compare?

People travel to destinations in different ways. They can use different forms (**modes**) **of transport**, different routes or different **transport providers**.

Different modes of transport that people commonly use to reach leisure and tourism destinations are:

- rail transport (trains, trams and metro systems)
- road transport (cars, buses and coaches, taxis and cycles)
- water transport (ferries, and other ships and boats)
- air transport.

Sometimes people can choose between different routes even if using the same mode of transport. For example a traveller who is driving her or his own car (or one they have hired) may be able to choose between a short, direct route through a town, or taking the bypass, which may be longer in distance but quicker in time. On other occasions the mode of transport chosen for a particular journey may decide the route. For example a rail passenger between London and Paris has no choice but to travel through the Channel Tunnel.

Even for the same mode of transport on the same route, the leisure and tourism customer may have a choice of provider. A tourist travelling between London and Paris by air will have a choice of several airlines – both flag-carrier airlines and **budget carriers**.

A *Ways to travel from London to Paris*

Mode	Route	Provider
Air	London Heathrow – Charles de Gaulle airport	British Airways
	London Luton – Charles de Gaulle airport	easyJet
Train	St Pancras, London – Gare du Nord, Paris	Eurostar
Car and train	London – Folkestone – Calais (via Channel Tunnel) – Paris	Eurotunnel
Car and ferry	London – Dover – Calais – Paris	P&O Ferries

Sources

Sources of information about ways to travel to leisure and tourism destinations include:

- timetables
- atlases and route maps
- travel providers and online travel companies, including their internet sites
- destination information providers such as tourism information centres

Key terms

Modes of transport: forms of transport, for example rail and air.

Transport providers: leisure and tourism organisations that operate travel services.

Budget carriers: transport providers that carry people at discounted fares. Budget airlines operate more basic services than flag-carrier airlines.

Remember

When you studied destinations in Chapter 1, you found out about the ways people can reach them.

AQA Examiner's tip

You may be asked to describe a route. Include details of each stage of the journey.

Think about it

The journeys people make to leisure and tourism destinations can be simple or more complex. A tourist's journey from home to a hotel in an overseas holiday destination may involve a number of stages, modes, routes and providers.

∞links

www.transportdirect.info is one of a number of websites that give information about ways to travel from one place to another.

- leisure facility and visitor attractions and their promotional materials, including websites
- travel guides: books and internet sites.

Background knowledge

The Channel Tunnel is 50km long. It connects Folkestone in Kent to Coquelles in northern France. The Channel Tunnel goes through the rocks that lie beneath the seabed of the English Channel. It is really three tunnels in one:

- northbound tunnel (France to the UK)
- southbound tunnel (the UK to France)
- service tunnel.

Eurotunnel shuttle and Eurostar passenger trains are the ways of travelling through the Channel Tunnel, which people use to help them reach leisure and tourism destinations.

Shuttle trains carry tourists and their cars through the Channel Tunnel. Eurostar trains carry passengers.

B   *A Eurostar train*

C   *The route of the Channel Tunnel*

Activities

1   Make a visual display to illustrate different passenger transport modes.

2   Choose one overseas leisure and tourism destination you have studied other than Paris. Describe a variety of travel options for people travelling there from your home area.

Group activity

Which way of travelling from London to Paris would you recommend for a single parent and two children under 5 years of age? Why? How difficult would the other ways be?

Summary questions

1   Outline four different types of transport modes.

2   Choose one UK leisure and tourism destination. Make a map to show different ways visitors can travel to the destination.

Summary

People travel to leisure and tourism destinations in different ways. These include different:

modes

routes

transport providers.

People can use trains to travel between most towns and cities in the UK. Most of the country's city destinations and larger beach (or seaside) resorts have rail links and stations. Rail passengers to leisure and tourism destinations in the UK may be travelling for leisure or business reasons or to visit friends and relatives.

Rail transport systems also exist within larger urban destinations, for example the London underground, the Tyne–Wear metro and Manchester's Metrolink. The Metrolink uses vehicles that are trams rather than trains. Other UK cities with tramway systems include Croydon, Sheffield and Nottingham. Such local rail systems help people make use of leisure and tourism facilities in different parts of cities. The trams of Blackpool's seafront are a heritage tourist attraction in themselves. They also provide a transport service along the shore and a means for visitors to view the annual Blackpool Illuminations.

A Metro train

Case study

Virgin Trains

Virgin Trains is a train operating company that runs InterCity passenger train services in the UK along the West Coast main-line railway between London and the west of Scotland via Birmingham. High-speed, electric Pendolino tilting trains draw their power from overhead electricity cables. The carriages tilt as the train rounds corners at high speed.

The principal route operated by Virgin Trains is the 650km West Coast main line that runs from London's Euston station to Glasgow Central. From this **artery**, tracks branch off to the West Midlands, Liverpool, Manchester and north Wales, where the port of Holyhead is a rail gateway to the UK. A ferry service operates across the Irish Sea from Holyhead to Dun Laoghaire in the Republic of Ireland.

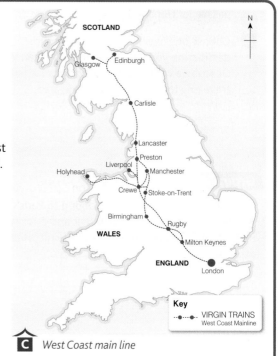

C West Coast main line

links

www.tfl.gov.uk is the internet address of Transport for London and gives information about all forms of transport in London.

B Virgin Pendolino train

Background knowledge

Virgin Trains is one of the UK's **train operating companies (TOCs)**. Others include National Express and Arriva, both of whom also operate road travel services (mainly coaches and buses, respectively).

Activities

1. Outline three ways in which people can make use of rail transport systems.

2. Use examples to illustrate the meanings of:
   a rail terminal
   b rail gateway
   c railway artery.

3. Suggest how a business tourist who lives in London might make use of at least two different train services to travel to a conference in Manchester.

Extension activities

1. Research a railway journey from your home area to a UK city destination in another part of the country that is not served by the West Coast main line. Find out the:
   a start and end railway stations
   b route between them
   c TOC(s) providing the train(s)
   d journey time
   e cost at two different start times for a single adult on an open return ticket.

2. Make a chart to illustrate different ticket types available for your journey.

Coursework activity

Evaluate how well different options for travelling by rail between your home area and a UK beach (or seaside) resort are likely to appeal to three different customer types. Options to consider include:
   a route and provider
   b time of travel and price.

Summary questions

1. Describe the West Coast main line and one other principal UK railway route.

2. Make a map or chart to illustrate the railway routes operated from London's main rail terminals.

3. Outline the rail services provided to and from two UK rail gateways.

D *London railway terminals*

Terminal	Areas served
Euston	Midlands, north-west England, north Wales and Scotland
Kings Cross	north-east England and Scotland
Liverpool Street	eastern England
Marylebone	Midlands
Paddington	western England and south Wales
St Pancras	east Midlands and the Channel Tunnel
Victoria	southern England
Waterloo	southern and south-west England

Key terms

Artery: a principal transport route such as a main railway line or motorway.

Train operating companies (TOCs): leisure and tourism organisations that run trains in the UK. Examples include Virgin Trains, National Express East Coast and Arriva Trains Wales.

AQA *Examiner's tip*

Think about how much help rail services are to people visiting UK leisure and tourism destinations you have studied.

Summary

Rail transport includes trains and trams.

Rail services operate between UK leisure and tourism destinations and within them.

People use road transport to travel to UK leisure and tourism destinations.

Different forms of road transport commonly used by tourists and by people going to local leisure facilities are:

- cars (own or self-drive hire)
- buses and coaches
- taxis.

Leisure and tourism organisations, including car hire firms, bus and coach operators and taxi companies provide road transport options for people on a commercial basis. Travellers who arrive at important rail terminals (such as those located in London) and UK gateways like airports, often change transport mode to complete their journeys. As a result, car hire desks, bus and coach stops and stations, and **taxi ranks** are facilities commonly found at such **transport interchanges**.

People's choice of road transport depends on accessibility, cost and convenience. In Cartoon **A** a business tourist explains the factors that affected her choice.

■ Sources

- road atlases and internet map and route planning websites
- websites and publicity materials of road transport providers such as car hire firms and bus and coach operators.
- leaflets, brochures, guides and internet sites that give information about how to travel to leisure and tourism facilities and destinations.

Objectives

Describe the principal road routes used by domestic and international tourists to move around, enter and leave the UK.

"Hiring a car at the airport is convenient and makes it quicker for me to travel to the places I need to go. There's only me so I don't need a big vehicle, which keeps the cost down a bit. I can manage my journey so I arrive for my appointments on time."

A A business tourist explains

Factors influencing this business tourist from Scotland who has flown in to Belfast International Airport on a 2-day trip to Belfast and Enniskillen and needs to be able move readily about Northern Ireland to visit these places.

Case study

Europcar

Europcar is a car hire company with operations around the world. In 2008 Europcar operated from 191 locations in the UK, including airports, railway stations and town centres. Customers, who must at least hold a valid driving licence, typically hire a car for a period of between 1 day and 2 weeks. Many are visitors who are willing to pay more than the cost of public transport in exchange for the flexibility that a self-drive car offers.

In Belfast, Europcar operates three car hire locations:

- Belfast City Centre (the Europcar desk is in the lobby of the Days Hotel)
- Belfast City Airport
- Belfast International Airport.

B Car-hire desk

Profiles of two typical customers at Europcar's car-hire desk at Belfast International Airport in Northern Ireland are:

a   a business tourist from Scotland who is on a two-day sales trip to Belfast and Enniskillen

b   a tourist couple from Manchester who are visiting Northern Ireland for a short-break holiday and who want to see the natural attractions of the Antrim coast, including the Giant's Causeway.

Background knowledge

Belfast International Airport is one of two airports that serve Northern Ireland's largest city. The other is the George Best Belfast City Airport, which is named after the famous footballer who came from Belfast. Access to both Belfast airports is by road. Neither has an integrated railway station like those of London Gatwick and Manchester airports, for example.

Activities

1   Give three different forms of road transport provided by leisure and tourism organisations.

2   Explain why car companies often have locations at transport interchanges such as airports and major railway stations.

3   Explain why hiring a car may be a good travel option for a business tourist.

Extension activities

1   Research and recommend a road route for the business tourist (profile a) featured in the Europcar case study.

2   Analyse the range of travel options available for the tourist couple profiled in the case study (profile b).

Coursework activity

Evaluate how well road transport meets the needs of people from three different age groups. Consider different forms of road transport in your answer.

Summary questions

1   Describe the principal road route a car driver would be likely to take from:

a   Belfast City Airport to Enniskillen

b   your local area to a UK leisure and tourism destination in another part of the country.

2   Outline the options available to a 14-year-old school student who wants to travel from a housing estate on the edge of a town near you, to a leisure facility in the town centre.

Remember

People can choose between modes of transport (such as rail instead of road), as well as between different forms of road transport.

links

www.theaa.com, the Automobile Association (AA) website is one that provides an online road route planning service.

AQA Examiner's tip

Some leisure and tourism facilities and destinations are accessible by a choice of transport modes. In some cases people's choices are more restricted. Stick to describing the forms of transport that customers and visitors actually and commonly use.

Key terms

Taxi ranks: roadside locations where people can hire a taxi.

Transport interchanges: points or facilities (such as a rail terminal or airport) where people can change from one mode of transport to another.

Summary

Leisure and tourism organisations provide different forms of road transport.

People may use road transport for the whole or part of a journey.

Road transport is often used to transfer from a transport terminal or gateway to a final destination.

People use ferries and other **marine transport** such as cruise ships to travel to and from the UK and among the islands that make up the British Isles.

Map **B** shows the principal seaport ferry terminals, which act as UK gateways for international tourists. Marine ferries also operate domestic routes across narrow stretches of sea within the UK, for example between Stranraer in Scotland and from Portsmouth across the Solent to the Isle of Wight.

Water transport in the UK is also found on rivers and lakes. Regular ferry services operate across major rivers like the Mersey and the Tyne, and river (or water) bus services run along others such as the Thames. Some of these services are used by commuters on their way to and from work, but they also help people travel to leisure and tourism destinations. In London, for example, Tate Boat (Photo **A**) is a river bus service that links the Tate Modern and the Tate Britain art galleries.

On lakes such as Windermere in the Lake District National Park, pleasure boat services provide a means of transport for visitors, as well as acting as visitor attractions in themselves. Canal boat trips and narrow boat navigation Photo **D**) for pleasure are further UK water transport examples.

Objectives

Describe the principal routes and facilities, including terminals and gateways, that are used by domestic and international tourists to move around, enter and leave the UK.

A Tate Boat

Case study

The Irish Sea

Passenger ferry services between the UK and Ireland in 2008 were provided by Irish Ferries, Stena Line and P&O Ferries. People using these services to travel to leisure and tourism destinations could choose between routes from these ports in England, Scotland and Wales:

- Liverpool and Fleetwood
- Stranrear, Cairnryan and Troon
- Holyhead, Fishguard and Pembroke.

Passenger ferries to Ireland also operated to Ireland from the Isle of Man, and some cargo ship operators (such as Norfolk Line) offered passenger accommodation on board their vessels.

B UK sea ferry ports

Fact

In recent years, particularly in the wake of the opening of the Channel Tunnel in 1994 and the growth of budget airlines (also from the 1990s), there have been frequent changes to ferry routes and providers.

⊘⊘ links

www.ferriesdirect.org is the website of one online booker for UK ferry crossings.

Key terms

Marine transport: water transport that crosses the sea rather than a freshwater body such as a river or lake.

Itineraries: detailed journey programmes.

Windermere
Lake Cruises

Home
Park and Sail
Cruises
Timetables
Fares and Special Offers
Fun Days Out
Special Events
Self Drive and Rowing Boats

Groups
Schools
Weddings
Private Charter
Gallery
About Us
How to find us
Contact and Brochures

Cruise & Walk

This is just one of our most popular walks - 3 boats & a walk! Sail on our traditional wooden launches from Ambleside to Wray Castle then take the shorline walk, south to Ferry house, board another wooden launch and sail back to Bowness. Stop off for a cake & coffee at the pier before sailing back to Ambleside

C   *Water transport as a visitor attraction*

AQA *Examiner's tip*

Ferry crossings are usually one part of longer journey **itineraries**, so think about the travel options to and from ferry terminals as well.

A narrowboat canal holiday is an example of a special-interest holiday.

Activity

Make a poster to illustrate different forms of water transport.

Group activity

How do people make use of pleasure boat services such as those provided on Lake Windermere? Think of as many different ways as you can.

Extension activity

Research and make a chart to summarise the ferry options for tourists wanting to cross the English Channel between England and France.

Coursework activity

Analyse and evaluate the suitability of ferry options for crossing the Irish Sea for these customers:

a   a business tourist from Scotland visiting Belfast and Londonderry by car

b   a couple from Manchester, also travelling by car, who want to spend their short-break holiday in Northern Ireland touring the Antrim coast.

Summary question

Describe the principal ferry routes and facilities, including terminals and gateways, that tourists use to move around, enter and leave the UK.

D   *Narrowboat*

Summary

Ferry terminals act as UK gateways when used by international tourists.

Examples of water transport include ferry crossings, as well as river bus services and pleasure cruises.

4.5 Air links

Airlines provide air transport that helps people reach leisure and tourism destinations. International flights operate into and out of the UK, while domestic flights are those between airports within the UK.

The main airports around London are:

- Heathrow – the first London airport, west of London
- Gatwick – the second largest, located south of the city
- Stansted
- Luton
- London City Airport (a smaller urban airport located in London Docklands).

Beyond the south-east of England, regional airports serve the UK's other cities and regions.

Objectives

Describe the principal air routes and facilities, including terminals and gateways, that are used by domestic and international tourists to move around, enter and leave the UK.

∞ links

www.stanstedairport.com is the official website for Stansted Airport.

www.durhamteesvalleyairport.com is the official website for Durham Tees Valley Airport.

A *Airlines and flights: different types*

Airline type	Description	Examples
Flag carrier	an airline which is seen as representing its country of origin	British Airways Air France
Budget	a low-cost airline offering cheaper fares and a no-frills service	easyJet Ryanair
Scheduled	an airline that operates timetabled flights with tickets sold to the public	British Airways easyJet
Charter	airline flights for a specific purpose such as to transport package tourists to a holiday destination. Some tickets may be sold to members of the public	Monarch Airlines Thomson Fly

Key terms

Scheduled: flights for which tickets are on sale to the public and which operate to a timetable.

Charter: flights that are arranged for the use of tour operators' customers.

Case study

London Stansted

Stansted is the UK's third busiest airport. Over 23 million passengers pass through its terminal every year. More than 30 airlines (charter and scheduled) operate flights from Stansted to destinations in more than 30 different countries abroad, as well as to UK regional airport destinations. Domestic routes from Stansted in 2008 were to Belfast (International and City airports), Edinburgh, Glasgow, Londonderry, Manchester, Newcastle and Newquay.

Most of Stansted's routes are to domestic or short-haul destinations. New York City's JFK Airport is one long-haul exception. Diagram **B** shows arrivals at Stansted during a one-and-a-half-hour period in September 2008.

London Stansted airport is located 75km north of London, near junction 8 on the M11. The Stansted Express is a shuttle train between Stansted Airport and Liverpool Street (one of London's main railway termini). The train runs every 15 minutes and takes 45 minutes to complete its journey. There is also a coach station from which express services operate to London, including to Victoria, London's principal coach station.

Airport terminals such as that at Stansted provide a range of leisure and tourism facilities for their customers. These include catering facilities like bars, cafés, restaurants and on-site hotels. At Stansted, catering facilities in the terminal are located in the arrivals hall and baggage reclaim area, as well as in the departures section, both before and after security. Catering outlets are operated under brand names that are familiar to customers from town and shopping centres. They include Est Est, Pret a Manger, and Wetherspoons. Hotel chains that are represented at the airport include Holiday Inn, Radisson SAS and Days Inn.

Scheduled Time	Flight No.	Coming from	Status
Fri 19 September 2008			
09:00	YK933	IZMIR	LANDED 0907
09:10	FR6112	BELFAST CITY	LANDED 0855
09:20	YK1191	BODRUM MILAS	LANDED 0943
09:25	FR206	DUBLIN	LANDED 0945
09:25	FR902	CORK	LANDED 0917
09:25	FR9272	EINDHOVEN	LANDED 0928
09:25	FR9903	NEWQUAY	LANDED 0921
09:30	A3600	ATHENS	
09:30	FR435	HAMBURG LUBECK	LANDED 0913
09:40	EZY3002	AMSTERDAM	LANDED 0946
09:45	FR3631	BREMEN	LANDED 0940
10:05	FR704	KERRY	EXPECTED 1020
10:10	FR612	DERRY	EXPECTED 1010
10:25	FR633	MONTPELLIER	EXPECTED 0957
10:25	FR8543	BERLIN SCHONEFE	EXPECTED 1020
10:25	FR9773	KARLSRUHE BADEN	EXPECTED 1040

B Arrivals board, Stansted Airport

Activities

1 a Explain what is meant by a regional airport.

   b Some airports, even quite small ones (for example Durham Tees Valley), are international airports. What do you think that means?

2 Describe the differences between these two pairs:

   a budget and flag-carrier airlines

   b charter and scheduled flights.

Coursework activity

Evaluate how well the routes available from one regional airport meet the needs of:

a business tourists

b inbound tourists to the UK.

Summary questions

1 Describe the range of air routes available from London Stansted Airport.

2 Explain how London Stansted Airport tries to meet the needs (other than for flights) of leisure and tourism customers.

Extension activity

Research and describe the air routes available from one UK airport other than London Stansted and Durham Tees Valley.

Group activity

What airports do people from your area most often use? Why? How could air links from your area be improved? Why does air travel raise environmental concerns?

Summary

The major London airports are Heathrow, Gatwick, Stansted, Luton and London City Airport.

Regional airports serve UK cities and regions other than the London area.

4.6 UK travel options

People travelling to leisure and tourism destinations choose between different **travel options**. These options are:

- modes and facilities
- routes
- providers
- prices.

Modes are the different forms of transport available.

Prices often vary among providers, routes and transport modes. The date and time of travel often plays a major part in the pricing of a trip. Leisure and tourism organisations providing travel are commercial businesses. They seek to make profits. At busy times, when demand for travel is high, prices can be raised to take in as much money as possible from ticket sales. In quieter periods, when demand falls, providers may reduce ticket prices to attract more customers and continue to take in money.

For this reason, the price of a budget airline flight, for example, can vary considerably depending on departure time. Peak and off-peak fares are charged for rail travel. For more local travel to a leisure facility, time may be less likely to affect the price of bus or metro travel, for example for a journey from a suburban housing estate to a town centre theatre.

Case study

Travel options between Belfast and London

A tourist travelling from Belfast to London could fly or take a ferry. The latter alternative would give further choices of driving (his or her own car or a hire car) or travelling by train or coach. There are two airports serving Belfast – Belfast International Airport and George Best Belfast City Airport. This gives a choice of facilities for air travellers.

There are often different possible routes between places, even by the same transport mode. The fact that there are two Belfast airports and four London airports served by flights from them (see Table **A**) by four different airline providers, gives customers a range of route and provider options from which to choose, even after deciding to fly rather than taking a ferry.

A *Air routes between Belfast and London*

Belfast Airport	London	Provider (airline)
International	Gatwick	easyJet
	Heathrow	Aer Lingus
	Luton	easyJet
	Stansted	easyJet
George Best City	Gatwick	Flybe
	Heathrow	Bmi
	Stansted	Ryanair

Transfers to the airport increase the range of options for people who choose to fly. Leisure and tourism organisations provide taxi and airport bus services, for example between Belfast International Airport and the city centre.

Objectives

Describe the range of different travel options to UK and overseas destinations:

| modes |
| routes |
| providers |
| prices. |

Remember

Different travel options are more likely to appeal to some customer types than they are to others. A pair of young students, for example, would be more likely to favour a cheaper option that involved a late-evening flight departure than would a family with young children.

∞ links

www.easyjet.com, **www.flybe.com** and **www.ryanair.com** are the websites of three low-cost airlines operating between Belfast and London.

AQA Examiner's tip

There is likely to be a variety of travel options available for any journey to a tourist destination. When describing a route, avoid over-detailed directions. Stick to the main points.

Key terms

Travel options: ways of travelling to a destination.

B *Airport bus*

Activities

1 **a** Outline the range of options that exists for a tourist who wants to travel between Belfast and London without flying.

  b Research and describe the range of price options that exists for travel between Belfast and London next Tuesday.

2 Analyse and evaluate the range of options that exists for you to travel between your home and a leisure facility of your choice.

C *Ferry*

Extension activity

Research the travel options available for a single elderly person from your local area, to a leisure and tourism destination in the UK:

a Recommend one of the options and explain why the customer should choose it.

b Which factors affect the choice most?

Group activity

Discuss how well different travel options between Belfast and London meet the needs of different customer types.

Coursework activity

Analyse the range of travel options that exists between your local area and a UK leisure and tourism destination for different customer types.

Summary

People can choose between a variety of travel options to reach a UK leisure and tourism destination. The options are choices of:

mode
route
provider
price.

Summary questions

1 Explain the meaning of each of these:

a transport mode

b transfer

c travel options.

2 Describe the range of travel options that exists between your home area and one leisure and tourism destination elsewhere in the UK.

4.7 Overseas travel options

People travelling to leisure and tourism destinations overseas choose how to reach their selected destinations. They choose between modes and facilities, routes, providers and prices.

The growth of the internet has helped more people to make their own travel arrangements, often using the websites of online travel companies such as Expedia, Travelocity and Opodo. Alternatively tourists can arrange travel using the internet sites of leisure and tourism organisations called **transport principals**. These are travel businesses that provide transport. Examples are airline, ferry, train and coach operators and car hire firms.

Budget airlines like easyJet, Ryanair and Flybe are examples of transport principals.

Objectives

Describe the range of different travel options to overseas destinations:

modes and facilities

routes

providers

prices.

Case study

Budget flights to Venice

Budget airlines easyJet and Ryanair both operate flights between the UK and Venice's Marco Polo Airport. EasyJet routes to Venice are shown by Map **A**. Table **B** gives information about its flights there from three UK airports, useful to a tourist from Birmingham who wanted to fly to Venice on one particular day in winter.

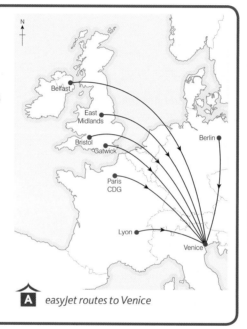

A easyJet routes to Venice

Think about it

1 Tourists can reach Venice by means other than budget airline flights. For example:
   - flag-carrier airline
   - cruise
   - self-drive
   - coach
   - train.

2 Some visitors use more than one transport mode in their journey to Venice.

B easyJet flight options to Venice

Date		26 December	27 December	28 December
From	price*	£54.99	no flights	£54.99
Bristol	Departure time	17h20		17h05
From	price*	£56.99	£109.99	£84.99
East Midlands	Departure time	13h00	13h00	13h00
From London	price*	£42.99	£52.99	£52.99
Gatwick	Departure time	13h05	06h45	07h40
	price*	£42.99	£64.99	£62.99
	Departure time	18h00	16h15	17h55

* prices as quoted on 9 November 2008 not including extras such as baggage charges and booking fees

◼ Background knowledge

Venice

Venice is a city destination in the north-east of Italy. The city is most famous for the picturesque canals. These act as streets in the old heart of Venice. Historic places and mansions built right next to the canals give the city an urban heritage unique to that in any of the world's other city destinations.

Three principal sights that tourists go to see in Venice are:

- St Mark's (described by Rough Guide as 'the most exotic cathedral in Europe')
- the Grand Canal
- Doge's Palace, where the most powerful of Venice's rulers lived.

Leisure activities that are popular among visitors to Venice other than sightseeing are:

- canal trips on traditional gondolas (Photo C) and other, usually cheaper, boats
- eating and drinking in street-side cafés called trattoria
- visiting Venice's art galleries and museums such as the Accademia, which contains many of the masterpieces that were painted in Venice
- visiting the Venice carnival that takes place each spring.

C *Gondolier in Venice*

AQA *Examiner's tip*

Journeys between places by air also involve transfers at both ends.

The cost, convenience, comfort, accessibility, reliability and relative environmental impact of transfer options may affect people's choice of route.

Key terms

Transport principals: leisure and tourism organisations that provide transportation products/services.

Group activity

Discuss the range of travel options from the UK to Venice other than those including a budget airline flight.

Coursework activity

Analyse and evaluate how well different travel options between your home area and an overseas leisure and tourism destination meet the needs of different customer types.

Activities

1. a Outline the range of options that exists for a tourist who wants to travel between the UK and Venice using easyJet services.

   b Research and describe the range of easyJet and Ryanair budget air flights available between the UK and Venice on a given date.

2. Analyse and evaluate the range of options that exists for you to travel between your home and a hotel in Venice city centre, using a budget airline for your flight.

Extension activity

Research the travel options available for a family of two adults and teenage children from your local area who want to visit Venice between Christmas and New Year. Recommend one of the options and explain why you chose it.

Summary

People can choose between a variety of travel options to reach an overseas leisure and tourism destination. The options are choices of:

mode and facility

route

provider

price.

Summary question

Research and describe a variety of different travel options between one UK location and one overseas leisure and tourism destination.

4.8 Local travel

One of the reasons people travel within their local area is to make use of local leisure facilities. These people are not tourists, but they are customers of the leisure industry.

Travelling locally presents people with a range of **public transport** and **private transport** options. These are shown in Table **A**.

Among public transport options, bus travel is generally available in UK towns and cities. However, for people living in the villages and countryside surrounding a town or city it can be much more limited. The growth of car ownership in the UK in the late 20th century has meant a fall in demand for local bus travel and the withdrawal of many rural services. The usefulness of local train services very much depends on the closeness of railway stations to the start and end points of journeys. In any case, like tram and metro options, local trains tend to serve cities and other large urban areas better. However, some areas such as some of the valleys of south Wales, do have relatively frequent services.

Travel by taxi is usually a relatively expensive option. As a result, it can be easily forgotten that taxis are public transport. Taxis present a convenient and comfortable option whose price per person falls considerably when several people are carried. Shared taxis are widely used in some localities where there is a tradition of doing so, for example in west Belfast.

Private transport options are generally more convenient. Cycling has the added advantages of no emissions and of providing exercise for the rider.

A *Local transport options*

Public	Private
Bus	Car
Tram	Cycle
Local train	Motorcycle/scooter
Metro	
Taxi	

To decide between local transport options, people consider these factors:

- how much money different options cost
- how much time they will take
- how convenient they are for them to use, and how comfortable
- how accessible they are for them
- the relative environmental impact of different transport options.

Sheb

Sheb is a single man in his 30s. He lives in Darlington, a town in the north of England. Sheb tries to keep fit and is a member of Bannatyne's Health and Fitness Club in the town. Sheb used to live in an apartment within easy walking distance of Bannatyne's, but he has recently moved to a house on an estate in the outskirts. His new house is 3km away from the club (as Map **C** shows).

In Cartoon **B**, Sheb explains his choice of transport for the journey between his home and Bannatyne's.

"I used to walk to the gym. Sometimes, in summer if the weather's fine I still do – or cycle. Either is free and helps keep me fit. Time is an issue, so I often drive. Bannatyne's has quite a big members' car park.

There is a bus, but that's to another part of the town centre so I have to walk for a few minutes anyway. It's time really – waiting for the bus, the stops it makes on the way in and then the walk after that. There's coming back too. It all adds up so it's just not convenient for me. Mind you, I wouldn't want to pay for a taxi."

B Sheb's choice

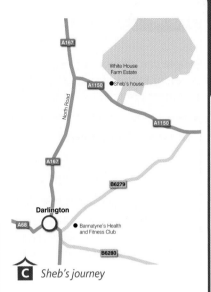

C Sheb's journey

Activities

1. Illustrate the difference between public and private transport.

2. Assess how much different factors have affected Sheb's choice of transport to the club.

Coursework activity

a. Survey different people to find out how they choose to travel to local leisure facilities.

b. Analyse your results.

Extension activity

Research the different ways you could travel from your home or school or college to three leisure facilities in different parts of your locality.

Summary question

Compare the advantages and disadvantages of different travel options for one journey in your local area for two different types of people.

Think about it

There is a variety of different local travel options in your local area. Depending where your local area is and what type of place it is, some travel options may not be available at all. The local travel options that are available are more suitable for some people and some local journeys than they are for others.

Group activity

What travel options would you advise different types of people to choose for journeys similar to Sheb's?

Summary

Even local journeys present people with travel options.

Travel options have advantages and disadvantages for different types of customers.

People can choose to travel to leisure and tourism destinations using different forms of transport. They can pick different routes, different transport providers and can often choose different prices to pay.

Case study

Glasgow to London

Business tourists wanting to travel from Glasgow to London have a variety of options open to them. Three transport modes they commonly use are:

- air – scheduled flights operate from Glasgow Airport to London's airports
- rail – train operators Virgin Trains and National Express run **express trains** between Glasgow and London's Euston and Kings Cross railway station terminals (see Map **C**)
- road – south via the UK's **trunk road** and **motorway** system.

There are advantages and disadvantages to each mode. These relate to journey time, convenience and comfort, price, and environmental impact. These are listed in Table **A**.

While business tourists are more likely to travel in a self-drive car (their own, their company's or a hire car), they could opt to use a coach. However, rail and air travel are usually much quicker options so this does not often happen.

A *Advantages and disadvantages of transport modes*

Transport mode	Advantages	Disadvantages
Air	speed of flight cheap budget fares	inconvenience and time of transfers cost of undiscounted fares concern over environmental impact
Rail	business tourists can work during journey discounted fares available speed between city centres relatively low environmental impact	journey may last several hours overcrowding at busy times may need to change trains
Road (car)	flexibility of departure time no transfers or changes privacy easy to transport luggage and equipment	unable to work en route cost of fuel environmental impact journey times can be long traffic jams, congestion, and road works delays

Glasgow to London Gatwick: all flights

Sat 28th March

£23.99
dep. 08:55, arr 10:25

£23.99
dep. 19:15, arr 20:40

Glasgow to London Luton: all flights

Sat 28th March

£25.99
dep. 07:00, arr 08:15

£25.99
dep. 10:40, arr 11:55

Glasgow to London Stansted: all flights

Sat 28th March

£25.99
dep. 07:15, arr 08:35

£25.99
dep. 18:00, arr 19:20

B *Glasgow to London flight options on 28.3.09*

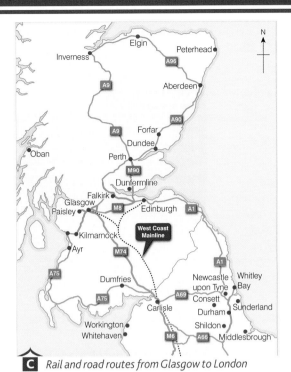

C   *Rail and road routes from Glasgow to London*

Activities

1   People choosing how to travel to a leisure and tourism destination can choose between different transport providers. Give three other transport choices they have.

2   Compare the advantages and disadvantages to a business tourist of travelling from Glasgow to London by air, with those of travelling by rail.

3   Evaluate how suitable the option of travelling by road would likely be for a business tourist.

4   Make a glossary of travel and transport key words and terms using your own words to explain the meaning of each.

Coursework activity

Evaluate how well different travel options between a UK city and an overseas leisure and tourism destination are likely to appeal to three different customer types.

Extension activity

Research and analyse the suitability of different ways of travelling between two leisure and tourism destinations in the same overseas country, for an early retired couple from the UK who are on holiday there.

Summary question

Explain the advantages and disadvantages of two different travel options to a leisure and tourism destination for two different types of customers.

Key terms

Express trains: long-distance, relatively fast trains that make only limited stops.

Trunk road: a main road that is not a motorway. In the UK these are normally A roads such as the A30.

Motorway: the top grade of road.

∞ links

www.nationalexpresseastcoast. com is the website for National Express's East Coast main-line train operations.

AQA   *Examiner's tip*

Within a category of tourist, think who they might be. Business tourists may include:

- single travellers
- groups of colleagues
- people of different adult age groups
- different ethnic and cultural groups
- people with special needs.

Group activity

What would be the range of appropriate travel options available to a single mother and her two children, aged 6 and 10, for a journey between two UK cities of your choice? Which would you recommend? Why?

Summary

For any journey to any destination for any type of customer, there is likely to be a range of travel options.

Travel options have a variety of advantages and disadvantages for different customers and journeys.

4.10 Getting there from here

A journey from home to a leisure and tourism destination can involve several different stages, perhaps using different transport modes. On the other hand, a simple door-to-door cycle or car journey may be all that is needed. This is especially likely to be true for a local trip or a journey to a domestic leisure and tourism destination.

Multistage trips may be long distance such as to an overseas leisure and tourism destination or they may simply be across a city. A long trip does not necessarily mean more stages. For example the journey made by a package holidaymaker from a suburban housing estate to a long-haul beach destination such as Phuket in Thailand, is quite likely to involve the same number of stages as a journey to a short-haul seaside resort such as Palma Nova in Mallorca, or even a journey from one side of a city to another.

An independent traveller is likely to investigate travel options using the internet. Surfing the websites of transport providers such as airlines, train operating companies, ferry operators and car hire firms allows people to compare and evaluate their own options from home. Online travel companies such as Expedia and Opodo allow easy comparison of a range of different (but not all) providers.

Objectives

Explain the advantages and disadvantages of different travel options from home to leisure and tourism destinations for different types of customers.

∞ links

www.theo2.co.uk is the O2 arena's website address.

www.traveline.org.uk is a website that gives information about public transport services.

Case study

Across London

Darren lives in Enfield, on the northern outskirts of London. Researching options for travel to the O2 arena in Greenwich, Darren began by investigating the O2's own website and discovered that the arena is very close to the North Greenwich railway station. Since he lives within walking distance of Enfield Town railway station, Darren decided to find out if he could travel conveniently by train. Making use of the **Transport for London** website Darren discovered that a four-stage journey beginning with a walk to Enfield Chase railway station, would allow him to travel to the O2 arena in about an hour, at the time he had in mind. Darren was satisfied with this way of travelling to the O2. He decided that it would be the one that he would choose.

A O2 arena

■ Sources

Sources you can use to find out about travel from your home area to leisure and tourism destinations include:

- websites of transport providers, online travel companies and travel information services provided by organisations such as the AA and **Traveline**
- road and travel atlases, maps
- travel guidebooks
- transport timetables
- tour operator brochures.

Key terms

Transport for London: the public sector organisation that oversees the provision of public transport in London.

Traveline: a partnership of transport providers and local councils, which provides information about public transport in the UK.

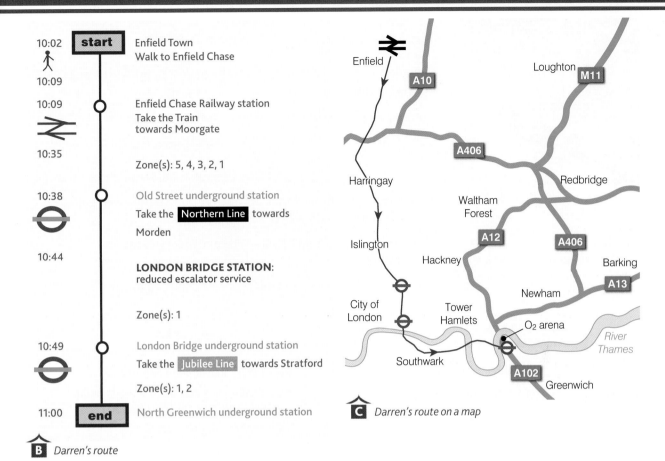

10:02	**start**	Enfield Town
	🚶	Walk to Enfield Chase
10:09		
10:09	○	Enfield Chase Railway station
	⇌	Take the Train
		towards Moorgate
10:35		
		Zone(s): 5, 4, 3, 2, 1
10:38	○	Old Street underground station
	⊖	Take the Northern Line towards
		Morden
10:44		
		LONDON BRIDGE STATION:
		reduced escalator service
		Zone(s): 1
10:49	○	London Bridge underground station
	⊖	Take the Jubilee Line towards Stratford
		Zone(s): 1, 2
11:00	**end**	North Greenwich underground station

B Darren's route

C Darren's route on a map

Activities

1 Describe Darren's route to the O2 arena, from Enfield to North Greenwich railway station.

2 a Research an alternative way for Darren to travel to the O2 from Enfield.

   b Find out and compare the current prices for making the journey in these two ways.

3 Research travel options for a journey from your home area to a UK leisure and tourism destination of your choice.

4 Describe the range of services provided by online travel companies such as Expedia.

Group activity

Why might Darren have wanted to visit the O2 arena? What type of visitor attraction is it? What leisure activities are available there? What customer types are they most suitable for?

Coursework activity

Evaluate how well different travel options for a journey from your home area to a UK leisure and tourism destination of your choice are likely to appeal to a range of different customer types.

Summary question

Explain the advantages and disadvantages for two different customer types of two different ways of travelling between your home area and one named leisure and tourism destination overseas.

Summary

Different ways of travelling to leisure and tourism destinations present a variety of advantages and disadvantages for different types of customers.

4

In this chapter you have learnt:

People travelling to leisure and tourism destinations choose between different travel options:

✔ modes and facilities   ✔ providers

✔ routes   ✔ prices

Different modes of transport include rail, road, water and air transport.

Transport facilities that may act as transport terminals or gateways include railway stations, ferry ports and airports.

Transport providers are leisure and tourism organisations that include:

✔ train operating companies   ✔ ferry operators

✔ car hire firms   ✔ airlines.

Revision quiz

1 Name three modes of transport.

2 What is a transport artery?

3 Give two examples of railway terminals.

4 What is meant by marine transport?

5 Name three London airports.

6 What is the difference between public transport and private transport?

7 What is Opodo?

AQA↗ Examination-style questions

1 Table A describes three types of people who are planning to travel to a destination.

    (a) Choose the type of transport listed below that would be best for each person:

        • car

        • full-size coach

        • train.   *(2 marks)*

    (b) Explain your choices.   *(6 marks)*

Description of three people who are planning to travel to a destination

A	B	C
A tour group of 40 elderly people	A student couple in their 20s who live a long way from the destination and do not have access to a car	A family of four, including school-age children

2 Which one of the following statements is true:

    • Eurostar trains operate from Dover.

    • Heathrow is a major London airport.

    • National Express operates trains on the West Coast main line?   *(1 mark)*

3 An elderly man in his late 70s and his friend want to travel from your local area to an overseas city destination that you have studied. Analyse and evaluate their travel options. *(9 marks)*

AQA   Make sure you revise the names of principal UK terminals and gateways.

Examiner's tip

◼ Introduction

Tourism's impact is on the environment, and on leisure and tourism destinations and the people who live in them. It is the set of effects that tourism has. Some of these effects are good but some can be harmful. Sustainability is the possibility of managing leisure and tourism now, so that possible harmful effects for the future are kept to a minimum.

◼ What is this chapter about?

This chapter is about the impact of tourism on local communities and on the environment. It is also concerned with the importance of sustainability in leisure and tourism, and with ecotourism.

Starter activity

- Think about a leisure and tourism destination you have visited or that you know about. What effects have visitors had on the place? Think about good effects and bad. Consider effects on jobs, buildings and development, the environment and on the lives of local people.

- Discuss with others what you know of the effects of travel on the environment. What can be done to limit travel's harmful effects on the atmosphere?

When tourists visit a destination they affect it. They affect its environment and they affect the local community who live there. The effects that tourists have are **tourism's impact**. Some effects are good for the environment or good for the local people. These benefits are the **positive impacts** of tourism. Other impacts of tourism are **negative impacts**. These effects of tourism are damaging to the destination's economy, to its society or to the environment.

Tourism impacts can be classified as:

- economic impacts that affect jobs, business and income in destinations
- social impacts that affect people themselves, their way of life and what facilities are available for them
- environmental impacts that affect not just the nature of the destination itself but the global environment as well.

Objectives

Understand the range of impacts tourism can have.

Classify tourism impacts as economic, social and environmental and explain what each means.

Case study

To the beach

Photo **A** shows a crowded beach in a seaside resort overseas. It is a sunny, summer scene and the sandy beach is packed with people. In the background are high-rise hotels. Such scenes are typical of seaside destinations located in tourist-receiving areas where there is mass tourism, for example in parts of the Mediterranean such as the east and south coasts of Spain, and in resorts in some long-haul areas such as Florida.

Most of the people on the beach in Photo **A** are tourists on holiday. The range of impacts of their visit to the resort is shown in Table **B**.

A *To the beach*

■ Background knowledge

Tourism is often seasonal. Seaside resorts in the UK and some overseas locations (such as around the Mediterranean Sea) attract tourists mostly in the summer. This is when the weather is most likely to be warm and sunny. The summer is the peak season (the busiest time). At other times of the year there are fewer tourists. In the winter a UK seaside destination may have hardly any tourists at all. Some facilities may close for a few weeks. Such a quiet period is described as 'out of season'.

Key terms

Tourism's impact: the set of effects that tourism has on the environment and on people who live in destinations.

Positive impacts: the benefits that tourism brings.

Negative impacts: the harm that tourism causes.

B   *Impact of tourism to the beach*

Type of impact	Direction of impact	
	Positive	Negative
Economic	Tourists spend money. This increases the income of businesses in the destination. Businesses employ more staff so there are more jobs.	Some tourists spend money in businesses that are not local to the destination. This money leaks away from the destination. Tourism is often seasonal. There are fewer jobs out of season.
Social	Leisure facilities that open in destinations because there are tourist customers, can also be used by local people. Tourism brings different people into contact with each other so they understand each other better.	Leisure facilities that cater for tourists may be too expensive for many local people to use and sometimes replace cheaper ones that they could use. Some local people (especially young people) copy tourists' behaviour instead of living their traditional ways of life.
Environmental	The environment of destinations can be improved to make it attractive for tourists. Tourists can become active in the conservation of beautiful places they visit.	Travel to destinations causes pollution.

Activities

1   Give the three types of impacts tourism can have.

2   What is the difference between positive and negative impacts?

3   Outline two impacts of tourism shown in Photo **A**.

4   Choose two impacts of tourism shown in Table **B**. Explain:

a   why each is an economic, social or environmental impact

b   how each is positive or negative.

Summary questions

1   Make a poster to illustrate the range of impacts tourism has on places and their people. Classify the types of impacts shown.

2   Explain what is meant by each of these impacts:

a   economic

b   social

c   environmental.

Group activity

Think about trips you have made to beach resorts. How much do you think your trip and others like it impact on the destination you visited? Why? How do you think you could limit the negative impacts and maximise the positive impacts of a similar trip in the future?

Summary

Tourism's impacts are the effects tourism has on the environment and on people who live in destinations.

Positive impacts are beneficial effects. Harmful effects are negative impacts.

Tourism impacts can be classified as economic, social or environmental.

5.2 Tourism's economic impact on local communities

The people who live in leisure and tourism destinations make up its host community. Members of the host community benefit economically from tourism because it provides:

- jobs
- money.

The money spent by tourists as they use destination facilities allows leisure and tourism and other businesses to prosper and grow, perhaps taking on more staff and creating more jobs. Job holders are paid wages. They spend their wages in other businesses in and around the destination and pay taxes to the local government. In this way, as Diagram A shows, the whole economy of the area benefits.

Many seaside resorts experience seasonal variations in tourism flow (see Diagram B). The number of visitors is likely to be high in the summer months (**peak or high season**), less in spring and autumn (**shoulder season**), and low in the out-of-season winter months.

Some leisure and tourism businesses located in destinations are not locally owned. The profits that destination facilities make are taken away from the destination and taxes paid on them elsewhere. This effect is called economic leakage.

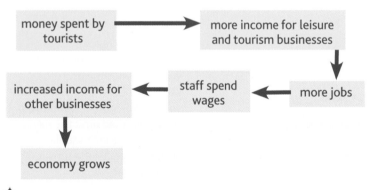

A Tourism's wider economic benefits

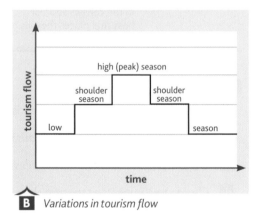

B Variations in tourism flow

Case study

Jess's family in Jamaica

Jess is 14 years old. She, her parents and her 19-year-old brother travel from their home near New York City (US) to Jamaica for a holiday every two or three years. This is because Jess's mother is originally from Jamaica and her sister (Jess's aunt) still lives there.

The family stay at the seaside resort of Negril, which is located at the west end of the island of Jamaica. Their favourite hotel is called Beaches. Beaches Negril is an all-inclusive hotel operated by the Sandals hotel chain. Although Sandals is a leisure and tourism organisation based in Florida (in the US), most of the staff employed at Beaches are Jamaican.

Jess's family is different from many of Beaches's customers because they like to visit several local restaurants outside the hotel during their holiday.

■ Background knowledge

All-inclusive hotels are large hotels that provide a wide variety of leisure and tourism facilities and activities. As well as accommodation, they typically provide:

- a choice of bars, cafés and restaurants
- child-care services
- a swimming pool or pools
- entertainment
- water sports and beach activities
- other sports facilities such as tennis courts.

C *Economic impacts of tourism*

a positive impact on a UK destination community	a negative impact on a UK destination community
a positive impact on an overseas destination community	a negative impact on an overseas destination community

Activities

1 Identify two purposes of Jess's family's visits to Jamaica.

2 Suggest and explain the positive and negative impacts of Beaches all-inclusive hotel on Negril, Jamaica.

3 Explain the likely views of the following people in Negril about all-inclusive hotels such as Beaches:

  a a young school-leaver who would like to continue living locally

  b the owner of a local restaurant.

4 How might Jess's family's behaviour help tourism's positive economic impact on Negril?

Summary questions

1 Describe one example each of the impacts shown in Table C.

2 Explain two different views about the costs and benefits of tourism to the economy of a destination community.

 links

www.sandals.co.uk is the website of the Sandals organisation.

www.negril.com and www.visitblackpool.com are websites that give destination information.

Group activity

To what extent can all-inclusive hotels:

a bring economic benefits

b be economically damaging to leisure and tourism destinations?

Coursework activity

Research and analyse different views about the costs and benefits of tourism to the economic well-being of a destination.

Summary

The host community is the population of a leisure and tourism destination.

Host communities benefit economically from tourism because of the money tourists spend, which in turn creates jobs.

Negative economic impacts of tourism include seasonal unemployment and economic leakage.

Tourism affects the ways of life of people. Destinations gain leisure facilities. Local people may make use of such leisure facilities. Their availability improves the quality of life of some local people and is a positive social impact of tourism. In addition tourists and local people can meet and learn from each other. Understanding the views and attitudes of people from different places and cultures is also a positive social impact.

However, traditional ways of life found in some destinations have been disrupted by tourism. With the arrival of tourism some local people have left farming in the countryside. Such people have often been younger adults. They have left an increasingly older population behind in the countryside.

Some long-haul destinations are in the less economically developed world. The traditional ways of life of the people who live there are interesting to many tourists. In destinations such as the Maldives (Photo **A**), for example, excursions to local villages are organised for hotel guests. Sometimes traditional dances and religious rites are performed for a tourist audience (Photo **B**). Some people view such trips and shows as a negative social impact. They see performing a religious ceremony just so tourists can watch it as devaluing its true meaning and significance.

Objectives

Describe examples of positive and negative social impacts of tourism on communities in destinations in the UK and abroad.

Explain different views about the costs and benefits of tourism to ways of life in destination communities.

Case study

Tourism Concern

Tourism Concern is a UK charity, which aims to promote tourism that benefits the local people who live in leisure and tourism destinations. Tourism Concern runs publicity campaigns and publishes books, videos and educational resources to try to achieve its aims.

In 2008 Tourism Concern was campaigning to make UK tourists aware of what it sees as the potential for tourism to make a greater positive impact in the Maldive Islands. The Maldives is a long-haul tourist destination in the Indian Ocean and receives more than 600,000 tourists a year. The country consists of over 1,000 small islands. Some of the islands have been developed for tourism. Typically, such an island is home to an all-inclusive hotel where guests enjoy beach and water sports based holidays. In 2008 there were 89 operational resorts in the Maldives.

A *The Maldives*

B *A visit to a local village*

Away from the resort islands and apart from the capital city of Male, local Maldivian people live largely in traditional fishing villages on the country's 185 inhabited islands.

According to Tourism Concern, 'Tourism is the major industry in the Maldives with the potential to stop poverty and improve local living conditions. But this is not happening. Nearly half of the local population are living on just over $1 a day. Maldivian people are suffering. Fresh fruit and vegetables go directly to tourist islands, by-passing local people. The UN recently found that over 30% of Maldivian children under the age of 5 are suffering from malnutrition'.

The Maldivian government says it is keen to keep developing tourism, to protect the environment and improve training for young Maldivians to allow them to take up jobs in the tourism industry.

Background knowledge

The countries of the world can be considered in two main groups:

- more economically developed world (MEDW) countries that have generally higher standards of living in Europe, North America, Japan and Australasia
- less economically developed world (LEDW) countries where many people are poorer in Africa, South America and the Caribbean, southern Asia and the island nations of the Indian and Pacific oceans.

Activities

1. Make a table to summarise positive and negative social impacts of tourism.

2. Why do some people think that performing traditional rituals for tourists is a negative social impact?

3. Explain the views of:
   a Tourism Concern
   b the Maldivian government about the social costs and benefits of tourism to the Maldives.

Coursework activity

Explain different views about the advantages and disadvantages of tourism to the ways of life of people in an overseas destination such as the Maldives.

Summary questions

1. Describe one example each of positive and negative social impacts of tourism:
   a overseas
   b in the UK.

2. Explain a range of different views about the disadvantages and benefits of tourism to the way of life in a destination community.

Key terms

Tourism Concern: a charity that campaigns against the negative impacts of tourism on local communities.

∞ links

www.tourismconcern.org.uk is Tourism Concern's internet address.

www.tourism.gov.mv is the Maldivian government's tourism website.

Examiner's tip

Remember that people have different views about the disadvantages and benefits of tourism and that these may differ from your own. You need to be prepared to explain both sides of the argument.

Group activity

Think about a UK leisure and tourism destination:

1. What positive social impacts does tourism bring?

2. What negative impacts of tourism are there likely to be?

Summary

Tourism affects the ways of life of people who live in destinations.

People hold different views about whether the costs of social change are too high a price to pay for the benefits that tourism can bring to host communities.

5.4 Environmental impacts

Travel and tourism affects the environment. One way this happens is through emissions. Emissions are exhaust gases that pollute the atmosphere. They add carbon to the air. The amount a traveller adds by a journey is their **carbon footprint**. Air travellers can offset their carbon footprint by paying extra for their tickets to support projects that take carbon out of the atmosphere, for example by planting trees.

Other negative impacts at destinations are:

- visual impact
- noise pollution
- waste
- loss of land from other uses
- consuming scarce resources such as water.

A *Examples of tourism's negative environmental impacts*

Tourism's negative impacts on the environment	
Type	**Impact**
Resources	land: tourism developments use land that might otherwise have been farmland or wild
	water: tourists and tourism facilities use water for drinking, washing, cooking and sanitation
	energy: fuel and power is used by travel and tourism facilities
Pollution	water: waste from tourism facilities can pollute rivers, lakes and seas
	land: rubbish generated by tourists may be dumped on the surface and in landfill sites
	noise: tourism facilities generate noise, as do transport vehicles
	visual: tourism developments can adversely affect the appearance of destinations

There are also positive impacts of tourism. Local councils in destinations may ensure that the street scene of the town is well landscaped. In 2008 Brighton's city council decided to try to make Brighton the UK's first urban biosphere reserve. Such a designation would help to promote Brighton as a '**green destination**'.

This is one way of improving the environment to encourage tourism. Equally, some tourists enjoy the environments of destinations they visit and want to be involved in conserving them. In the UK the National Trust is a voluntary sector leisure and tourism organisation that seeks to conserve landscapes and historic buildings that are important to the country's heritage.

Objectives

Describe examples of positive and negative impacts of tourism on the environment.

Explain different views about these.

∞ links

www.yha.org.uk is the Youth Hostel Association's website.

Key terms

Carbon footprint: the amount of carbon a person or activity adds to the environment.

Green destination: one which appeals to visitors because of its clean, natural environment.

The National Trust

The National Trust conserves the natural and the built environment by owning scenic landscapes and historic sites that are important to the country's heritage. The trust owns over 350 historic sites, including large country houses and industrial buildings such as mills. It cares for a wide variety of attractive landscapes that includes woods and forests, wetlands, beaches, farmland, moors and downs, islands, and nature reserves.

The National Trust is funded by money from the fees its members (3.5 million of them) pay, from donations that people make and through the profits it generates from operating some of its properties as visitor attractions. National Trust properties had 62 million visitors in 2007–8. Twelve million of these were to visitor attractions for which entry fees are charged.

An example of a National Trust property is Charlecote House in Warwickshire (see links). Charlecote House is a large Tudor country house. Inside the house there is a collection of portrait paintings. In its grounds are extensive landscaped gardens in which visitors can walk and picnic and where there is a children's play area. In 2008 admission prices at Charlecote House ranged from £1.50 for a child, just to the grounds, to £8.20 for full adult admission, including Gift Aid. Gift Aid is an extra 10% voluntary donation to the National Trust that is added to the entry price. Under the UK government's Gift Aid scheme, the National Trust can reclaim tax it pays from the money it makes by charging for admission.

 Examiner's tip

Do not confuse the National Trust with national parks. The National Trust is a voluntary organisation. It is not owned by the government. National parks are large areas of countryside that are protected by law.

Group activity

Can tourism really have a net positive impact on the environment? Why (or why not)? What more could be done?

Activities

1. Outline three ways in which tourism development can damage the environment.

2. Describe how the National Trust tries to make a positive environmental impact.

Extension activity

Research how the Youth Hostel Association (YHA) deals with environmental issues. To what extent do you think the YHA has a positive impact on the environment?

Coursework activity

For one overseas destination, explain the relative impacts on the environment of two different ways to travel there from the UK.

Summary

Tourism has positive and negative impacts on the environment.

Travel and transport can lead to negative environmental impacts, for example through aircraft emissions.

The National Trust is a UK leisure and tourism organisation that seeks to make positive environmental impacts.

Summary questions

1. Describe one example each of the positive and negative impacts of tourism on the environment.

2. Suggest and explain two different views about whether a seaside resort like Brighton can be a 'green destination'.

5.5 Sustainability matters

Sustainability is very important to leisure and tourism, not just in the UK but internationally as well. Sustainability in leisure and tourism means meeting the needs of today's customers while not spoiling the future for others. Some examples of sustainable behaviour in leisure and tourism are:

- reducing carbon emissions
- using renewable energy and conserving energy
- hotels using locally sourced food
- employing local staff and using local suppliers
- recycling and reducing waste
- limiting visitor numbers.

Behaving sustainably minimises the negative impacts of leisure and tourism. It helps to protect the future of the environment and of destinations and their people. This is important for the economic future of destinations. People will not want to visit places that have been spoilt by tourism's negative impacts in the past.

Sustainable development in the leisure and tourism industry is about making changes that improve activities and facilities for customers in ways that minimise negative impacts – this means in ways that protect the environment and local people's ways of life for the future. Visitors will still be able to enjoy destinations and local populations' ways of life in the future.

Objectives

Explain the meaning of sustainability.

Explain why sustainability is important not just in the UK but internationally too.

Describe the aims of sustainable development.

Describe how destination changes satisfy the aims of sustainable development.

A *Sustainability matters because...*

"Conserving the nature and beauty of destinations matters because it affects the quality of life of local people and visitors, now and in the future.

Travelling in more sustainable ways matters because emissions damage the atmosphere and contribute to global warming.

Future tourists won't want to visit destinations if the environment is spoilt today. So, sustainable tourism matters because it keeps future tourist numbers high. Tourists bring money and jobs to destinations, so the economic well-being of local people in the future depends on sustainability now."

Case study

Going to the gym

How sustainable is the leisure activity of going to the gym?

Many customers of health and fitness clubs drive the few kilometres from their homes. Most health and fitness clubs provide car parks for their members. Providing such car parks meets customer demand. However, it also encourages people to travel to the facility by car. Cars emit exhaust gases, which negatively impact the environment.

B *Health and fitness club*

The pollution they cause is harmful to health, yet people go to the gym to develop their health and fitness. Having driven to the health and fitness club, customers engage in physical exercise. They may, for example, swim or run on treadmills or ride stationary cycles. Some gym activities like running and cycling can be done outside without going to the gym, where exercise machines use electricity, as do the facility's lights. The central heating and air conditioning systems of health and fitness club buildings consume more resources.

C *Examples of sustainable development*

Examples of sustainability	
UK	Overseas
Eden Project, Cornwall (Photo 5.6A) – a visitor attraction based on a conservation theme. The Eden Project aims at sustainability by encouraging visitors to use public transport, employing local staff and using locally grown food in its catering outlets. It also shows visitors how they can help to conserve the environment themselves.	Khao Sok eco-lodge, Thailand (see Photo 5.9A) – acts sustainably by buying supplies locally, including food, recycling its rubbish and paying local taxes. It also employs local people both in the lodge itself and as guides to the national park where it is located.
National Trust (see 5.4) – conserves historic and heritage buildings and attractive landscapes for the benefit of future generations, as well as for today's visitors to enjoy.	Black Sea Gardens, Bulgaria (see Photo 5.7B) – a planned tourism development that intends to be sustainable. For example cars would be banned as part of its effort not to pollute the atmosphere.

Hotel operators such as the Rezidor Park Inn hotel chain operate both in the UK and overseas. Many of their hotels promote their energy and water saving measures (see Photo 5.8C) as evidence of their sustainable approach.

Key terms

Sustainability: the ability to sustain or conserve the environment and people's ways of life into the future by minimising negative impacts.

Sustainable development: growth that is planned to minimise negative impacts on the environment and on people's lives.

Activities

1   Outline two ways in which sustainable development aims to minimise tourism's negative impacts.

2   Why is going to the gym not necessarily a sustainable leisure activity?

3   a   Find out about two changes to leisure and tourism provision in a destination you have studied.

   b   Assess the sustainability of these changes.

Think about it

Sustainable development involves minimising negative impacts so that what happens now does not significantly harm the environment and people of the future. It may not be possible to reduce negative impacts to zero. However, ensuring that they are slight has increasingly been considered to be possible in recent years. Will this be enough to protect the future?

Coursework activity

Explain the likely environmental impacts of one named leisure facility.

Group activity

How could the leisure activity of going to the gym be made more sustainable? Think about measures the gym could take, as well as those that customers could take.

AQA Examiner's tip

You need to be able to explain what sustainability is and why it is increasingly thought to be important. Work out what you would say in advance of the exam in case such a question arises.

Extension activity

Choose a leisure activity other than going to the gym. How sustainable is this activity? To what extent could it be made more sustainable, in your view?

Summary questions

1   Explain what is meant by sustainability.

2   Explain why sustainability matters.

3   a   Describe two aims of sustainable development.

   b   Describe how one example of change in a destination satisfies the aims of sustainable development.

Summary

Sustainability in leisure and tourism means operating facilities and managing activities so that they have a minimal negative impact on the environment and people's ways of life.

5.6 Sustainable development: UK

Changes in UK leisure and tourism destinations such as the development of new visitor attractions, cause tourism impacts. It is important that developments are managed sustainably so as to protect the future of the environment and the local community.

Case study

The Eden Project

The Eden Project (Photo **A**) is a large-scale built attraction in the south-west of England, which is an important tourist-receiving area in the UK. Visited by more than one million people per year, the Eden Project is located near St Austell in Cornwall (see Map **B**). Developed on the site of a disused china clay pit, the Eden Project is promoted as a 'global garden'. Large dome-shaped conservatories called 'biomes' – one of them claimed to be the largest greenhouse in the world – enclose plants from different environments around the world, creating a series of simulated environments ranging from Mediterranean, with citrus and olive trees, to the cacti of the semi-arid American south-west and rainforest plants of the tropics. Outside the 'biomes' in the grounds are crops, including tea and hops, bamboo and flowers.

Visitors can explore and learn about the variety of nature around the world. There are children's play areas, story-telling sessions, cafés and restaurants, a visitor centre and gift shop. The Story Compass is a handheld electronic **global positioning system (GPS)** device that customers can hire from the visitor centre. It shows video clips relevant to the customer's location within the Eden Project, for example when the visitor walks through one of the biomes it shows clips on how the 'biomes' were built. As well as aiming to showcase nature worldwide, the Eden Project tries to be a sustainable development itself. Ways in which it does this are by:

- educating visitors, through exhibits, events, workshops, and projects working with schools, in how they can help to conserve the environment
- promoting public transport and cycling as ways to travel to the attraction
- seeking to ensure that the Eden Project benefits the local economy
- sourcing food for its cafés and restaurants locally
- managing waste disposal carefully.

A *The Eden Project*

Objectives

Describe examples of positive and negative social impacts of tourism on communities in destinations in the UK and abroad.

Explain different views about the costs and benefits of tourism to ways of life in destination communities.

Key terms

Global positioning system (GPS): a means of accurately fixing a location on the earth's surface using a satellite signal. GPS devices can act as handheld electronic guides to visitor attractions in leisure and tourism destinations.

⃝links

www.edenproject.com is the Eden Project's internet address.

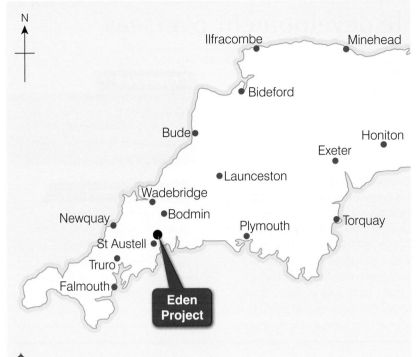

B   *The location of the Eden Project*

Activities

1   Make a poster to promote the Eden Project as a sustainable visitor attraction.

2   Outline one way in which the Eden Project uses modern technology to improve its service to customers.

Extension activity

Research different ways tourists can travel to the Eden Project and assess their relative local economic and environmental impacts.

Coursework activities

1   Suggest and explain two different views about the advantages and disadvantages of the Eden Project to the economic well-being of the local community.

2   Explain and evaluate the likely environmental impacts of the Eden Project.

Summary question

Describe how tourism development can satisfy the aims of sustainable development.

Group activity

Discuss how sustainable the Eden Project is. Think about travel to the attraction, as well as what visitors can do there.

Summary

Changes in destinations cause impacts.

Changes that satisfy the aims of sustainable development minimise negative impacts.

The Eden Project is an example of a UK tourism development that tries to satisfy the aims of sustainable development.

Sustainability in leisure and tourism is important in overseas destinations, as well as those in the UK. Sustainability matters to:

- local people
- tourists
- leisure and tourism organisations.

Sustainable tourism developments minimise negative impacts on the environment so that destinations remain pleasant places to live and work, as well as to visit. Destinations that are developed sustainably will have sufficient resources in the future so that local ways of life and tourism can keep going. In recent years, tourists have become increasingly aware of the potential negative impacts of their travel. Many want to play their part in keeping negative impacts as low as possible. Leisure and tourism organisations, including airlines, hotel accommodation providers and tour operators, are aware of this. As a result, they promote sustainable leisure and tourism products/services.

Objectives

Explain what sustainability is and why it is important in leisure and tourism internationally.

AQA Examiner's tip

People can have different views about whether a tourism development is sustainable or not. You may have your own. In an exam you should be able to give both points of view even if you disagree.

Case study

Black Sea Gardens, Karadere, Bulgaria

Karadere is in Bulgaria. It is on the Black Sea coast, in the north-east of the country (Map A). Karadere's beach has traditionally attracted domestic tourists in Bulgaria, for camping holidays.

A   *The location of Karadere, Bulgaria*

B   *Black Sea Gardens*

In 2008 a major tourism development was proposed for Karadere (Diagram **B**) to build a beach resort consisting of five villages grouped around leisure facilities, including a **marina**. The whole development is called Black Sea Gardens. Sustainability has been considered in its planning.

The use of local building materials is one sustainable aspect of the project. Black Sea Gardens is intended to be Bulgaria's first **carbon-neutral resort**. Conventional cars will be excluded. Instead electric cars and shuttle buses will provide transport within the destination.

However, the proposal has attracted strong local opposition (Cartoon **C**). Opponents say that Black Sea Gardens will:

- damage one of the few undeveloped stretches of the Black Sea coast
- destroy wildlife habitats and reduce local **biodiversity**
- spoil a traditional and natural leisure and tourism destination for local people.

D   *Recent tourism development on Bulgaria's Black Sea coast*

"Karadere is a magnet for those wishing to spend time away from civilisation and to enjoy nature, but soon it will be lost forever and we'll only realise the consequences once it's too late."

C   *Biliana's view*

Key terms

Marina: a harbour used for yachts and other pleasure craft.

Carbon-neutral resort: does not add net carbon to the atmosphere.

Biodiversity: the variety of species.

▇ Background knowledge

Recently the Black Sea coast of Bulgaria has seen a boom in tourism development. Much of the 350km shoreline has been built up with resorts such as Sunny Beach and Golden Sands (Photo **D**), attracting inbound tourists from western European countries, including the UK.

∞ links

www.guardian.co.uk/travel/bulgaria is an online newspaper feature about travel to Bulgaria.

Activity

Design a poster to promote Black Sea Gardens Karadere as a sustainable leisure and tourism destination.

Summary questions

1   What is sustainability in leisure and tourism?

2   Why is sustainability important in leisure and tourism?

Summary

Sustainability in leisure and tourism matters overseas, as well as in the UK.

People's views vary about how sustainable some tourism developments are.

5.8 Responsible tourism

Responsible tourism is visiting destinations in ways that harm the environment and local people as little as possible. Tourism that is responsible is therefore sustainable. Responsible tourists act in destinations in ways that maximise the positive impacts of tourism. For example UK visitors to long-haul Less Economically Developed World (LEDW) destinations can act responsibly by buying products and services directly from local people. In this way they are passing the economic benefit of tourism straight to members of the host community.

Objectives

Explain what responsible tourism is.

Assess how well examples of responsible tourism recognise similarities and differences of attitudes and cultures between visitors and members of destination host communities.

Case study

Negril, Jamaica

Jess, a 14-year-old girl, and her family, like to holiday at Beaches, which is an all-inclusive hotel in Negril, a seaside destination in Jamaica (see 5.2). Felix, Jess's father, believes that their family holiday will benefit local people more if some of the family's spending money goes to locally owned leisure and tourism businesses (Photo **B**).

Beach vendors (Photo **A**) walk along the shore selling goods such as local craft products and CDs of Jamaican music to tourists on the beach. Felix likes to buy from 'the guys on the beach' because he feels he is behaving as a responsible tourist and benefiting local people. The hotel management organises weekly markets in the grounds of Beaches. Local people sell craft products that include carvings, paintings and printed T-shirts at these markets.

Few of the guests staying at Beaches leave the hotel compound other than on organised excursions. The hotel management promotes the weekly craft market as a responsible tourism event.

Beaches all-inclusive hotel has its own gift shop. The shop sells a range of Jamaican, as well as imported, goods. Jamaican products include craft products similar to those sold on the beach and at the weekly market by the vendors. Beach vendors work in the informal economy. The gift shop staff, like most of the hotel's employees, are local people who have formal contracts of employment with the hotel.

A *Jah, a beach vendor*

In a destination such as Negril local people have a range of attitudes towards tourism. Some will favour it because of the jobs and income it brings. Employees of leisure and tourism organisations, and people such as beach vendors who work in the informal economy, are likely to welcome tourism. However, others, often older people, may regret the loss of traditional ways of life or, for cultural reasons, object to the noisy behaviour and informal dress of some tourists.

Leisure and tourism organisations can encourage responsible tourism behaviour by their customers (see Diagram C).

B *Locally owned tourist businesses, Negril*

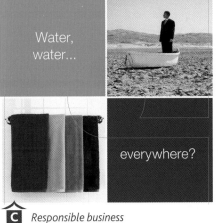

Water, water...

everywhere?

If you would like your used towels replaced, please leave them on the floor in the bath area.

Towels you have hung up to dry will be left for you to re-use.

As part of our efforts to reduce our water consumption, sheets are only changed every three days or upon departure, whichever occurs first.

If you would like your bed linen changed today, please leave this card on your pillow in the morning.

Thank you. Your contribution goes towards saving up to 15 litres of water per towel or sheet.

responsible business

park inn

C *Responsible business*

Activities

1   Explain the meanings of:

a   sustainability

b   responsible tourism.

2   Describe how Jess and her family aim to be responsible tourists.

3   Assess the responsible tourism value of the Beaches weekly market.

Extension activities

1   In what ways are the terms sustainability and responsible tourism similar and different in meaning?

2   a   Research an example of responsible tourism at a destination in a More Economically Developed World country other than the UK.

b   Evaluate the extent to which it shows responsible tourism behaviour.

Group activity

What similarities and differences about responsible tourism are shown in the Beaches case study?

Coursework activity

Assess how well one example of responsible tourism recognises similarities and differences of attitudes and cultures between visitors and members of a destination's host community.

Summary question

Design a comic strip that uses examples to explain what responsible tourism is.

links

www.beachesresorts.co.uk is the gateway internet site for Beaches hotels.

AQA *Examiner's tip*

Before the exam, clarify in your own mind the meaning of each of these terms:

■   sustainability

■   responsible tourism.

Summary

Responsible tourism is behaviour that does not harm local people and the environment.

Leisure and tourism organisations, and tourists can behave responsibly by having the:

maximum possible positive impact

minimum possible negative impact on host communities and the environment.

5.9 Ecotourism

Ecotourism is a type of tourism. It is visiting a leisure and tourism destination because of the appeal of its natural environment while negatively affecting the environment as little as possible. Ecotourism is normally tourism on a small scale because mass tourism is likely to affect a destination's natural environment. Ecotourists try to be responsible tourists and to benefit the local communities they visit socially and economically.

The aims of ecotourism are to:

- help people enjoy and learn about the natural environment in leisure and tourism destinations
- conserve the natural environment of leisure and tourism destinations by minimising the negative environmental impacts of tourism
- make positive impacts that improve the environment and the lives and well-being of local people.

Background knowledge

Eco-lodges (Photo A) are small-scale ecotourism hotels or guest houses. Typically, eco-lodges are owned and run by individual people. Owners make real efforts to protect the environment by conserving natural resources and limiting waste.

Eco-lodges are also sustainable because owners benefit the local community economically and socially. They do this by buying food from local producers and by employing local staff.

Case study

Khao Sok National Park, Thailand

Khao Sok National Park is in rural Thailand – a LEDW country in south-east Asia (Map **C**). The national park takes its name from the river Sok, which flows through it. The eco-lodge in Photo **A** stands beside the river.

The national park is in a mountainous, rainforest environment. Ecotourists to Khao Sok enjoy the spectacular scenery of limestone cliffs, waterfalls and dense jungle. Apart from viewing the scenery and observing the wildlife, visitors take part in a variety of leisure activities:

- trekking in the jungle with local guides
- elephant trekking
- canoe trips
- night-time wildlife safaris
- lake tours
- tubing down the river Sok.

The owners of the Khao Sok eco-lodge practise sustainable tourism because they employ local people both in the lodge and as guides, buy all their supplies locally, including food, and pay local taxes on their profits.

A *Khao Sok eco-lodge*

One way in which guests are encouraged to behave as responsible tourists is by not feeding the animals they encounter, including gibbons, lemurs and jungle squirrels, so that they do not become dependent on human handouts, thus remaining wild.

The lodge's rubbish (plastic, paper, aluminium, glass) is recycled, and the owners help local people do the same. To reduce the spread of plastic drinking water bottles, for example, they refill local people's for half the price of a new bottle of water. They do this so as to make a positive environmental impact.

B   *Elephant trekking in Khao Sok National Park*

THAILAND

Andaman Sea

●Bangkok

●Khao Sok National Park

Phuket●

Strait of Malacca

South China Sea

N

C   *The location of Khao Sok*

∞links

www.i-to-i.com is the address of i to i (eye-to-eye), which promotes and sells ecotourism holidays based on volunteering.

Think about it

Many hotels that are not ecotourism facilities nevertheless promote themselves as responsible tourism businesses (see Photo 5.8C). Hotels like Park Inn belong to large hotel companies. Each hotel accommodates hundreds of guests per night and is a mass tourism feature.

Activities

1   Describe what is meant by:
   a   an eco-lodge
   b   mass tourism.

2   Explain why mass tourism is not ecotourism.

3   Describe how the Khao Sok eco-lodge practises or promotes:
   a   ecotourism
   b   sustainable tourism
   c   responsible tourism.

AQA   Examiner's tip

Be clear in your mind about the meanings of:
- sustainable tourism
- responsible tourism
- ecotourism.

How are they the same? How are they different?

Group activity

Discuss why the Khao Sok eco-lodge is deliberately kept as a small-scale facility and whether this is beneficial to the local community.

Coursework activity

Explain and evaluate likely impacts on the environment of:

1   travel to Khao Sok

2   the Khao Sok eco-lodge and the leisure activities that its visitors enjoy.

Summary

Ecotourism is visiting a destination to enjoy its natural environment without spoiling it.

Ecotourism is small-scale tourism, not mass tourism.

Ecotourists want to benefit the local community economically without upsetting their traditional ways of life.

Summary question

Design a poster to promote the idea of ecotourism that includes an explanation of the meaning and aims of ecotourism.

5.10 Managing impact

Like all economic activities, leisure and tourism impacts on the environment. Travel to destinations causes pollution through transport emissions and by consuming fuel resources. Leisure activities that are enjoyed by people in their own locality and while they are staying in destinations use natural resources, produce waste and lead to emissions of their own. All this is happening at a time when people and governments are very much aware of the need to conserve planet earth because people are:

- using up the world's natural resources
- polluting the land, water and air with their waste and emissions
- causing the climate to change
- damaging the habitats of other creatures
- spoiling the appeal of destinations for future visitors.

In addition to negatively affecting the environment, leisure and tourism can damage societies and the economic well-being of some people. For example the traditional ways of life of host communities can be disrupted and seasonal unemployment can result.

However, at the same time, leisure and tourism brings positive benefits for the environment and for the social and economic well-being of destination communities. As a result, the public and government increasingly think that:

a leisure and tourism should be developed but should be developed sustainably
b tourists should behave sensitively in destinations, be aware of their impact and understand that host communities may have different attitudes and cultures from their own.

Background knowledge

Greenwashing

Because ecotourism is seen as such a good thing by so many people, leisure and tourism organisations can be tempted to promote products/services as being more environmentally friendly or more sustainable than they really are. This is called greenwashing.

Examples of greenwashing are:

- hotels claiming to be eco-lodges just because they are set in the countryside
- some safaris being promoted as ecotourism even though they do not help conserve the environment.

Tourism in the natural environment is not necessarily ecotourism, responsible tourism or sustainable tourism.

Homestay

Homestay may be with a friend or relative (like Hannah's holiday) or it may be as a paying guest. Some responsible tourists to LEDW countries

Objectives

Explain why it is increasingly thought important by the public and government:

to develop leisure and tourism sustainably

that tourists behave with sensitivity towards local populations

to understand how different approaches link together to manage tourism impact.

Key terms

Homestay: accommodation in someone's home.

A *Hannah's homestay holiday in France*

see homestay as a way of directly benefiting local people. Homestay helps people learn about the lives of others in other countries at first hand.

Case study

Hannah's homestay holiday

Katie invited her friend Hannah to stay with her at her family's house in France. Katie's French house is in the countryside of Provence in southern France.

Diagram **B** shows the postcard Hannah sent home to her parents.

Dear Mum and Dad

Having a great time. The weather's really hot and sunny. The flight over here was on time and Katie's parents drove to collect us from the airport – it was about an hour's drive to their house.

We've been cycling in the lanes around here and walking in the hills nearby. You can walk up a mountain straight from the house. We picked figs and the people next door have given us grapes and apples. We've been in the car to a farmer's market, where we bought fruit and cheese from local producers.

Back next week. See you at the airport.
Love
Hannah

B   Hannah's postcard home

Activities

1 Explain what is meant by:

a greenwashing

b homestay.

2 Analyse how Hannah's homestay holiday was:

a ecotourism

b responsible tourism.

Coursework activity

1 Explain a range of different views about the advantages and disadvantages of tourism to the:

a economic well-being of destination communities

b ways of life of local people.

Summary questions

1 Explain why it is increasingly thought important by the public and by government:

a to develop leisure and tourism sustainably

b for tourists to behave with sensitivity towards local populations who may have similar or different attitudes and cultures from their own.

2 Draw a poster to illustrate how different approaches link together in managing the impact of tourism.

links

www.worldwidehomestay.com links people in over 30 different countries.

AQA   Examiner's tip

Ecotourism, responsible tourism and sustainable approaches can link together to manage tourism impacts. When they do they can help maximise the positive benefits of tourism while keeping the negative ones to a minimum.

Group activity

Is ecotourism always positive for local communities? Why might some local people in LEDW destinations welcome mass tourism instead? Can mass tourism be green?

Extension activity

This chapter includes a variety of approaches to managing tourism's impact. Make a chart to show how different approaches contribute to managing the impact of tourism.

Summary

The public and government increasingly want leisure and tourism to be sustainable.

Ecotourism, and responsible and sustainable tourism can link together to help maximise leisure and tourism's positive impacts on the environment and on local people.

5

In this chapter you have learnt:

✔ Tourism impacts affect the environment and leisure and tourism destinations. There are positive and negative impacts, as shown by the table below.

✔ Different approaches have been adopted to minimise negative impacts of tourism and maximise the positive ones. The public and government increasingly think that it is important that leisure and tourism should be sustainable.

✔ Responsible tourism and ecotourism are two approaches to managing the impact of tourism so that it is sustainable.

Revision quiz

1 Give one example of each of the following impacts of tourism:

  a positive economic   d negative social

  b negative economic   e positive environmental

  c positive social   f negative environmental.

2 What is meant by each of these:

  a sustainability   c ecotourism?

  b responsible tourism

3 What is greenwashing?

AQA Examination-style questions

Tourism's impact	
positive economic	negative economic
positive social	negative social
positive environmental	negative environmental

1   Traditional ways of life can be damaged by tourism. Which type of tourism impact is this statement referring to? Draw a ring around the correct answer:

     economic   social   environmental.   *(1 mark)*

2   Outline one way that tourism can have a negative impact on a destination.   *(2 marks)*

3   What is meant by responsible tourism?   *(2 marks)*

4   A tourist couple in their 30s want to take an ecotourism holiday in a destination you have studied. Recommend where they should go and how they should behave as responsible tourists while they are there. Justify your choices.   *(9 marks*

6 Why people use leisure and tourism facilities

Objectives

To be able to:

explain what leisure is

explain what tourism is and the main reasons for it

describe how people make use of leisure and tourism facilities.

Introduction

Leisure is all the different kinds of activities that people enjoy in their spare time. Tourism means visiting other places and includes travel to destinations, as well as the facilities there that meet people's needs. Going on holiday is both leisure and tourism because it is an enjoyable, spare time experience and because it involves travelling away from the visitor's home/work area to enjoy leisure activities at a destination that is located elsewhere.

Leisure and tourism organisations operate as businesses that promote their products/services, employ staff, deliver customer services and deal with health and safety issues.

What is this chapter about?

Chapter 6 is about the nature of both leisure and tourism – what each of them is. It is also about the reasons for tourism and about how people make use of leisure and tourism facilities in their local area, while they are travelling and in the destinations they visit.

Starter activity

- Think about what activities you do in a day other than sleeping. Some of these activities are to do with work and some with the necessities of life such as eating your usual meals, taking a shower or shopping for your daily needs. Other spare time activities that you do for fun are your leisure activities. What are they? How do they differ on weekdays, in the evenings, at weekends and during the holidays?

- Discuss with a partner why it is that people travel to places other than those where they normally live and work. To help you, think about visits that people you know about have made.

- Survey members of your class. What types of leisure and tourism facilities have they used in the last few months? What did they use them for? Make a bar chart to show your results and analyse what it shows.

People enjoy **leisure activities**. They are the fun things they do in their spare time. Watching television, reading, playing football, swimming, going to the cinema or theatre and cooking for pleasure are all examples of leisure activities.

Case study

Katie's leisure

Katie is a 15-year-old school student. During term she goes to school each day, travelling on the school bus. School is Katie's work not her leisure. School day mornings are about life's necessities – taking a shower, dressing and eating breakfast. These activities are not Katie's leisure either. Nor is the homework she does in the evenings. So, what is Katie's leisure?

During the week (Cartoon **A**) Katie attends her local youth club on Monday evenings, plays the piano most evenings, reads, watches television and uses the internet to chat with friends. These are leisure activities. On Saturdays she spends the afternoon singing, dancing and doing drama at a theatre arts club. Katie thinks of this as her main hobby. She often goes to sleepover parties at her friends' homes, usually watching a movie there. Occasionally she and her friends enjoy going to the cinema to watch a newly released film and sometimes meet up at a coffee shop in the local town centre.

On holiday Katie enjoys swimming, reading in the sun, cycling, walking and eating out in restaurants.

Key terms

Leisure activities: spare time relaxation that is fun to do. Examples include reading, swimming and going to the cinema.

Leisure tourism: visiting a destination to relax, take part in leisure activities and have fun, for example going there on holiday.

TUESDAY EVENING...

THURSDAY EVENING...

SATURDAY AFTERNOON...

SATURDAY EVENING...

A *Katie's leisure week*

Remember

Leisure activities are fun and relaxing. People go on holiday to relax and enjoy themselves. Holiday activities that are fun are just as much leisure activities as those that people enjoy at home and in their local area. Holidays are **leisure tourism** (Diagram **B**).

Heritage Golf & Spa Resort, Mauritius

Possibly the best all inclusive package in the Indian Ocean ...

* Free watersports
  Windsurfing, Sailing,
  Rowing, Pedaloes,
  Waterski, Glass bottom
  boat and Snorkelling

* Tennis courts 2 Free .
  Court surface - Hard

* Fitness club Yes. Free

* Volleyball Yes

* Bicycle rental Yes. Free

* Other activities Scuba
  Diving can be
  arranged locally

* Scuba Diving

* Snorkelling Free.

* Golf

* Heritage Golf Club

* Location On site

* Course Heritage Golf
  Club

* 18 holes, par 72

* Between
  mountain and
  sea, this
  spectacular
  international
  golf course
  is built on
  more than
  100 acres of
  land.

  Green fees
  Local charge

B   *Resort activities*

AQA *Examiner's tip*

Be prepared to describe examples of leisure activities that people do:

■ at home

■ in the local area

■ in leisure and tourism
  destinations.

Think about it

Leisure activities can be active or passive. Reading and using the internet for chat are two of Katie's passive leisure activities. Cycling and dancing are more active.

Activities

1. Draw a comic strip or make a leisure diary to show your own leisure activities.

2. Describe with examples the difference between active and passive leisure activities.

3. When are the following not leisure activities?:

   a playing football
   b cooking.

4. What is meant by leisure tourism?

Group activity

Talk about people you know from different age groups. What are their leisure activities? Which do they do most? How much leisure time do they have? To what extent do you think leisure activities depend on people's ages?

Extension activity

Interview a number of different people in your school or college to discover their leisure activities and how much time they spend on them. Graph and analyse your results.

Coursework activity

Describe the range of activities that is leisure.

Summary question

Make a poster to illustrate the variety of leisure.

Summary

Leisure is what people do in their spare time, to have fun and to relax.

People enjoy leisure activities locally and when they are on holiday.

Some leisure activities are physical in nature. Of these, some are **sports** (for example football, cricket, netball, horse racing and tennis). They are competitive. Others involve **physical recreation**. Jogging is an example of a non-competitive physical recreation.

People can enjoy sport by taking part in races, games, matches or other competitions. Alternatively people can enjoy sport by watching it. **Sports spectating** is a leisure activity but it is not a physical one – not a physical recreation. Sports participants are not necessarily engaged in leisure. A professional footballer, for example, plays football not just for fun but as a job. Professional sportsmen and women may enjoy their sports but their participation is their work not their leisure.

Case study

Edgbaston Indoor Cricket Centre

Edgbaston Indoor Cricket Centre (Photo **A**) is a sport and physical recreation leisure facility in Birmingham. It is one of Warwickshire County Cricket Club's facilities. Another is the Edgbaston cricket ground, which is Warwickshire's home ground and which hosts international cricket test matches. The indoor cricket centre provides:

A *Edgbaston Indoor Cricket Centre*

- cricket nets
- cricket coaching
- a hall for different recreational uses, including five-a-side football and dances
- birthday party and conference facilities, including a café and bar
- educational visits and guided tours
- physiotherapy provided by **partner organisation** Physiokinetic
- a cricket shop.

B *Edgbaston Indoor Cricket Centre*

⚭ links

www.edgbaston.com is the website of Edgbaston, home of Warwickshire County Cricket Club.

Key terms

Sports: organised physical leisure activities that are competitive.

Physical recreation: a physical leisure activity that participants enjoy non-competitively.

Sports spectating: watching sports events.

Partner organisation: an organisation that works with a leisure and tourism organisation to jointly provide products/ services.

Think about it

Some people enjoy physical leisure activities as competitive sports. Other people participate in the same activities just for fun. Swimming is an example of a physical leisure activity that is a sport for some participants but which is a simple, non-competitive physical recreation for others.

2009 Festival of cricket

Thursday 30th July – Monday 3rd August 2009*

Few sporting occasions match the intensity, excitment and competition of the Festival of cricket.

The Festival of cricket is well known for its electric atmosphere, especially when it comes to International cricket. 2008 had a real cliffhanger of a final day with the home team surviving a last-ditch International All-Stars fight back to complete a thrilling two-run victory.

This is now your chance to experience the thrill of this year's amazing event.

Match day hospitality includes the following:

- Personalised match day ticket
- VIP fast track entrance
- Reserved seating
- Breakfast rolls and tea/coffee on arrival
- 3 course luncheon
- Afternoon tea
- Complimentary bar (excluding spirits and champagne)
- Hostess service
- Commemorative match day programme and scorecard

Demand is very high to experience our first class Corporate hospitality facilities and we urge you to call 0845 711 1177 to book your places now.

*All dates are provisional and subject to change

 C *Festival of cricket*

Activities

1   Use examples to explain what is meant by:

a   sports participation

b   sports spectating

c   physical recreation.

2   Describe how people make use of the Edgbaston Indoor Cricket Centre for leisure activities.

3   a   Find out about sports spectating opportunities in your local area next week.

 b   Make a flyer or other advertisement to promote one of them.

Summary question

Outline a variety of leisure activities that is:

a   sports

b   physical recreation.

Coursework activity

Make a guide to sports and physical recreation facilities in your local area.

Group activity

To what extent are sports participation, sports spectating and physical recreation leisure activities provided for separately?

Extension activity

Research online and analyse the range of leisure activities provided by Warwickshire County Cricket Club other than at Edgbaston Indoor Cricket Centre.

Summary

Physical leisure activities include physical recreation and sports participation.

Watching sport (sports spectating) is also a leisure activity but not a physical one.

Entertainment facilities and visitor attractions are two types of leisure facilities. Theatres and cinemas are entertainment facilities while museums and historic sites are visitor attractions.

Objectives

Describe one overseas example of a ski/snowsports resort.

Case study

Guildford

Guildford is a city in Surrey in southern England. Among Guildford's leisure facilities are the Spectrum leisure complex, the Odeon cinema, two theatres, and visitor attractions.

The Odeon in Guildford is a multiplex cinema. It has nine screens, which means that it can show a range of different films to suit different customer types. During the week beginning Wednesday 29 October 2008 the Odeon was showing 15 different films ranging from U to 18 in classification. They included children's cartoons, adult horror, and musical and action films. A particular highlight was the then newly released James Bond movie *Quantum of Solace*.

Guildford's two theatres are the Electric Theatre and the Yvonne Arnaud Theatre. The Electric Theatre (Photo **A**) is so-called because it is housed in a former electricity power station. It began to operate as a theatre in 1997 and is managed by Guildford Borough Council, which also provides **funding**. The theatre's main role is to be a professionally run facility for local amateur theatre groups to stage shows. However, professional artists, including stand-up comedians, also perform there when they are on tour around the country. Like many leisure facilities the theatre provides extra leisure facilities beyond its main function such as a temporary ice skating rink outside the Electric Theatre.

Guildford Castle, a historic site (Photo **B**), and Guildford Museum, are visitor attractions in the town.

Key terms

Entertainment facilities: leisure facilities such as cinemas and theatres where customers enjoy shows.

Funding: financing for a leisure and tourism facility. Sources of funding may be, for example, public, from ticket sales or from voluntary donations.

Remember

Visitor attraction types are:

- natural attractions
- historic sites
- theme parks
- major sports/entertainment venues
- built attractions.

Some or all of these may be found in your local area.

A *Electric Theatre, Guildford*

B *Guildford Castle*

C   *Visitor opinion of attractions in Guildford, 2007*

	Guildford 2000	Guildford 2003	Guildford 2007	All historic towns	All destinations
Mean	4.75	4.19	4.10	4.31	4.15
Very good	80%	39%	30%	45% (max 74%)	39% (max 74%)
Good	16%	44%	52%	43%	42%
Average	3%	14%	16%	10%	16%
Poor	1%	3%	2%	2%	3%
Very poor	_	_	_	_ (max 2%)	1% (max 3%)

Tourism South East

Activities

1   Describe why people use entertainment facilities and visitor attractions.

2   a   Find out what films the Odeon Guildford is showing this week.

   b   Compare the range of films currently on show with that described in the case study.

3   a   Research the leisure activities available at either Guildford Castle or Guildford Museum.

   b   Design a piece of promotional material for the facility you have researched.

4   Comment on what Table C tells you about what visitors to Guildford thought of the city's attractions and places to visit.

∞ links

www.guildford.gov.uk/ guildfordweb/tourism is Guildford Borough Council's official welcome website.

www.yvonne-arnaud.co.uk is the internet address for Guildford's Yvonne Arnaud Theatre.

> **AQA** *Examiner's tip*
>
> Chapter 3 has a section about visitor attractions that you can draw on.

Group activity

Research and discuss the range of entertainment facilities and visitor attractions provided in your local area. Is it a broad range? Why/why not? How well does it cater for people of different ages?

Coursework activity

Describe how people make use of entertainment facilities and visitor attractions in your local area.

Summary question

Outline a variety of examples of leisure activities that involves:

a   using entertainment facilities

b   visiting attractions.

Summary

Entertainment facilities and visitor attractions are types of leisure facilities.

Towns, cities and other localities provide a range of such facilities for local people and for visitors.

Entertainment facilities include cinemas and theatres.

Visitor attractions include historic sites and museums.

6.4 Eating out and socialising

Eating an everyday meal at home is not a leisure activity. This is because people have to eat to live whereas leisure is what they do to have fun beyond the necessities of life. However, going out for a meal with friends or family is leisure because it is a fun thing that people do not have to do. Cafés, restaurants and pubs are leisure facilities that provide for the leisure activity of eating out.

Socialising is a leisure activity that can centre around enjoying a meal out, but need not. Simply chatting with friends or other people is a leisure activity that many enjoy. Public house bars, coffee shops and youth centres are examples of leisure facilities that provide for the leisure activity of socialising without customers needing to eat a meal.

Objectives

To be able to outline examples of leisure activities that involve eating out and socialising.

Key terms

Socialising: going out of the home to spend leisure time with other people.

Community centre: a building in a community that consists mainly of rooms that can be hired for leisure activities.

Case study

Bishopton

Bishopton is a village in the north of England. Opportunities for eating out are provided by the village's two pubs – the Blue Bell (Photo **A**) and the Talbot Inn (Photo **B**). The village hall (Photo **C**) acts as the village **community centre**. Socialising activities held there include the weekly youth club, Brownies and the African drum circle (Figure **D**).

B Talbot Inn, Bishopton

A Blue Bell, Bishopton

C Bishopton village hall

D   Drum circle

"The best time I've had in ages"

"So relaxing, I would recommend this to anyone"

"It's been absolutely COOL!!"

"Absolutely, totally, utterly fantastic family fun!!!"

"I've thoroughly enjoyed myself"

"That was drumtastic!"

Positive Beats wants to share their joy of drum circles with everyone!

Drumming together is fun, creative, inspiring, empowering and motivating. It is light-hearted exercise, promotes health and well-being and a sense of community.

It is described as the new approach for team building and has been proven to have benefits at both psychological and physical levels.

E   Chinatown

Activities

1   Outline the leisure activities of:

a   eating out

b   socialising.

2   a   Describe with examples the provision of eating out and socialising facilities in Bishopton.

b   Compare the range of provision in Bishopton with that of your locality.

Coursework activity

Describe the range of eating out facilities in a city destination.

Group activity

Discuss the provision of eating out and socialising facilities in your local area. How well does it cater for customers of different ethnic and cultural backgrounds?

Extension activity

Chinatown (Photo E) is the part of a town/city where people of Chinese ethnicity and culture come together to socialise and to run businesses, including leisure and tourism facilities such as restaurants. Many UK cities have Chinatowns, for example Birmingham.

Research and analyse the range of eating out and socialising facilities provided for people of different ethnic and cultural backgrounds in one UK town/city.

Summary

Eating out and socialising are leisure activities.

The leisure and tourism industry provides a variety of facilities for different people to enjoy such leisure activities.

Summary question

Make a poster to illustrate a variety of examples of leisure activities that involves eating out and socialising.

6.5 Home-based and special-interest leisure activities

Home-based leisure activities are leisure activities that people enjoy at home. Examples are:

- reading for pleasure
- computer gaming
- listening to music
- using the internet
- gardening
- cooking for enjoyment.

The leisure and tourism industry provides facilities that support home-based leisure activities. For example libraries and bookshops provide products/services that help people read for pleasure at home.

Special-interest leisure activities relate to pastimes, hobbies and leisure pursuits that play a key role in the leisure lives of participants. Examples of special-interest leisure activities are:

- birdwatching
- angling.

Case study

Home-based leisure

Facilities that support home-based leisure (Table **A**) are found in any locality in the UK. They are the facilities that are provided by the leisure and tourism industry to support people's enjoyment of home-based leisure activities. Leisure and tourism organisations also support home-based leisure online.

A *Home-based leisure facilities*

Home-based leisure activity	Leisure facilities
Reading for pleasure	Libraries Bookshops
Computer gaming	Computer game shops
Listening to music	Libraries Music stores
Using the internet	Computer shops
Gardening	Garden centres and plant nurseries

Objectives

To be able to outline examples of leisure activities that are:

- home based
- special interest.

Key terms

Home-based leisure: spare time activities people take part in at home.

Special-interest leisure: spare time activities people take part in as a hobby or pastime.

links

www.rspb.org.uk is the web address of the Royal Society for the Protection of Birds (RSPB).

Think about it

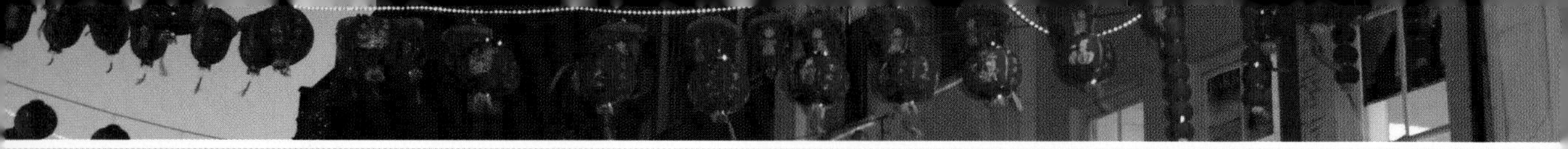

Home-based and special-interest activities like all leisure activities have participants who have special needs. The British Disabled Angling Association (BDAA) supports anglers who have special needs (Photo **B**).

B   *A disabled angler*

Activities

1   Explain the difference in meaning between home-based and special-interest leisure.

2   a   Survey people in your class. What are their home-based and special-interest leisure activities?

   b   Make a graph of your results and analyse your findings.

3   a   Find out what the BDAA does to support anglers with special needs.

   b   Write a newspaper article about the BDAA's work.

Group activity

What special-interest leisure activities is the group aware of? Which, if any, can be classified as leisure activities other than special interest? How can truly special-interest activities be classified further? Record your thoughts on a flip chart or A3 piece of paper and report back to the class.

Extension activity

Research the range of facilities that supports home-based leisure in your local area. Evaluate how well it meets the needs of:

a   teenagers

b   retired people.

Coursework activity

Describe the range of facilities in a leisure and tourism destination that supports special-interest leisure activities.

Summary question

Outline a variety of examples of leisure activities that are:

a   home-based

b   special-interest.

Summary

Home-based and special-interest leisure are two types of leisure activities.

Leisure and tourism organisations support home-based leisure through local facilities and online.

Special-interest and other leisure activities are enjoyed by all types of people, including those who have special needs.

Tourists travel away from the place where they usually live and work to a leisure and tourism destination that is located somewhere else. The three main reasons why they do this are for:

- leisure (such as going on holiday)
- business
- visiting friends and relatives.

Many tourists stay away from home overnight. Some definitions of tourism insist that it must involve at least one night away. At the same time, tourism is a temporary movement. Tourists intend to return home after their trip is over. This distinguishes tourism from **migration**, which is people moving away from home to live somewhere else permanently.

Objectives

To be able to explain what tourism is.

Key terms

Migration: the permanent movement of people away from their home area.

Case study

Making a weekend of it

Dave and Steve are old friends who work for the same organisation. Dave lives in Lancashire in north-west England and Steve lives in north-east England. Once or twice a year either Steve or Dave travels with his family across the Pennines to spend the weekend together (Map **A**). Travelling by car the journey takes about four hours. Sometimes, usually in the school holidays, they meet up at a leisure and tourism destination that is located about halfway between their homes. Hawes and Harrogate (Photo **B**) are two destinations where they have met previously.

Unusually, in November Dave and Steve both need to attend the same business meeting in London on a Saturday. They plan to take their families with them and spend the weekend at a hotel there. The meeting will take a few hours on Saturday, and the rest of the time Dave and Steve can be at leisure with their families.

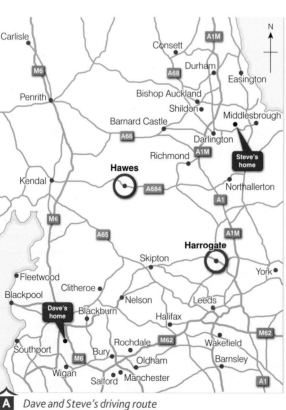

A Dave and Steve's driving route

⬭⬭ links

www.yorkshiredales.org is a website that gives tourist information about the Yorkshire Dales National Park and Harrogate.

Remember

Leisure activities can be enjoyed locally or in a destination. Tourism must involve people being away from their home area.

Think about it

Tourism means going away from home and coming back again. Tourists may be away for a short time or for a longer period. Business tourists often take trips of a few days. A family's main annual holiday is more likely to be a week or two but short-break second and third holidays have become more popular recently.

B *Harrogate*

Activities

1   List four key characteristics of tourism.

2   Assess the extent to which Dave and Steve's trips are:
   a   leisure tourism
   b   business tourism
   c   visiting friends and relatives.

Extension activity

Choose one of the following destinations: Hawes, Harrogate or London.

a   Research three Sunday morning leisure activities that would suit Dave and Steve and their families (wives and two teenagers) in your chosen destination.

b   Justify your choices.

Group activity

Talk about the tourism experiences that you, and your friends and families have had. Where have you travelled? Why did you go there?

Coursework activity

Describe how people make use of leisure and tourism facilities in one UK destination.

Summary questions

1   Explain what tourism is clearly and carefully. Use examples to illustrate your explanation.

2   a   How is tourism different from leisure?
    b   How different is it?

Summary

Tourism is visiting other places.

Leisure can be local but tourism has to be outside the home area.

Tourists often stay overnight and always intend to return home.

Tourism is temporary.

Leisure tourists visit destinations in their spare time. Leisure tourism is undertaken for fun and enjoyment. It includes going on holiday and visiting tourism attractions.

VFR means visiting friends and relatives. It is a reason for tourism and means travelling to another place to spend time with family members or other people the tourist already knows.

Case study

Brigitte and Michel

Brigitte and Michel are a middle-aged French couple who live in a village about an hour's car journey from Paris. Every year they travel to Bandol (Photo **A**), a seaside resort on the Mediterranean coast of France, for their summer holiday. Last year in Bandol they met another couple (Martine and Vicent) of similar age who live in the southern French countryside.

A   *Bandol*

Michel and Brigitte later invited Martine and Vicent to stay with them in their house near Paris and promised to take them into the city for a day's sightseeing. Martine and Vicent particularly wanted to include a boat trip on the Seine in their day visit to the city (Photo **B**).

▨ Background knowledge

Many French people stay in France for their holidays because of the variety of different tourist-receiving areas there.

Paris is one of the most important city destinations in the world. Other French destinations popular with French domestic tourists and with inbound tourists from other countries include:

- coastal regions of France where beach (or seaside) destinations such as Bandol are located. La Rochelle on the Atlantic west coast, and the glamorous resorts of the French Riviera like St Tropez and Cannes, are other such destinations
- mountain ranges such as the Alps and the Pyrenees, which are popular for their skiing and snowsports in winter, attractive scenery and leisure activities such as trekking and rock climbing in the summer
- countryside areas such as the Dordogne and Provence, which attract tourists for their scenery, traditional rural life and outdoor leisure activities such as cycling and horse riding.

Objectives

To be able to explain:

leisure tourism

visiting friends and relatives (VFR).

Key terms

VFR: going away from home to stay with friends and relatives.

∞ **links**

www.worldtravelguide.net/beach_resort/15/beach_resort_guide/Europe/Bandol.html is a webpage that gives some information about Bandol.

Remember

Tourism can be:

- inbound – into a country
- outbound – out of a country
- domestic – within a country.

Martine and Vicent's trips to Bandol and Paris are both domestic tourism.

B *Bateaux mouches, Paris*

Activities

1   Explain how the trips made by Brigitte and Michel and by Martine and Vicent illustrate:

  a   leisure tourism

  b   VFR.

2   Give one example each of:

  a   inbound tourism (travelling into a country to visit a leisure and tourism destination)

  b   outbound tourism (travelling out of a country to visit a leisure and tourism destination).

Summary question

Explain why each of the following is one of the main reasons for tourism:

a   leisure

b   VFR.

Coursework activity

Discuss the leisure and tourism facilities a VFR tourist to your local area would most likely use.

Group activity

Discuss examples of VFR tourism the group has made or know of. Where were these trips to? Who were they to visit? Were they inbound, outbound or domestic trips?

Extension activity

Research and explain a programme for a day trip to Paris that would suit Martine and Vicent.

Summary

Leisure and VFR are two of the three main reasons for tourism.

6.8 Business tourism

People who travel away from home and from where they normally work for work-related reasons are business tourists. Examples of **business tourism** are:

- attending a meeting or conference
- touring around an area to visit several customers in order to sell products/services
- visiting a branch factory/office project elsewhere in the country or overseas.

Business tourism is very important. Leisure and tourism organisations are keen to attract business tourist customers whose companies are often willing to pay premium prices for products/services that will help their employees do their business better. Travel can be a stressful and tiring experience. Companies do not want their employees to arrive at important meetings stressed and tired. So they are prepared to pay a little more for staff to have more comfortable travel and accommodation facilities. Providers such as airlines often offer **business class** travel, which is more comfortable than standard or economy class while avoiding the additional expense of more luxurious first class.

Hotel providers such as Rezidor Park Inns (Photos **B** and **C**) offer business guests business-friendly bedrooms, which offer more space and facilities than standard rooms.

Key terms

Business tourism: being away from the usual home/work area for work-related reasons.

Business class: a more comfortable and expensive class than economy.

Corporate hospitality: companies entertaining customers, for example by organising tickets and a party at a major sports event.

Case study

Traveller's Friend

Traveller's Friend is an online travel agent (Diagram **A**) specialising in business tourism. Traveller's Friend:

- acts as a consultancy to advise companies about business tourism
- arranges travel for business tourists, including airline flights, Eurostar and other rail journeys, and car hire
- advises on the range of hotels and conference venues available and makes bookings
- arranges **corporate hospitality**, including theatre and event tickets
- makes discount holiday bookings for organisations' business customers
- arranges insurance.

The Travellers' Friend

Welcome

A very big welcome to the Travellers' Friend web site. As one of the UK's leading Corporate Travel Agents with many years experience in the business travel industry, our experienced travel consultants are ideally placed to handle our clients' full business travel management requirements, from consultancy through to business travel reservations and associated services.

A Traveller's Friend

∞ links

www.travellersfriend.com is the homepage address of Traveller's Friend.

www.rezidorparkinn.com is the internet address for Rezidor Park Inns.

Think about it

Leisure and tourism providers operate as businesses so their intention is to make money. They offer higher-class accommodation to business travellers to help make more money. They know that employers usually pay business tourists' expenses. Employers want an economical but comfortable, relaxing standard for their staff. They are often prepared to pay more than the standard class price.

Rooms

The park Inn London, Russell Square offers a wide variety of guest rooms from standard and Business Friendly rooms to one and two bedroom suites which are ideal for long stays and families on a city break.

Standard rooms:
- Work desk
- Wireless high-speed Internet access
- Coffee & tea-making facilities
- Free access to the gym
- Plasma TV with 40 Pay TV movies and Internet
- Electronic laptop-sized safe
- Voice mail
- Same day dry cleaning/laundry service
- Hair dryer
- Individual climate control
- Iron and ironing board

Business Friendly rooms feature all the amenities found in standard guest rooms including the following:
- Extra large Plasma TV screen
- Direct-dial telephone
- Fridge
- Fluffy bathrobe and slippers
- Complimentary Full English breakfast
- Complimentary bottled water

C   *Park Inn, Russell Square, London*

B   *Rooms at Park Inn*

Activities

1   Outline two examples of business tourism.

2   a   Explain what is meant by: i premium price ii discount.

    b   Outline how both are used by business tourism providers.

3   Make a table to summarise three different travel classes.

4   Explain why business tourism is important to leisure and tourism organisations.

Extension activity

Research a range of business class travel options for a business tourist who works for a firm in London and needs to travel to a conference in Paris.

Summary question

Explain the reasons for business tourism.

Group activity

Should leisure and tourism organisations provide different classes of accommodation? Would it be better to have just one class? Would it be cheaper? Why are there different classes? Who benefits?

Summary

Business tourists stay away from home for work-related reasons such as attending meetings or conferences.

Coursework activity

Describe the facilities provided for business tourism in a large UK seaside resort.

Business tourists are often prepared to pay a premium price for better than standard class accommodation.

Why do people use leisure and tourism facilities?

People use leisure and tourism facilities for different reasons:

- In their local area people use leisure and tourism facilities in order to enjoy their leisure activities. The facilities they use depend on what is available and on what their leisure activities are. They may, for example, use a leisure centre to swim and keep fit and a local library to support their home-based activity of reading for pleasure. These are facilities that are provided by the leisure and tourism industry with the local **leisure market** in mind.

- Other facilities in a locality may be provided for the **tourism market** but may still be used by local people. In a village in a UK national park, for instance, the local hotel may see its main role as being to provide accommodation and meals for tourists but local people may book a function room for a social occasion such as a marriage or birthday party.

- People are tourists when they visit leisure and tourism destinations. The leisure and tourism facilities they use there provide for their needs as tourists, for example visitor attractions. People also need to use leisure and tourism facilities in order to reach leisure and tourism destinations. Airports and railway stations are such examples.

Objectives

Describe how people make use of leisure and tourism facilities to:

support and help them enjoy their leisure activities

travel to leisure and tourism destinations

provide for their needs as tourists.

Key terms

Leisure market: the set of customers of leisure and tourism organisations who are local.

Tourism market: the set of customers of leisure and tourism organisations who have travelled to a destination.

Case study

Dorothy

Dorothy is a retired widow. She cannot drive so she travels by bus to her local town centre. Dorothy's leisure activities in the town centre are socialising with friends, dancing and occasional visits to the town's theatre to see a show, for example the Christmas pantomime. She uses cafés to meet friends for coffee and a local hall that people can hire, to attend her afternoon dance club. Dorothy also uses leisure and tourism facilities when she goes on holiday to the seaside or on coach trips organised by the over-60s club to which she belongs. Table **A** shows the types of facilities Dorothy uses and why.

A Dorothy's leisure facilities

Facility type	Dorothy's leisure activity
Cafés	Eating out and socialising
Hall hired by dance club	Dancing
Theatre	Watching stage shows
Hotel	Holiday: sleeping, eating in the restaurant, being entertained
Visitor attractions	Sightseeing
Bus and coach	Local travelling and touring

AQA Examiner's tip

Customer types you need to think about are:

- single people
- couples
- families with children
- groups travelling together
- different age groups
- different ethnic and cultural groups
- people with special needs.

Think about it

Over-60s clubs are examples of voluntary organisations. They arrange visits and events for their members on a non-profit basis. For local coach companies and the visitor attractions to which they take groups, clubs and societies are important customer types.

Find a coach company

Select an Area, city, port or airport by clicking on the map to find a quality coach company.

Featured coach company

BUZZLINES

We take pride in a job well done and firmly believe that we offer levels of customer care found only in a family business. With modern, high specification vehicles and friendly and well-trained drivers, Buzzlines really are different.

B *Guild of British Coach Operators website*

Activities

1 Describe the uses that Dorothy makes of leisure and tourism facilities:

a for local leisure

b as a tourist.

2 Compare the ways Dorothy uses leisure and tourism facilities with those of a person you know.

Group activity

Survey a variety of different types of people to find out the use they make of leisure and tourism facilities. Discuss your findings.

Coursework activity

Describe the uses people make of leisure and tourism facilities in a small rural locality or destination.

Summary question

Describe how people make use of leisure and tourism facilities to:

a support and help them enjoy their leisure activities

b travel to leisure and tourism destinations

c provide for their needs as tourists.

∞links

www.coach-tours.co.uk is the website of the Guild of British Coach Operators (Diagram **B**).

Extension activity

Recommend and justify a programme for a one-day coach trip for an over-60s club from your local area.

Summary

People use leisure and tourism facilities for different reasons. These are to:

support and help them enjoy their leisure activities

travel to leisure and tourism destinations

provide for their needs as tourists.

6.10 Leisure and tourism: the same or different?

'Leisure' and 'tourism': are they the same thing or are they different? Jugjit and Leon discuss this question in Cartoon **A**.

Some leisure activities can be tourism as well. People's special-interest activities are common examples of this. Keen bird watchers, golfers and **ramblers**, for instance, may enjoy their favourite activity in their home area (leisure) so much that they make it the focus of a **special-interest holiday**.

> Leisure's about people having fun. Holidays are fun and going away's tourism, so tourism must be the same as leisure.

> Not quite. People can enjoy leisure activities locally – they don't have to go away and sometimes people go away as business tourists. Business tourism isn't leisure.

A *Jugjit and Leon discuss*

Case study

A night at the opera

A visit to the Grand Theatre in Leeds (Photo **B**) to watch a performance by Opera North can be both leisure and tourism. Watching the opera is an entertainment, which is a leisure activity. Members of the audience may enjoy a drink or meal as part of their evening out even if they are local to Leeds.

Some members of the audience are likely to have travelled to Leeds from another part of the country and some of them may have decided to spend the night in a hotel. Such visitors are engaged in leisure activities as tourists.

Objectives

Understand how leisure and tourism fit together.

⊙⊙ **links**

www.operanorth.co.uk is the website for Opera North.

Key terms

Ramblers: people who walk in the countryside as a leisure activity.

Special-interest holiday: one whose main focus is a particular leisure activity.

Remember

A night at the opera is a leisure activity involving visiting an entertainment facility (a theatre). Other leisure activities are:

- taking part in and watching sport
- physical recreation
- eating out and socialising
- visiting attractions
- home-based leisure activities
- special-interest activities.

Think about it

People can do any type of leisure activity when away from home as tourists. Reading for pleasure is a home-based leisure activity but people also read when they go away. So home-based leisure activities can be enjoyed outside people's homes and local areas.

Special-interest activities that are hobbies are often enjoyed at home. People take part in them elsewhere in the local area too, as well as when away on holiday.

B   *Grand Theatre, Leeds*

AQA   *Examiner's tip*

Many leisure and tourism organisations are exactly that. They provide products/services to people who enjoy local leisure and to people who are tourists. Such organisations are not just leisure organisations nor are they simply tourism organisations.

Activities

1   Explain why Jugjit and Leon think that leisure and tourism:

a   have different meanings

b   are nearly the same.

2   Explain how a visit to see an Opera North performance at the Grand Theatre in Leeds can be both a leisure and a tourism activity.

3   Give one example each of a leisure activity that is not tourism, and a tourism activity that is not leisure.

Group activity

Discuss examples of organisations in your local area that have tourist, as well as local customers. Are there many? Why/why not? Are the tourists mainly leisure, business or VFR tourists? Are the tourists causing positive or negative impacts?

Extension activity

Suggest a range of examples of visits that can be both leisure and tourism.

Coursework activity

Describe the range of leisure facilities in a tourist destination that has local customers, as well as tourist customers.

Summary question

Discuss how similar and how different leisure and tourism are.

Summary

Leisure can be local but tourism is being away somewhere else.

Leisure and tourism fit together closely.

Many tourists are leisure tourists or enjoy leisure activities while away from home.

Many leisure and tourism organisations have both leisure and tourism customers.

6

In this chapter you have learnt:

People use leisure and tourism facilities to:

✔ support and help them enjoy their leisure activities

✔ travel to leisure and tourism destinations

✔ provide for their needs as tourists.

Leisure is the set of people's spare time activities:

✔ taking part in and watching sport

✔ visiting entertainment facilities

✔ physical recreation

✔ eating out and socialising

✔ visiting attractions

✔ home-based leisure activities

✔ special-interest activities.

Tourism is going away from home for a temporary visit to another place. People become tourists mainly for these reasons:

✔ leisure

✔ business

✔ VFR.

Revision quiz

1 What is?:

a leisure

b tourism

c leisure tourism.

2 What is the difference between sport and physical recreation?

3 Give two examples of special-interest leisure activities.

4 What is VFR?

5 Why do people pay for business class when it is more expensive than economy?

6 Give an example of an activity that can be both leisure and tourism.

AQA Examination-style questions

1   Describe how people make use of two different leisure and tourism facilities to travel to a leisure and tourism destination overseas.

(6 marks)

Travel and transport facilities are examples of leisure and tourism facilities.

7 Different types of leisure and tourism organisations and facilities

Objectives

Describe and account for the range of leisure and tourism facilities provided:

in one place

by one leisure and tourism organisation.

■ Introduction

Leisure and tourism organisations are the businesses that run leisure and tourism facilities, including:

- ▦ leisure centres, health and fitness clubs
- ▦ theatres, cinemas, arenas, museums and galleries
- ▦ sports venues and facilities
- ▦ home-based leisure providers
- ▦ visitor attractions
- ▦ restaurants, cafés and takeaways
- ▦ hotels and self-catering accommodation
- ▦ travel agencies and online booking websites
- ▦ tourist information centres
- ▦ transport.

■ What is this chapter about?

Chapter 7 is about two different ranges of leisure and tourism facilities – those that are provided:

- ▦ in a place
- ▦ by a leisure and tourism organisation.

Places where leisure and tourism facilities are provided include:

- ▦ towns
- ▦ rural areas
- ▦ suburbs
- ▦ city centres
- ▦ leisure and tourism destinations overseas.

Leisure and tourism organisations which operate facilities include:

- ▦ local leisure providers
- ▦ leisure and tourism organisations in a destination
- ▦ leisure and tourism organisations that operate facilities in different places.

Starter activity

- ■ Make a chart to show the leisure and tourism facilities you can think of that are found in one place.
- ■ Name a leisure and tourism organisation.

- ■ Design a website homepage for your chosen organisation that presents the range of leisure and tourism facilities it operates.

7.1 Leisure in a place

Leisure and tourism facilities in a place provide for the needs of:

- local people
- visitors.

In UK towns, leisure and tourism organisations provide leisure and tourism facilities for both of these groups of people.

Leisure centres and health and fitness clubs, for instance, provide products/services mainly for people who live locally. However, visitors to a town may also use these facilities while they are staying there. In the same way, a town's main hotel does not only meet the needs of the tourists it accommodates. It also provides products/services for local people, for example use of the hotel's restaurant for meals, bar for socialising, and function rooms for social events such as wedding receptions and birthday parties.

Case study

Galashiels

A Galashiels

B Location of Galashiels

Galashiels (Photo **A**) is a town in Scotland. Map **B** shows its location in the Scottish Borders. Like many inland UK towns it has a range of leisure facilities that is provided to meet the needs of the local population (Table **C**). Galashiels tennis courts form part of a leisure complex that includes the swimming pool and which is run by the local council. As well as the Sizzling Pig mobile barbecue, leisure and tourism organisations provide a range of pubs, cafés, restaurants and takeaways.

Although not particularly a **tourist town** Galashiels does have visitors, and tourist facilities are provided to meet their needs, for example the hotels listed in Table **C**. There are also travel and transport facilities that local people can use to visit destinations elsewhere (Table **C**). Eildon Travel acts as a tour operator by arranging accommodation and excursions for visitors to the town, and as a travel agent by arranging travel and holidays elsewhere for local people.

C *Leisure and tourism facilities in Galashiels*

Mostly for local leisure	Mostly for visitors	Mostly for local people to travel elsewhere
Catering: • Sizzling Pig mobile barbecue	Hotels: • Abbotsford Arms • Clovenfords Country Hotel • Kings Hotel • Kingsknowes Hotel	
Sport and physical recreation: • Gala rugby club • Gala Fairydean football club stadium • Torwoodlee golf course • Galashiels swimming pool • Galashiels tennis courts	Tour operator: • Eildon Travel	Travel agent: • Eildon Travel
Entertainment: • Pavilion cinema		Transport: • Galashiels bus station

Activities

1 Give two groups of people for whom leisure and tourism facilities are provided.

2 Explain why travel and tourism facilities are provided in a town such as Galashiels, which is not particularly a tourist town.

Extension activity

Compare the range of leisure and tourism facilities provided by:

a a town or city local to you

b a tourist town or city.

Coursework activity

Describe and account for the range of products/services provided by one leisure and tourism organisation in a town.

Summary question

Describe and account for the range of leisure and tourism facilities provided in a UK town.

⬮⬮ links

www.galashiels.border-net.co.uk is the Galashiels town website.

www.pavilioncinema.co.uk is that of the Pavilion cinema in Galashiels.

Think about it

It is possible to think of all UK towns or cities as tourist towns or cities. They all have facilities that visitors use. However, towns or cities that are generally regarded as tourist towns or cities rely on tourism for economic prosperity.

Group activity

To what extent is your local town or city a tourist town or city?

Summary

A town has a range of leisure and tourism facilities.

While some towns are regarded as tourism towns and others are not, all towns have facilities that meet the needs of visitors.

7.2   Types of leisure and tourism organisations and facilities in a rural area

Different types of places have different ranges of **leisure and tourism facilities**. Fewer people live in a rural area than in a town. As a result, the level of local demand for leisure and tourism facilities is lower. However, the people that do live there still have leisure needs, and leisure and tourism organisations provide facilities for local people, as well as visitors, to use.

Rural populations are more scattered – among small towns, villages and farms. Therefore local people often have to travel further to access leisure and tourism facilities.

On the other hand, rural areas appeal to many tourists. Leisure and tourism organisations provide facilities to meet the needs of visitors.

Objectives

Describe and account for the range of leisure and tourism facilities in a rural area.

Key terms

Leisure and tourism facilities: resources, including buildings, attractions and outdoor areas such as playing fields, that are provided by leisure and tourism organisations.

Case study

The Amman valley, Wales

The Amman valley (Photo **A**) is a rural area in Carmarthenshire, south-west Wales (Map **B**). Ammanford, a small market town, is the main settlement and its leisure and tourism facilities provide for people from the town, surrounding villages such as Betws and for tourists who are visiting the area. The town is located about 20km north-east of the city of Swansea.

In Ammanford there is a range of leisure and tourism facilities comparable with that in any small UK town (such as Galashiels), for example cafés, bars, restaurants and takeaways. There is a local library, small theatre (Miners' Theatre) and the Amman valley leisure centre that includes two swimming pools.

A   *The Amman valley*

Carreg Cennen Castle is a ruined fortress near Ammanford and dates from the 13th century. The castle and Llyn Lech Owain (a lake in the town's nature reserve) are visitor attractions. Places to stay include the Wernoleu Hotel and the Black Lion caravan park. Glyn Hir Estate Mansion House and Pen-y-Banc Farm provide bed and breakfast accommodation in the nearby countryside.

Amman Valley Paddlers (Photo **C**) is a kayak canoe club based in the Amman valley. The river Amman itself is a natural facility for the club. However, Amman Valley Paddlers also makes use of Ammanford swimming pool for practice and coaching sessions.

links

www.ammanfordtown.co.uk is a website that gives information about leisure and tourism facilities in Ammanford and the Amman valley.

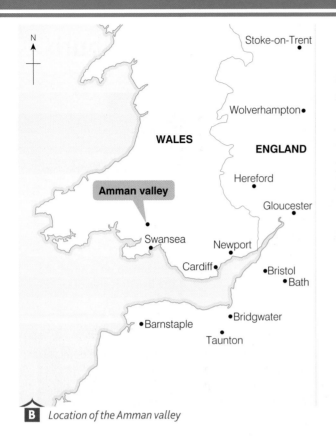

 Amman Valley Paddlers

B *Location of the Amman valley*

Activities

1   Outline how the provision of leisure and tourism facilities in a rural area may be different to that in a town.

2   Compare the provision of leisure and tourism facilities in the Amman valley with that in a town such as Galashiels.

Extension activities

1   Investigate the range of leisure and tourism facilities provided in a rural area other than the Amman valley.

2   Compare the range of leisure and tourism facilities provided by one rural and one urban area.

Coursework activity

Prepare a visual presentation to illustrate the range of leisure and tourism facilities provided in a rural area.

Summary question

Describe and account for the range of leisure and tourism facilities in a rural area.

Remember

Leisure activities include:

- taking part in and watching sport
- visiting entertainment facilities
- physical recreation
- eating out and socialising
- visiting attractions
- home-based leisure activities
- special-interest leisure activities.

AQA Examiner's tip

Be clear about what are facilities and what are organisations. Make a table of these for a place you have studied.

Group activity

Discuss whether the range of leisure and tourism facilities provided in a rural area meets the needs of young people better or worse than the range in a town local to you. How do you account for similarities and differences in the range of facilities provided?

Summary

The range of leisure and tourism facilities in a rural area provides for a smaller local population (than a town), as well as for visitors.

Suburbs are parts of towns or cities. They are the residential parts of towns or cities where people live. Leisure and tourism facilities are provided in suburbs, and local people often find it more convenient and cheaper to use them rather than travel into the town or city centre to use facilities there. This is particularly true for the suburbs of larger towns or cities such as Leeds.

Many suburban leisure and tourism facilities provide products/services mostly for local customers. However, there are exceptions, for example:

- Some hotels take advantage of suburban locations partly because of relatively easy access for customers travelling by car.
- Visitor attractions such as historic houses may be located in suburbs which were built around them.

Objectives

Describe and account for the range of leisure and tourism facilities in a suburb.

∞ links

www.beeston.co.uk is a website about the Beeston area of Leeds.

Case study

Beeston, Leeds

Beeston (Photo **A**) is an inner city suburb in south Leeds (Map **B**). The range of leisure and tourism facilities provided there is primarily aimed at the needs of the local community and includes the:

- south Leeds sports centre
- Burger King takeaway
- Glenns restaurant and guest house
- Whistle Stop public house
- Old Peacock public house
- Cross Flatts Park adventure playground
- Old White Hart public house
- Beeston Hill social club.

A *Beeston*

Like many inner urban areas Beeston is not a locality that attracts many tourists. Of course, there are people from elsewhere who travel to the suburb to visit friends and relatives who live there. Such tourists use the same leisure and tourism facilities in Beeston as local people do and may travel to other parts of Leeds, including the city centre, as well as to the surrounding area to make use of leisure and tourism facilities there.

Elland Road football stadium is located on the west side of Beeston. It is the home ground of football league club Leeds United and also stages other events such as concerts, as well as providing conference facilities. The stadium brings visitors to this part of Leeds, some of whom make use of Beeston's facilities such as the Old Peacock public house.

B *Location of Beeston*

Background knowledge

Outer suburbs are several kilometres distant from town and city centres. Many residents of outer suburbs make use of locally provided leisure facilities rather than travel to the town or city centre. Journeys to the centre are time consuming and cost money. Car parking in town and city centres can be quite difficult and expensive.

Inner suburbs of UK towns or cities are closer to the town or city centre but average standards of living are often relatively low. Local people often find the leisure and tourism facilities provided in the town or city centre too expensive for them. The range of leisure and tourism facilities provided in some inner suburbs is narrow because of the lower **disposable income** of many local people.

Key terms

Disposable income: the money left over after paying for the necessities of life such as housing, energy and food. Leisure and tourism products/ services are paid for from disposable income.

Activities

1. Outline two sources of demand for leisure and tourism facilities in a suburb.

2. Describe a range of leisure and tourism facilities in Beeston.

AQA Examiner's tip

The range of leisure and tourism facilities provided in a suburb largely depends on how well off local people are. People living in outer suburbs tend to be better off than those living in inner suburbs.

Extension activity

Analyse the similarities and differences in the range of leisure and tourism facilities provided in one inner and one outer suburb of a UK town or city.

Group activity

How do you think the range of leisure and tourism facilities in an outer suburb is likely to compare with that found in Beeston? Why?

Coursework activity

Compare and contrast the range of leisure and tourism products/services provided by two leisure and tourism organisations in a suburb.

Summary

Leisure and tourism facilities in suburbs provide mostly for the local population although there are exceptions, for example some visitor attractions and hotels.

Summary question

Describe and account for the range of leisure and tourism facilities provided in one named suburb of a UK town or city.

Leisure and tourism organisations provide wide ranges of leisure and tourism facilities in town and city centres. This is especially so in large cities such as Sheffield, Bristol, Cardiff and Belfast.

Leisure and tourism facilities in a city centre such as Birmingham meet the needs of people who live in the city, suburbs, surrounding rural areas, and smaller towns within easy travelling distance. People who live in a small or medium-sized town may be attracted by newer, better or more fashionable leisure and tourism products/services provided in a nearby city centre. For example a city centre theatre may stage shows that are newer productions, featuring more famous performers, than those on offer at a smaller local theatre.

City centre leisure and tourism facilities are likely to include larger numbers of visitors among their customers. Business tourists who stay in city centre hotels are also customers of city centre leisure facilities such as restaurants, bars and entertainment facilities.

Objectives

Describe and account for the range of leisure and tourism facilities in a suburb.

∞ links

www.visitbirmingham.com is an information site for people who are thinking about visiting Birmingham.

Key terms

Boutique hotels: small luxurious hotels with individual character. They normally charge premium prices.

Leisure complex: a building or site where several leisure and tourism facilities are located.

Case study

Birmingham

Birmingham city centre (Photo **A**) has a very wide variety of leisure and tourism facilities. These are used by local people and by visitors to the city, many of whom are business tourists. City centre accommodation includes large hotels provided by major hotel chains such as Accor, Jury's Inn and Radisson, as well as smaller **boutique hotels** such as the Hotel du Vin (Photo **B**).

Birmingham is widely promoted as 'England's second city'. Venues for artistic and cultural events, entertainment and nightlife are found throughout the city centre. They include the Museum of the Jewellery Quarter, and Gas Street Basin. The Jewellery Quarter is the part of the city centre where jewellery has historically been made. It still has around 500 jewellery related businesses. Gas Street Basin is a restored canal basin with cafés and bars where canal boat trips can be taken: Birmingham has historically been the hub of England's canal transport system.

A Birmingham city centre

The city has been a major centre for manufacturing in the UK since the Industrial Revolution. Heritage attractions in the city centre include the:

- Birmingham Hippodrome Theatre, which stages drama, musicals, pantomimes and ballet productions – it is home to the Birmingham Royal Ballet
- Symphony Hall
- clubs and bars of Broad Street, and the Arcadian **leisure complex**.

Brindley Place is an urban regenerated leisure complex in the city centre just off Broad Street. Facilities here include the Ikon art gallery, as well as a variety of bars, clubs and restaurants.

B   *Hotel du Vin, Birmingham*

The multicultural make-up of Birmingham's population is reflected in the breadth of cuisines from around the world that is found in the city centre's many restaurants.

Activities

1. Who are city centre leisure and tourism facilities provided for?

2. Outline a range of city centre leisure and tourism facilities that meets the needs of business tourists.

3. Make a leaflet to promote the leisure and tourism facilities of Birmingham city centre.

Extension activity

Investigate and report on the range of leisure and tourism facilities provided in a city centre other than Birmingham.

Group activity

How well do city centre leisure and tourism facilities meet the needs of people of different ages?

Coursework activity

Explain the different range of products/services provided by two city centre leisure and tourism organisations.

Summary question

Describe and account for the range of leisure and tourism facilities provided in the centre of a major UK city.

Think about it

Towns and cities vary considerably in size. The centres of large cities such as Birmingham tend to have more leisure and tourism facilities than do the centres of smaller towns although the range of types may differ less.

AQA Examiner's tip

Consider how and why the range of leisure and tourism facilities in city centres differs from that found in:

- small to medium-sized towns
- rural areas
- suburban areas.

Summary

The range of leisure and tourism facilities found in city centres is affected by the:

size of the city

need to provide for visitors to the city, as well as for local people.

Leisure and tourism facilities in an overseas destination

Leisure and tourism facilities in overseas destinations are provided for local people and for visitors. Visitors include domestic and inbound tourists. Some inbound tourists may be from the UK. Tourists may visit the destination for leisure reasons (such as for a holiday), on business or in order to visit friends and relatives.

Objectives

Describe and account for the range of leisure and tourism facilities in a leisure and tourism destination overseas.

Case study

La Rochelle

La Rochelle (Photos **A–C**) is a town on the west coast of France. A well-preserved historic port with beaches nearby, it is popular with both domestic and inbound tourists.

Transport facilities are provided for visitors to travel to La Rochelle, as well as around the destination. These include a major railway station and a bus/coach station. The 'Autoplus' public transport system includes local buses and free cycle parks. It is used by local people, as well as by visitors. Hire cars and taxis are other options. Water transport includes a summer time 'bus de mer' (sea bus) and there are various boat trips from the harbour.

The historic harbour and its towers give the whole of the old town **heritage tourism** appeal.

Individual visitor attractions include a variety of museums (for example the Musée Maritime), aquarium and beaches, including the Plage des Minimes.

There are numerous places to stay (hotels, apartments, youth hostel and campsites) and to eat and drink in and around La Rochelle.

A *La Rochelle – harbour at night*

B *La Rochelle – the town*

C *La Rochelle – harbour*

Activities

1. Outline three groups of people for whom leisure and tourism facilities are provided in an overseas leisure and tourism destination such as La Rochelle.

2. Compare the transport facilities in La Rochelle with another place you have studied.

3. a Research the range of accommodation and eating and drinking facilities in La Rochelle.

   b Write guidebook entries for each.

Extension activity

Compare the range of leisure and tourism facilities found in La Rochelle with that of another overseas destination.

Coursework activity

Investigate the range of products/services provided by a leisure and tourism organisation in an overseas destination of your choice.

Summary question

Describe and account for the range of leisure and tourism facilities in a leisure and tourism destination overseas.

∞ links

www.ville-larochelle.fr is the official website of La Rochelle. It can be read in various languages, including English.

Group activity

To what extent do you think the range of leisure and tourism facilities at an overseas destination such as La Rochelle provides for the needs of local people rather than the needs of visitors?

Types of leisure and tourism organisations

Leisure and tourism organisations run leisure and tourism facilities where customers can buy or use leisure and tourism products/services.

There are many different types of leisure and tourism organisations:

- sport and physical recreation providers, including local council leisure departments and health and fitness clubs
- home-based leisure providers such as libraries, and computer gaming and DVD rental shops
- entertainment providers such as theatres and cinemas
- visitor attraction providers
- catering and accommodation providers such as **restaurateurs** and **hoteliers**
- travel agents and online travel bookers
- tourist information providers, including regional tourist boards
- transport providers such as airlines, ferry companies, train and coach operators and car hire firms.

The size or scale of leisure and tourism organisations varies from small businesses run by individuals (Photo B), families or partners, to large international companies. Hotels, for example, may be run as small family enterprises (Photo A) or be links in chains that can stretch around the world. Hotel companies like Accor, which owns the Ibis and Novotel brands among others, Holiday Inn and Radisson SAS run establishments in all parts of the world.

Objectives

Describe and account for the range of leisure and tourism facilities that is provided by one leisure and tourism organisation.

Key terms

Restaurateurs: people who own and run restaurants. Restaurants may be run by individuals or by catering companies.

Hoteliers: people who own and run hotels. Hotels may be run by individuals or by companies.

◯◯links

www.swtourism.co.uk is the homepage for one of the UK's regional tourist boards.

Remember

Transport providers are leisure and tourism organisations that provide options for people choosing how to travel to destinations (see Chapter 4).

AQA Examiner's tip

Be clear that the organisation is the set of people (whether a family, council department or private company) that runs leisure and tourism facilities.

A *Lundy House Hotel, Mortehoe, Devon*

B   A catering outlet

Activities

1   Explain the meaning of each of the following:

a   leisure and tourism organisation

b   leisure and tourism facility

c   leisure and tourism products/services.

2   Make a flyer to promote the range of leisure and tourism facilities run by one home-based leisure provider.

Extension activity

Research and analyse the range of leisure and tourism products/services that is provided by one leisure and tourism organisation.

Group activity

Produce a poster to illustrate the range of catering and accommodation providers operating in one leisure and tourism destination of your choice.

Coursework activity

Describe and account for the range of leisure and tourism facilities that is provided by the leisure and tourism organisation listed in the links section.

Summary questions

1   Choose a leisure and tourism organisation that runs at least one facility in your local area.

2   Describe and account for the range of facilities that your chosen organisation operates in different places.

Summary

Leisure and tourism organisations own and run leisure and tourism facilities.

There is a wide variety of leisure and tourism organisations.

Investigating a local leisure and tourism organisation

In any **locality** a range of leisure and tourism organisations will provide facilities for local people and visitors to buy and use leisure and tourism products/services.

A public sector provider of local leisure services is the local council. Facilities that local councils often operate include:

- leisure centres and swimming pools
- parks, playing fields and playgrounds
- sports facilities such as tennis courts and bowling greens
- community centres and village halls.

Local leisure facilities such as cinemas, health and fitness centres and restaurants are usually operated by commercial organisations.

Case study

Chelmsford

Chelmsford is a town in Essex in the south-east of England. The local council is Chelmsford Borough Council and it provides a variety of leisure and tourism facilities.

`http://`

Parks and Green Spaces

Parks & Green Spaces >>
Parks in the Borough >>
Allotments >>
Play in the Park >>
Green Flag Award >>
Heart and Sole Healthy Walks >>

Museums and Attractions

Hylands House and Estate >>
Virtual Tour of Hylands House >>
Chelmsford Museums Service >>
The Essex Regiment Museum >>
Sandford Mill: Science for Schools and Gateway to Chelmsford's Unique Industrial Heritage >>

Arts and Entertainment

Chelmsford Civic and Cramphorn Theatres >>
View All Shows by Date >>
Cramphorn Film >>
Arts Development >>

Tourism

Visiting Chelmsford >>

What's On

Cultural Events >>
Leisure, Parks and Tourism Calendar >>
Project Support >>

Sports and Leisure

Riverside Ice and Leisure Centre >>
Chelmsford Sport & Athletics Centre >>
South Woodham Ferrers Leisure Centre >>
Dovedale Sports Centre >>
Sports Development >>
Sports and Leisure Calendar >>

A *Chelmsford Borough Council website extract*

Activities

1   Outline the range of sports and leisure facilities provided by Chelmsford Borough Council.

2   a   Research the range of leisure and tourism products/services provided by one of Chelmsford Borough Council's museums/attractions.

    b   Assess how well the museum/attraction meets the needs of one type of customer.

3   a   Find out what visitors to Chelmsford might find to see and do.

    b   Make a visual presentation called 'The appeal of Chelmsford as a leisure and tourism destination'.

Extension activity

Compare the range of local leisure services provided by the councils in Chelmsford and your local area.

Group activity

How well do the leisure facilities provided by the local council meet the needs of local elderly people? How could they be improved?

Coursework activity

Describe how people use the leisure facilities provided by your local council.

Summary questions

1   Use a map to illustrate the location and range of leisure and tourism facilities that are provided by one leisure and tourism organisation in your local area.

2   Suggest why these facilities are provided where they are.

Summary

Local leisure and tourism facilities are provided by a variety of organisations.

Local councils are public sector organisations that provide for people's leisure needs.

links

www.chelmsford.gov.uk is Chelmsford Borough Council's web homepage.

AQA Examiner's tip

Leisure and tourism organisations are largely commercially owned (private) organisations. However, there are also public and voluntary sector leisure and tourism organisations. The Youth Hostels Association (YHA) and the National Trust are examples of voluntary sector leisure and tourism organisations.

Think about it

Commercial leisure and tourism organisations are privately owned. Owners can be companies or they can be individuals. Such organisations normally aim to make a profit. All leisure and tourism organisations are businesses that try to meet the needs of their customers as efficiently as they can.

Remember

Leisure and tourism organisations that belong to the public sector are publicly owned through bodies that include local councils. While the facilities they run may not need to make a profit, they are expected to show best value by providing the best possible customer service as economically as possible.

Facilities provided by a leisure and tourism organisation in a destination

A leisure and tourism organisation may provide facilities in various different locations. In some cases, especially in the case of larger organisations in larger destinations, an organisation may have several facilities in a single destination.

For example in a single destination:

- A provider of cafés, pubs or restaurants may have several different outlets in a single destination.
- A hotel company may operate a range of different hotels.

A leisure and tourism organisation may operate several facilities in a single larger destination for these reasons:

- Several facilities in different parts of the destination will attract more customers.
- The organisation's different **brands** may appeal to different types of customers.

So coffee bar chains such as Costa, Starbucks and Caffé Nero frequently have several outlets in single destinations. Hotel companies such as Accor often trade under several brand names that are intended to appeal to different customer types. Ibis, Novotel and Etap are examples of Accor brands which may all be found in the same destination. The UK city destination of Leeds is one such example. Marrakech, in Morocco, is an overseas destination where Accor was operating five hotels in 2008 (Photos A and B).

Objectives

Describe and account for the range of leisure and tourism facilities that is provided by one leisure and tourism organisation in a destination.

Key terms

Brands: trade names under which products/services are provided.

Partner organisation: a leisure and tourism organisation that works with another such business while retaining its independence.

∞links

www.accorhotels.com is the Accor website address.

www.costa.co.uk, www.starbucks.co.uk and www.caffenero.com are all coffee shop chain websites.

Case study

Accor in Marrakech

In 2008 the hotel company Accor operated five hotels in Marrakech under different brand names, including Ibis and Sofitel. In addition Accor promoted four further Marrakech hotels in its website. These four hotels were run by **partner organisation** brands Club Med and Hotels Barriere.

A Sofitel Agadir Royal Bay, Morocco

B *Hotel Ibis Moussafir Marrakech Palmeraie*

> **Remember**
>
> Leisure and tourism destinations include beach (or seaside) resorts, city destinations, ski/snowsports resorts and national parks.
>
> Destinations are located in the UK and overseas (short and long haul).
>
> Short-haul destinations lie within Europe and the Mediterranean basin; long-haul destinations are found further afield, for example in North America and in Asia.

Activities

1 Explain two reasons why leisure and tourism organisations sometimes operate several facilities in a single destination.

2 Analyse how Accor hotels in Marrakech try to meet the needs of these customers:

a three student friends wanting to enjoy the city's nightlife

b a retired couple looking for a relaxing break.

Extension activity

Research and analyse the range of facilities provided by one leisure and tourism organisation other than Accor in one overseas city destination other than Marrakech.

Coursework activity

Describe and account for the range of leisure and tourism facilities provided by one leisure and tourism organisation in a destination of your choice.

Group activity

Choose a UK leisure and tourism destination. What examples are there in your destination of leisure and tourism organisations which run more than one facility? How well do you think these organisations are meeting the needs of visitors to the destination?

Summary question

Describe and account for the range of leisure and tourism facilities that is provided by one leisure and tourism organisation in one destination.

> **Summary**
>
> Leisure and tourism organisations sometimes operate several facilities in a single destination.
>
> Leisure and tourism organisations may operate facilities under different brand names.

7.9 Leisure and tourism facilities provided in different places by one leisure and tourism organisation

Some leisure and tourism organisations operate facilities in a range of different places. This is true of larger leisure and tourism organisations of all types. Leisure and tourism businesses that run chains of facilities have branches in a variety of different locations, for example:

- Health and fitness providers such as Bannatyne run health and fitness clubs across the UK.
- Cinema chains like Cineworld have movie theatres in different parts of the country.
- Hotel **companies** like Accor run hotels in different destinations, as well as sometimes having several establishments in the same destination.
- Transport operators like car hire firm Europcar have facilities in a range of different places.

Larger leisure and tourism organisations may operate businesses of different types, for example the Bannatyne group.

Case study

The Bannatyne group

The Bannatyne group is a set of leisure and tourism organisations that provides leisure products/services for customers through facilities and companies that include:

- health and fitness clubs (Bannatyne Fitness)
- hotels (Bannatyne Hotels) (Diagram **A**)
- bars (Bar Bannatyne) (Diagram **B**).

A *Bannatyne Spa Hotel, Hastings*

BAR BANNATYNE

Welcome Promotions Menu Link

Welcome to Bar Bannatyne

Located on the ground floor of The Gate complex in Newcastle city centre, Bar Bannatyne is the perfect venue for day and night.

Our central location makes an ideal meeting spot at the start of your night out, a great place to rest weary legs during your shopping trip or to enjoy a bit to eat before the cinema.

Mediterranean Luxury

Strong Morrocan influences, with draped alcoves and hanging chandeliers, provide a luxurious Mediterranean setting in the heart of Newcastle. Ideal for enjoying good food, fine drinks and great friends.

Traditional Pub Food

Our menu offers a great selection of freshly cooked, traditional meals such as Sandwiches, Steaks and Snacks.

Every Sunday we have a traditional lunch menu including three courses for only £10.00!

Our extensive 'happy hour' drinks offers make Bar Bannatyne an affordable 'pre-bar' to kick off the start of your night but with our dance floor, regular DJ and 1 o'clock licence, we've got the middle and end covered too!

Bar Bannatyne is open all day long and we look forward to seeing you soon.

B *Bar Bannatyne*

■ Background knowledge

Larger leisure and tourism organisations may operate as groups of companies. For example the Bannatyne group operates leisure and tourism businesses through separate companies such as Bannatyne Fitness and Bannatyne Hotels. The Virgin group is another example of this way of structuring business activity.

⚭ **links**

www.**bannatyne.co.uk** is the internet landing page for the Bannatyne group of companies.

Activities

1 a Make a map to show the locations of facilities run by one of these leisure and tourism organisations: Bannatyne Fitness, Cineworld, or Europcar.

   b Describe the distribution of locations shown on your map.

   c Suggest reasons for this distribution.

2 a Describe the structure of the Bannatyne group.

   b Suggest why Bannatyne Fitness and Bannatyne Hotels are organised as separate companies.

AQA **Examiner's tip**

What is an appropriate size of leisure and tourism organisation for study for GCSE? The answer is an organisation that is:

■ large enough to have several different facilities (in one place or several)

■ small enough to be manageable.

Extension activity

Research the range of locations used by one leisure and tourism organisation other than Bannatyne, Cineworld, Accor or Europcar.

Coursework activity

Describe how people make use of the leisure and tourism facilities provided in different places by one leisure and tourism organisation.

Group activity ▰▰▰▰

To what extent do you think the Bannatyne Spa Hotel (Hastings) and Bar Bannatyne are likely to appeal to the same types of customers as Bannatyne health and fitness clubs? Why?

Summary

Leisure and tourism organisations may operate facilities in different locations.

Leisure and tourism organisations that are companies may belong to larger groups of businesses.

Summary question

Describe and account for the range of leisure and tourism facilities that is provided in different places by one leisure and tourism organisation.

A broad range of leisure tourism facilities can be found in any one place. A variety of commercial, public and voluntary leisure and tourism organisations runs these facilities. Some of the organisations concerned may operate more than one facility in the same place and/ or facilities in other places too.

The size and make-up of the **market** for leisure and tourism products/ services in a place are important factors in accounting for the range of provision. Leisure and tourism organisations try to gain as many customers as possible by catering for different types of customers. If the market (of local people and visitors) is sufficiently large, organisations compete against each other to gain the biggest **market share** they can.

Case study

Windsor

Windsor is a leisure and tourism destination in the south-east of England. A famous visitor attraction in the town is the royal residence of Windsor Castle (Photo **A**). Leisure and tourism facilities in the town vary. They include provision for local people such as Windsor leisure centre's leisure pool (Photo **B**) and for visitors.

The many hotels in Windsor include the Royal Adelaide Hotel, shown in Photo **C**, which is an example of commercially run accommodation for tourists. Youth hostels are accommodation provided by a voluntary organisation (YHA). Jordans youth hostel at Beaconsfield is in the Windsor area (about 12km to the north).

A *Windsor Castle*

Objectives

Understand the breadth of leisure facilities provided in a place and by organisations.

Key terms

Market: the set of people who may buy leisure and tourism products/services.

Market share: the fraction of the market that a leisure and tourism organisation wins for its products/services.

∞links

www.theroyaladelaide.com is the internet address of the Royal Adelaide Hotel in Windsor.

Remember

Leisure and tourism organisations can be commercial, public or voluntary organisations.

Commercial organisations are run privately with the aim of making a profit.

Bodies such as local tourist boards run public sector leisure and tourism facilities on behalf of the public, who own them.

Voluntary organisations have a charitable status and are run to provide leisure and tourism products/services that are seen to be beneficial to people or the environment.

AQA Examiner's tip

When you describe the range of facilities provided in a place, remember the wide variety of leisure and tourism facilities (Diagram **D**).

B *Leisure pool at Windsor leisure centre*

C *Royal Adelaide Hotel*

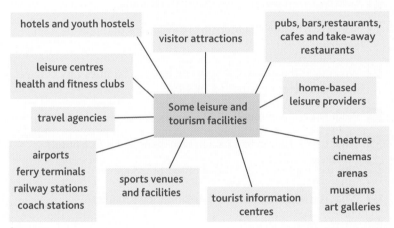

D *Breadth of leisure facilities*

hotels and youth hostels

visitor attractions

pubs, bars, restaurants, cafes and take-away restaurants

leisure centres
health and fitness clubs

home-based leisure providers

travel agencies

Some leisure and tourism facilities

theatres
cinemas
arenas
museums
art galleries

airports
ferry terminals
railway stations
coach stations

sports venues and facilities

tourist information centres

Activities

1 Explain why a broad range of leisure and tourism facilities can often be found in one place.

2 a Research the breadth of leisure and tourism facilities found in Windsor.

 b Make a poster to illustrate this breadth.

Extension activity

Describe and explain the breadth of leisure and tourism provision in one leisure and tourism destination other than Windsor.

Summary question

Describe and account for the breadth of leisure and tourism facilities provided in an overseas leisure and tourism destination by two leisure and tourism organisations.

Coursework activity

Describe the range of leisure facilities provided in your local area.

Group activity

How broad is the leisure and tourism provision in your local area? How well does it meet the needs of local people, as well as visitors? How does it compare to provision in Windsor? How much competition are you aware of between similar leisure and tourism organisations?

Summary

A broad range of leisure and tourism facilities may be found in any one place.

Leisure and tourism facilities in a place may be provided by commercial, public and voluntary organisations.

Chapter summary

7

In this chapter you have learnt:

Leisure and tourism facilities are provided in places by leisure and tourism organisations. In any one place such as a town, rural area, city centre or suburb, a broad range of different types of leisure and tourism facilities can be expected.

Leisure and tourism organisations operate facilities:

✔ as local leisure providers

✔ in leisure and tourism destinations (UK and overseas)

✔ in a variety of locations.

Revision quiz

1. Give two examples of entertainment facilities.

2. Name two leisure and tourism organisations that provide train services.

3. Why might the range of leisure and tourism facilities vary between the inner and outer suburbs of a UK city?

4. What is a restaurateur?

5. What name is given to a person who owns and runs a hotel?

6. Give two examples of catering outlet brand names.

7. What is a leisure and tourism organisation's market?

8. What is market share?

AQA Examination-style questions

1 Describe and account for the range of leisure and tourism facilities provided by one leisure and tourism organisation you have studied. *(8 marks)*

 AQA Examiner's tip A leisure and tourism organisation is a business that provides leisure and tourism facilities. It may do that in one place or several.

■ Introduction

Leisure and tourism has changed a lot in the last twenty years. The pace of change continues to be rapid today.

■ What is this chapter about?

Chapter 8 is about the changes that have happened and are still happening in leisure and tourism. These changes are in:

- the provision of leisure locally
- travel opportunities and holiday booking patterns
- response to environmental concerns.

Starter activity

- Discuss in a small group, changes you already know about to one of the following:
  - a leisure facilities that are provided in your local area
  - b how people book holidays and travel to destinations
  - c how leisure and tourism has changed as people have become more environmentally aware.
- Summarise your discussion on a flip chart.
- Report back to the rest of the class.

Leisure provision for local areas of the UK has changed a lot in the last twenty years. There are, for example, more health and fitness clubs, drive-through fast food outlets, coffee bar chains, and restaurants that were previously traditional pubs, than there used to be.

Many people have witnessed changes in leisure provision in their local area. They are a valuable source of information about the changes that have happened.

Objectives

Describe and explain changes in leisure provision that have taken place locally over the last twenty years.

Case study

Claire

Claire has lived in the same local area all her life. Now in her 30s, Claire has seen a number of changes in local leisure provision since she was in her teens.

In Cartoon **A** Claire describes one of the main leisure changes that have affected her. Diagram **B** is an extract from a questionnaire that Claire completed for a GCSE Leisure and Tourism student who was researching changes to leisure provision in Claire's local area. There are two types of questions in a questionnaire: **open questions** and **closed questions**.

> I never used to go the gym. Well, hardly anyone did really. Some people went jogging I suppose or to keep fit and aerobics – that sort of thing. There just weren't the health and fitness clubs you see now – not then.

A Claire remembers

Do you think people eat out more now than 20 years ago?

Yes.

How do you think eating out has changed in the last 20 years?

There are lots more places to go and eat now. More pubs serve food and there's a much bigger choice of restaurants in the town centre – Thai and Indian food as well as Italian and Chinese.

What is your special leisure interest?

Music really. I've a big collection of pop music tracks – well over 20 years worth.

How has provision for it changed locally in the last 20 years or so?

In the past I would buy CDs from a music shop in town. I don't now. I download it from the internet. There are less music shops than there were – smaller ones have disappeared altogether.

B Claire's answers

Key terms

Open questions: questionnaire or interview questions designed to allow the subject to answer in some detail.

Closed questions: questionnaire or interview questions that may be answered briefly – yes or no, for example.

Remember

Types of facilities that may have changed as part of changes in local leisure provision over the last twenty years are:

- leisure centres
- health and fitness clubs
- theatres and cinemas
- museums and art galleries
- sports facilities
- home-based leisure facilities
- restaurants, cafés and takeaways.

AQA Examiner's tip

Do not take twenty years too literally. It is change over that kind of period that you need to be able to describe and explain. Beware that some changes described in older textbooks may already have begun twenty years ago.

C *Local restaurants*

Activities

1 Outline two changes in local leisure provision that Claire has witnessed.

2 Write two more questions for the GCSE student's questionnaire. These questions should ask Claire about changes in local leisure provision other than those shown in Cartoon **A** and Diagram **B**.

3 Suggest reasons for:

    a the reduced numbers of town centre shops selling recorded music

    b people eating out more often.

Extension activity

Research changes in leisure provision in a place other than your local area. Compare these changes to those that have happened in your local area.

Coursework activity

Describe and explain changes in leisure provision that have taken place in your local area over the last twenty years.

Summary question

Make a chart to show the variety of changes in leisure and tourism in the last twenty years and the reasons for them.

Group activity

Survey a range of local people to find out about changes to leisure provision in your local area in the last twenty years. Make a display to illustrate your findings.

Summary

Changes in local leisure provision have taken place in the last twenty years.

Local people are witnesses to the changes that have happened.

Changes in local leisure provision over the last twenty years have been broadly similar in different parts of the UK.

The growth in the number of health and fitness clubs and town centre restaurants offering different cuisines, and the smaller number of shops selling recorded music, are changes that are repeated across the UK. They reflect current national trends in people's leisure activities:

- increased participation in health and fitness activities such as going to the gym, running for pleasure and hill walking
- more people eating out more often in a greater variety of different restaurants
- more people ordering food to be delivered from takeaways
- more people cooking for pleasure
- increased use of computers and other electronic devices for leisure at home, including downloading movies and music, social networking and gaming.

These trends are based on a greater awareness among the public of the health and fitness benefits of physical recreation, increased levels of disposable income and on changes in social behaviour and technology.

Background knowledge

The variety of different cuisines available in UK city destinations is one of the most important factors in attracting inbound tourists. Many visitors are keen to sample the food of countries other than their own. Others are grateful for the chance to relax and eat familiar food in what is to them a foreign country.

A Evenings out

B *Changes in leisure provision that reflect national trends*

Types of leisure facilities	Recent changes
Health and fitness clubs	These have increased in number, size and range of provision.
	These are more likely to be newly and purpose built with easy car access.
Cinemas	Although multiplex cinemas began to be developed more than 20 years ago, more have continued to be built.
Arenas	More indoor arenas have developed to host events such as concerts that were previously held in concert halls.
Home-based leisure providers	More chains have replaced smaller, independent suppliers of electronic and computer games, recorded music and books.
	DVD rental replaced videotape hire within the last 20 years.
	More home-based leisure products/services are provided via the internet. There was no internet in the 1980s.
Restaurants, cafés and takeaways	These have increased in number and variety with more restaurant, café and takeaway chains.
	Coffee bar chains such as those run by Starbucks and Costa have developed within the last 20 years.

Activities

1 Suggest three current national trends in people's leisure activities.

2 Explain how changes in leisure provision, shown in Table **B**, reflect current national trends in people's leisure activities.

Group activity

How likely do you think recent changes in leisure are to continue? What positive and negative impacts do they have? What future changes do you predict?

Coursework activity

Find out about and describe recent changes in leisure and tourism in a leisure and tourism organisation.

Summary question

Describe and explain how changes in leisure provision in your local area reflect current national trends.

Summary

Changes in leisure provision at local level reflect national trends.

Since the 1990s the range of travel opportunities available to people has broadened. A key change has been the development of budget airlines such as easyJet and Ryanair.

Objectives

Describe and explain changing travel opportunities.

Case study

easyJet

The growth of easyJet typifies the rapid growth of budget airlines from the 1990s into the early 21st century. EasyJet was founded by individual businessman Stelios Haji-Ioannou in 1995. Ten years later the airline had provided flights for 100 million people (Table **A**).

A *History of easyJet*

Year	Key event for easyJet
1995	1st domestic flights (from London Luton to Scotland)
1996	1st international flights (from London Luton to Amsterdam)
1997	easyjet.com website launches with 1st online bookings in 1998
	2nd UK easyJet base airport (Liverpool)
1999	internet sales reach 1 million (10 million by 2001)
2001	2nd largest scheduled airline using London Gatwick Airport
2002	stepping down of founding chairman Stelios Haji-Ioannou
2005	100 millionth passenger **dynamic packaging** introduced to easyjet.com by easyJet and Europcar
2006	**fast-track** boarding ('speedy boarding') introduced for passengers who pay a premium price
2007	website allows customers to offset the carbon emissions of the flights by paying a supplement, which goes to a hydroelectric energy project in Ecuador

Key terms

Dynamic packaging: customers creating their own travel package by combining trip elements usually chosen on a website.

Fast track: a means of allowing customers to avoid queuing by paying a premium price.

B *easyJet's growth*

◼ Background knowledge

Dynamic packaging allows a customer to put together their own travel or holiday package from a menu of elements.

A traditional package holiday is put together by a tour operator and sold as a ready-made product either through a travel agent or directly to the customer.

The internet has made dynamic packaging possible. The customer uses websites such as Expedia.com to assemble a self-customised travel package for which the travel provider then charges a single price.

AQA *Examiner's tip*

Compare the budget and conventional air flights between the same two airports. Consider the advantages and disadvantages of each for customers.

Activities

1 **a** Using Diagram **B** describe the growth of easyJet's passenger numbers between 1995 and 2007.

b Compare the pattern of growth with the key events in easyJet's history that are shown in Table **A**.

2 Explain what is meant by carbon offsetting and suggest why easyJet introduced such a scheme in 2007.

Extension activity

Research updated passenger statistics for easyJet. Do they show continued growth? Why/why not?

Group activity

What recent changes have there been in how people can travel other than the growth of budget airlines? Do you think budget airlines like easyJet will grow as fast in the future as they did in their first ten years?

Coursework activity

Describe and explain changing travel opportunities such as the growth of budget airlines.

Summary question

Make a poster to illustrate the breadth of change there has been in people's travel opportunities over the last twenty years.

Summary

Transport opportunities have broadened in recent years.

The growth of budget airlines has been a key change since the 1990s.

A key recent change in holiday booking patterns has been the expansion of dynamic packaging. This is also known as **self-packaging**. It is a change that has paralleled the growth of budget airlines and the spread of the internet.

Self-packaging involves customers assembling their own trips. They put them together from a number of component parts such as:

- travel (an air flight or a rail journey, for example)
- transfer (transport from a gateway point of arrival such as an airport to accommodation)
- possible car hire
- accommodation
- excursions.

∞ links

www.travelocity.co.uk and www. opodo.co.uk are UK websites of online travel providers.

Case study

Expedia

Expedia is an online travel provider. Customers access the Expedia website either to book a single travel component or to self-package a trip from more than one component (similar to Diagrams **A** and **B**). In addition to flights, hotels and car hire, Expedia customers can opt to include extras such as excursions and, on skiing holidays, ski hire and ski lift passes in their package.

As an online travel provider, Expedia works with partner leisure and tourism organisations. The lists of airlines and hotels which appear on the Expedia website are not the full range of what the market has to offer. They are menus provided by leisure and tourism organisations who have entered into a partnership arrangement with Expedia.

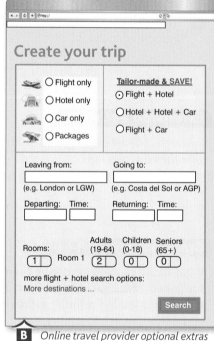

B Online travel provider optional extras

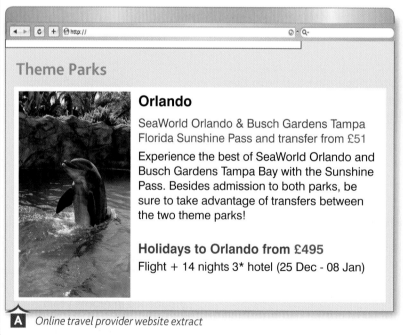

A Online travel provider website extract

The resultant self-package may include as few as two of the above or as many as all of them. What makes it a package is that the customer pays the provider one price for the whole.

Self-package providers include:

- online travel companies such as Expedia and Travelocity
- tour operators such as Thomson and Kuoni
- travel providers such as airlines (easyJet, for example), and train operators such as Virgin Trains and National Express East Coast.

■ Background knowledge

Package holidays abroad became very popular in the 1960s. The traditional package included air flights from the UK and transfer from the gateway arrival airport to hotels or self-catering accommodation. Traditional package holidays were assembled by tour operators and sold by travel agents. While **tailor-made holidays** and **independent travel** both existed, it was not until after the advent of the internet in the 1990s that self-packaging became very important.

AQA *Examiner's tip*

Online travel providers and tour operators are competitors. Established tour operators such as Thomson and Kuoni offer their customers self-packaging options so as to stop them buying from an online provider such as Expedia instead.

Key terms

Self-packaging: customers assembling their own package deal from a menu of optional components.

Tailor-made holidays: holiday packages especially assembled to meet a customer's individual needs.

Independent travel: tourists making their own travel and accommodation arrangements.

Activities

1. Use the internet to design a self-package holiday for your family to one leisure and tourism destination overseas.

2. Compare the cost of the self-package holiday that you designed in activity 1 with a traditional package holiday to the same destination.

Group activity

Make a poster to illustrate the advantages and disadvantages for customers of self-package holidays.

Extension activity

Use your knowledge of leisure and tourism organisations to identify examples of airline and hotel providers that are not listed on the Expedia website.

Coursework activity

Describe and explain the role of online travel providers in changing holiday booking patterns.

Summary question

Describe and explain two recent changes to the holiday booking patterns of people living in the UK.

Summary

The growth of self-packaging has been a major recent change in holiday booking patterns.

This change has happened alongside the expansion of the internet and the growth of budget airlines.

Change and the UK travel and tourism industry

Changing travel opportunities (such as the growth of budget airlines) and holiday booking patterns (such as the expansion of self-packaging) have affected the UK **travel and tourism industry**. Tour operators and travel agents, for example, have made changes to the ways in which they do business. Similarly providers of hotel and self-catering accommodation, and transport providers such as airlines, ferry companies and car hire firms have altered their practices (Table **A**).

The development of the internet has been at the root of much of the recent change that has affected the UK travel and tourism industry because it has enabled customers to:

- easily access the products/services of budget airlines
- self-package their trips by combining the component parts themselves.

This has put pressure on all the types of travel and tourism organisations listed above in ways shown by Table **A**.

■ Background knowledge

Travel and tourism organisations are linked in a chain, shown by Diagram **B**. It is called the chain of distribution because it is the chain of organisations through which travel and tourism products/services are distributed to customers.

Travel and tourism organisations from different stages in the chain may merge. This is called vertical integration.

Horizontal integration is when travel and tourism organisations from the same level in the chain of distribution join together.

A *Changes to the UK travel and tourism industry*

Types of travel and tourism organisations	Changes
Travel agencies	• fewer travel agent shops on high streets • many have merged with tour operators to form integrated travel companies such as Thomson • adopted internet booking systems
Hotels	• developed websites to allow internet booking • some have become partners of online travel providers such as Expedia
Airlines	• developed websites to allow internet booking and self-packaging by customers • some have become partners of online travel providers such as Expedia

Activities

1 Outline two ways in which the development of the internet has affected the UK travel and tourism industry.

2 Suggest reasons for each of the following changes:
   a fewer high street travel agent shops
   b more hotel websites.

Extension activity

Research examples of vertical and horizontal integration in the UK travel and tourism industry.

Group activity

Does internet booking suit everyone? Who does it suit more (or less) than others? Will travel agent shops all be forced out of business by the internet? Why/why not?

Coursework activity

Describe and explain how changing travel opportunities and holiday booking patterns have affected the UK travel and tourism industry.

Summary question

Describe and explain how changes in either travel opportunities or holiday booking patterns have affected the UK travel and tourism industry.

Customer

↑

Travel agent

↑

Tour operator

↑

Principal

B *Chain of distribution in travel and tourism*

Summary

Changing travel opportunities and holiday booking patterns are affecting the UK's travel and tourism industry.

The growth of the internet is at the root of many of these changes.

8.6 Leisure and tourism and the environment

People are more environmentally aware than they used to be. There has been growing public and government concern about the negative impact of leisure and tourism on the environment, as well as on local communities in destinations. Leisure and tourism has changed in response to such growing environmental concerns with:

- more sustainability
- the growth of ecotourism.

Sustainability in leisure and tourism is brought about by the ways in which leisure and organisations behave. Leisure and tourism is sustainable when organisations behave in ways that do not:

- damage the environment for the future
- harm the future of the communities who live in leisure and tourism destinations.

Sustainable leisure and tourism minimises negative economic, social and environmental impacts so that the future of the environment and of destinations and their people is protected. This is important for the economic future of destinations: visitors will not want to travel to places that have been spoilt by leisure and tourism's negative impacts.

Examples of the ways in which today's leisure and tourism organisations are behaving sustainably are:

- airline, train, coach and bus operators using vehicles with low-carbon emission engines and arranging carbon-offset schemes (Diagram A)
- leisure and tourism facilities using **renewable energy sources**, conserving energy and water, and recycling as much waste as possible
- catering and accommodation providers using locally sourced food to avoid unnecessary transportation and damage to the environment
- employing local staff and using local suppliers in destinations to protect the **economic well-being** and ways of life of local communities
- tour operators providing more ecotourism holidays.

Objectives

Describe and explain changes that are taking place in leisure and tourism in response to environmental concerns.

Remember

Sustainability is the ability to sustain or conserve the environment and people's ways of life into the future. Sustainability in leisure and tourism is made possible by minimising the negative impacts of:

- people's leisure activities – at home, in the local area and in leisure and tourism destinations
- travel to leisure and tourism destinations
- operating and developing leisure and tourism facilities.

Key terms

Renewable energy sources: ways of obtaining power from sources that can be replaced.

Economic well-being: how financially well off people are. How much money they have and whether they have secure employment are aspects of economic well-being.

Activities

1 Give two examples of changes in leisure and tourism that are responses to environmental concerns.

2 Explain why sustainability matters to the future of leisure and tourism destinations.

3 Outline two ways in which leisure and tourism organisations are behaving sustainably.

AQA Examiner's tip

Leisure and tourism organisations may want to be sustainable because their owners and managers see the importance of sustainability. However, they should also be seen to be acting sustainably in order to attract customers.

http:// 🔍 Q▾

easyjet and the environment

We have an environmental code, based on three promises

1.   To be environmentally efficient in the air
2.   To be environmentally efficient on the ground
3.   To lead in shaping a greener future for aviation, for example:
   - carbon offsetting
   - shaping future aircraft design - for example, the ecoJet

   easyJet high efficiency = lower emissions = low fares

easyJet carbon offsetting-eco
Carbon offset with easyJet

We balance the effect of the carbon emitted from your flight by supporting UN certified projects like Perlabi Hydroelectric in Ecuador.

Learn more about Perlabi Hydroelectric Project

How it works

easyJet buys credits from UN-certified schemes like Perlabi, there's no middle man in our not-for-profit scheme.

Learn more about the easyJet carbon calculator

On the ground

We're reducing emissions on the ground too by:
-   Using less ground equipment
-   Using more airports with good public transport links

What we do on the ground

Our Promises...
In the air

A traditional airline flying the same route as us, using the same plane, emits 27% more carbon per passenger km. easyJet is proud to fly:
-   Newer planes - our average fleet age is 3.4 years
-   Fuller planes - we sell on average 85% of the seats on our higher seat density planes
-   Short-haul, direct trips only

What we do in the air

For a greener future

We are leading the way to a greener future through initiatives like carbon offsetting and our ecoJet aircraft design (see Press Release)

Carbon offsetting

Learn more about Corporate Social Responsability

Carbon Offsetting Resources
-   Press Releases
-   UN Project Audit
-   UN Project Description Document
-   FAQ's
-   Terms and Conditions

 A   *easyJet's sustainability claims*

Extension activity

Research and report on how one leisure and tourism organisation other than easyJet is behaving sustainably.

Group activity

Study Diagram **A**. How sustainable do you think easyJet is? Are there ways in which easyJet could be more sustainable? Is it possible for a low-cost (budget) airline like easyJet to be fully sustainable? How can easyJet customers behave sustainably?

Coursework activity

Describe recent changes that one leisure and tourism organisation has made in response to environmental concerns.

Summary question

Describe and explain two changes that are taking place in leisure and tourism in response to environmental concerns.

Summary

Leisure and tourism changes in response to growing environmental concerns are:

organisations behaving more sustainably

the growth of ecotourism.

Public and government concern about the environment has created a need for sustainability in leisure and tourism. Leisure and tourism organisations have made changes in response to this concern.

The public and government are concerned that leisure and tourism can affect the environment negatively for the reasons shown in Table **A**.

A *How leisure and tourism harms the environment*

Cause	Comment
Greenhouse gas emissions	Gases are emitted from the exhausts of engines that power the forms of transport that tourists use. These gases enhance the world's greenhouse effect and contribute to global warming.
Noise and visual pollution	Leisure activities can be noisy, and some tourism developments are unsightly. This can make destinations less attractive for future tourists.
Consuming resources	Resources that may be in short supply in some destinations such as energy and land are put under pressure by tourism.
Waste disposal	Improper disposal can pollute the land and bodies of water such as rivers.

Such negative impacts can harm the future of leisure and tourism destinations and their communities. So sustainability is needed in leisure and tourism. Sustainability is the ability to live and work today without harming the future, and means, in leisure and tourism, reducing to the lowest possible level the negative impacts of leisure and tourism that are listed in Table **A**.

Objectives

Explain the need for sustainability in leisure and tourism.

Key terms

Conservation groups: voluntary organisations who try to keep the environment as natural as possible and to protect it from negative tourism impacts.

⊕links

www.thetravelfoundation.org.uk is the Travel Foundation's website.

Case study

The Travel Foundation in Tobago

The Travel Foundation has run sustainable tourism projects in leisure and tourism destinations largely in LEDW countries since 2004. On the Caribbean island of Tobago, the Travel Foundation has been working on several sustainable tourism projects. It is doing so in co-operation with the government of Trinidad and Tobago, the local tourism industry and local **conservation groups** and is supported in some of its work by the UK tour operator Virgin Holidays.

One of the Travel Foundation's Tobagan projects has been 'Adopt a Farmer'. This links hotels on the island with local farmers (Photo **B**) thus creating income and reducing the Tobago tourist industry's dependency on expensive imported food. Farmers have been encouraged to grow crops that the hotels want to serve to their customers. This has meant that they are able to earn at least 30 per cent more from selling their produce than they did before.

B   *Member of the Travel Foundation's Adopt a Farmer scheme in Tobago*

AQA *Examiner's tip*

Revise Chapter 5's case studies of sustainable leisure and tourism:

▪ going to the gym sustainably (5.5)
▪ the Eden Project (5.6)
▪ Black Sea Gardens (5.7).

◼ Background knowledge

The Travel Foundation is a charity that aims to develop tourism sustainably. The organisation is a partnership of the UK government and UK travel and tourism organisations, including major tour operators such as First Choice and Thomas Cook.

Activities

1   Describe how leisure and tourism can harm the environment.

2   Explain why the Travel Foundation's Adopt a Farmer scheme in Tobago is an example of sustainability in leisure and tourism.

Group activity

Why do you think UK tour operators like Virgin Holidays support sustainable leisure and tourism projects? Do you think that what they do is sufficient? What else could be done?

Coursework activity

Describe recent changes in leisure and tourism in your local area or in a destination that aims to be sustainable.

Summary question

Explain why sustainability in leisure and tourism is now seen as very important.

Extension activity

Research other sustainable leisure and tourism projects run by the Travel Foundation and make a display to illustrate their work.

Summary

Public and government concern about the environment has encouraged leisure and tourism organisations to become more sustainable.

The Travel Foundation is an example of a leisure and tourism organisation that promotes sustainability.

8.8 The growth of ecotourism

Rising environmental awareness among the public, governments and leisure and tourism organisations has encouraged the growth of:

- sustainable leisure and tourism
- ecotourism.

Ecotourism is visiting a leisure and tourism destination because of the appeal of its natural environment while negatively making an impact on the environment as little as possible. Ecotourists also try to benefit the local community in destinations.

Case study

Ireland Eco Tours

Ireland Eco Tours is a leisure and tourism organisation that operates 1, 3, 5 and 8-day ecotourism trips in Ireland – partly in Northern Ireland (which is in the UK) and partly in the Republic of Ireland. The tours feature cycling and walking activities in north-west Ireland's 'Greenbox' (Map **B**). Customers are accommodated in local eco-friendly bed and breakfast establishments.

Ireland Eco Tours uses a **carbon neutral** bio-fuelled minibus (Photo **A**) to transport its customers between destinations. The fuel used is plant oil that is derived from rapeseed crops grown in Ireland. The carbon emitted from the minibus exhaust is balanced by the amount absorbed by the rapeseed as it grows.

A Eco-bus

Objectives

Describe ecotourism and explain its growth.

Key terms

Carbon neutral: an equal balance between carbon added to and absorbed from the atmosphere.

Ecotourist-receiving area: a region visited by people taking part in ecotourism.

links

www.greenbox.ie is the internet homepage for ecotourism in Ireland's Greenbox.

Remember

The aims of ecotourism are to:

- help people enjoy and learn about the natural environment in leisure and tourism destinations
- conserve the natural environment of leisure and tourism destinations by minimising the negative environmental impacts of tourism
- make positive impacts not only on the environment but also on the lives and well-being of local people.

AQA Examiner's tip

Revise 5.9's case study of ecotourism in Thailand. Compare your ecotourism case studies – how are they similar and how are they different?

◼ Background knowledge

The Greenbox is in north-west Ireland. It is an **ecotourist-receiving area** (Map **B**).

Ireland is traditionally referred to as the 'Emerald Isle' because of its lush, green countryside. So, green is a description of both the Irish countryside and of ecotourism.

Both the Republic of Ireland and UK (Northern Ireland) governments support ecotourism in the Greenbox financially.

B *The Greenbox*   *www.greenbox.ie*

Coursework activity

Research and describe examples of ecotourism in an area of the UK other than in Ireland's Greenbox.

Group activity

Ecotourism is small-scale low-impact tourism. Is such tourism always beneficial to leisure and tourism destinations and their communities?

Extension activity

Research examples of ecotourism in Ireland's Greenbox (Map **B**). Write a newspaper article about them.

Activities

1 What is ecotourism?

2 Outline two ways in which Ireland Eco Tours holidays are examples of ecotourism.

3 a Explain why using local bed and breakfast establishments is sustainable tourism.

   b Suggest how accommodation providers can be eco-friendly.

Summary

Ecotourism has grown in response to growing environmental concerns.

Ecotourism is supported by governments and operated by leisure and tourism organisations.

Summary questions

1 Describe examples of ecotourism in the UK and overseas.

2 Explain why ecotourism has grown recently.

How much has leisure and tourism changed in the last twenty years? A lot! Chapter 8 shows that there have been major changes:

- to **local leisure provision** that have reflected **national trends**
- to the travel opportunities that are available to people
- in response to environmental concerns.

There are now more health and fitness clubs. This is partly because there has been a rising national trend in people's health consciousness. Fashion also plays a part. People join gyms because other people have joined. Health and fitness clubs compete with each other to attract customers. So rising demand has encouraged them to be as up to date as possible. The result is that most health and fitness clubs are in new or nearly new buildings and offer their customers the latest possible fitness machine technology.

Key terms

Local leisure provision: leisure facilities that are provided in a place mainly for the people who live in it.

National trends: patterns of change over time that affect a whole country.

Case study

Helen

Helen is an adult who lives in the UK. In Cartoon **A** Helen describes changes she has seen in leisure and tourism over the last twenty years.

I'm quite health conscious I suppose. I've always tried to keep fit. Twenty years ago I just used to jog a bit and go to an aerobics class. Now I'm a member of a health and fitness club – there weren't any of those around here then.

One of the biggest changes for me has been the growth of cheap air travel. I remember when even a short trip to Europe seemed hugely expensive. Now there's a wide choice of budget airline flights to short-haul destinations. It's not unusual for my friends and me to take city breaks on the continent now.

We've taken two long-haul trips in the last couple of years or so – to Cuba and Australia. We did try to be responsible tourists on those trips.

A Helen's changes

Think about it

The last twenty years have seen both increased travel opportunities and environmental concerns. Airlines such as easyJet have increasingly promoted themselves as low cost in two senses:

- cheap fares
- reduced carbon emissions.

Customers want both travel and the chance to be carbon neutral. Leisure and tourism organisations face a major challenge in trying to meet these two demands.

AQA *Examiner's tip*

Be aware of changes in leisure and tourism that have affected:

- different places in your local area
- people's travel options
- leisure and tourism destinations in the UK and overseas.

Activities

1 Suggest two likely changes to leisure provision in Helen's local area other than the development of health and fitness clubs.

2 Explain why more people take European city-break holidays now than twenty years ago.

3 Describe how long-haul tourists can limit the negative impacts of their trips.

Extension activity

Interview a sample of different adults to research leisure and tourism changes they have seen over the last twenty years. Make a visual presentation to illustrate your findings.

Group activity

How do you think leisure and tourism will change over the next twenty years? Which of today's trends will continue? Are there changes happening now that will slow down or stop in the future?

Coursework activity

Describe recent changes in leisure and tourism that have taken place in one place or that have affected one leisure and tourism organisation.

Summary question

Make a visual presentation to explain key changes in leisure and tourism over the last twenty years.

Summary

Leisure and tourism has changed a lot over the last twenty years.

Changes in technology, in what people can afford and in environmental awareness have been important factors in leisure and tourism's changes.

8

In this chapter you have learnt:

Over the last twenty years there have been many changes in leisure and tourism.

Changes to local leisure provision in the UK have included more:

✔ health and fitness clubs

✔ drive-through fast food outlets

✔ coffee bar chains and a greater variety of restaurants.

Tourists have a greater choice of travel options than was the case in the past. The growth of budget airlines has been a major trend since the 1990s. Also there has been growing awareness among the public and by government of the negative impacts of tourism on the environment and on local people who live in leisure and tourism destinations particularly those in LEDW countries. As a result, leisure and tourism has become more sustainable, and ecotourism has grown.

Revision quiz

1 Give two examples of recent changes in local leisure provision in the UK in the last twenty years.

2 a What is a multiplex cinema?
b When did the UK's first multiplex cinema open?

3 Name two budget airlines.

4 How has the internet helped budget airlines to grow?

5 Give one major transport change of the last twenty years other than the growth of budget airlines.

6 What does sustainability mean?

7 What is ecotourism?

8 Why has ecotourism grown recently?

AQA Examination-style questions

1   Describe and explain how one leisure and tourism organisation has responded to recent changes in leisure and tourism. *(10 marks)*

AQA
Examiner's tip Leisure and tourism organisations compete with each other. How they respond to change depends on the changes their rivals have already made or are likely to make.

9 Leisure and tourism organisations as businesses

Objectives

Explain how leisure and tourism organisations benefit from operating as businesses

Explain the importance to organisations of selling products/services

Account for and evaluate the range of promotional materials and techniques used by organisations.

■ Introduction

Leisure and tourism organisations are businesses. Each has been set up to provide a range of leisure and tourism products/services to its customers.

Some leisure and tourism businesses are privately owned commercial enterprises, for example travel agents and hotels. Such businesses are owned by individuals or companies. They aim to make a profit from their activities.

Public sector and voluntary leisure and tourism organisations are businesses too. They are established to provide a range of leisure and tourism products/services to their customers. They may not aim to make a profit but to provide:

■ best value products/services for their local communities

■ a subsidised benefit to people or the environment – to do good.

■ What is this chapter about?

Chapter 9 is about how leisure and tourism organisations benefit from operating as businesses by:

■ using up-to-date business systems

■ promoting their products/services

■ recognising different attitudes and cultures among their customers

■ dealing with health and safety issues.

As well as providing an outline of each of the above, the chapter deals in more detail with:

■ marketing in leisure and tourism

■ health and safety issues faced by leisure and tourism businesses and how risks are managed.

Starter activity

■ Discuss why you think leisure and tourism organisations need to sell products/services.

■ Consider examples you have seen of promotional materials (for example advertisements, brochures and leaflets) for leisure and tourism organisations. What are they like? How good do you think they are at encouraging customers to buy products/services?

9.1 A business system

Leisure and tourism organisations are run as businesses. They provide a range of leisure and tourism products/services to their customers through two sets of activities or **business operations**:

- front-of-house (sometimes called front office) operations
- back office operations.

Front of house is the part of the business that deals directly with customers. In a hotel, for example, staff who work in reception, the restaurant or bar or as housekeeping staff often come into direct contact with the hotel's customers. These **customer-fronting** staff members are engaged in the business's front-of-house activities.

In the same hotel other business operations take place behind the scenes. Examples of these back office functions are:

- administration – keeping records of the business's activities, for instance
- finance – dealing with money that comes into and goes out of the business
- human resources – managing the business's employees.

Back office functions may literally be carried out in the office at the back of reception but may be undertaken elsewhere.

Leisure and tourism organisations carry out business operations using set procedures. They try to design ways of doing things that are efficient and effective. These are the organisations' business systems. In the 21st century the most efficient ways of carrying out business operations are often by using **ICT systems**.

Efficiency means providing products/services as quickly and as economically as possible. To provide products/services economically, businesses keep their costs to a minimum. Staff wages is one example of a business cost that can be kept down by using ICT. Providing leisure and tourism products/services to customers as effectively as possible is also important as customers are more likely to be satisfied. As a result, they will probably:

- spend more money because they are relaxed and enjoying themselves
- make a return visit
- recommend the organisation to other people.

Objectives

Explain in outline, examples of how leisure and tourism organisations benefit from operating as businesses by using up-to-date business systems.

Key terms

Business operations: an organisation's activities that help it provide products/services to its customers.

Customer-fronting: business activities that involve dealing directly with customers.

ICT systems: ways of carrying out business operations using information and communications technology.

AQA Examiner's tip

When investigating business systems such as ICT systems that a leisure and tourism organisation uses find out about back office, as well as front-of-house operations.

Activities

1 Describe the difference between front-of-house and back office business operations.

2 Explain why:

a satisfied customers are important to leisure and tourism organisations

b ICT systems can help leisure and tourism organisations to satisfy their customers.

⚭ links

www.virginactive.co.uk and www.fitnessfirst.co.uk are addresses for health and fitness clubs.

Bannatyne health clubs

Bannatyne operates more than 60 health and fitness clubs (Photo **A**) in different parts of the UK. Customers are members of the club. The company uses its website to promote club membership (Diagram **B**).

Bannatyne uses an ICT system to manage its membership records efficiently. Membership cards are also swipe cards that are used to gain entry to the club through automatic barriers similar to the ticket barriers used at many railway stations. The swiping of membership cards provides Bannatyne with comprehensive data about who is actually using club facilities and when. Management can make use of such information to ensure the club is efficiently staffed and run at different times of the day and week.

If a member does not visit the club for a few weeks, the ICT system notices. A postcard is then sent to the member's address to invite them to return and remind them of the benefits of their membership of the club.

A *A Bannatyne health club*

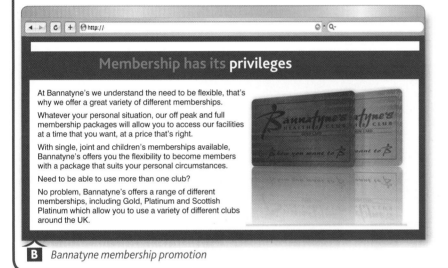

B *Bannatyne membership promotion*

Which leisure and tourism organisations has the group used as customers? What ICT systems did group members notice? How efficient were these organisations? Which would you recommend to each other? Why?

Research and analyse how a business system such as an ICT system is used by a leisure and tourism organisation other than Bannatyne health clubs.

Using one or more examples, outline how leisure and tourism organisations benefit from operating as businesses by the use of up-to-date business systems such as an ICT system.

Evaluate the success of a business system such as an ICT system that has been recently introduced by a leisure and tourism organisation.

Business systems are what an organisation uses to help it provide its customers with products/services.

ICT systems are often efficient and effective.

Efficient and effective systems help businesses serve their customers well and so they do well themselves.

9.2 Promoting products/services

Leisure and tourism businesses exist to provide products/services to their customers. They use promotion to let their customers know:

- what products/services they have to provide
- where and when these products/services are available
- how much they cost.

Leisure and tourism organisations are more successful businesses when customers know what products/services are available. This is because they are more likely to use the organisations' facilities, spend money and let other people know what is available too.

Case study

Park Inn

Park Inn is a hotel chain. From Monday to Friday it attracts largely business tourists. The flyer in Photo A is promoting Park Inn hotels to weekend leisure customers.

Great Weekend Breaks with Park Inn Hotels

2 nights B&B, 1 evening meal

From £65 pp

What a weekend!

We arrived at the Park Inn hotel on Friday evening to a warm welcome and enjoyed a delicious dinner in the hotel restaurant. The next day we enjoyed a hearty breakfast, then explored and discovered the city before returning to the hotel for a visit to the leisure centre. Slept like a baby that night! What a great hotel, great location and really great value!

For special deals in great locations around the UK click on **parkinn.co.uk** or call free on **0800 056 0591** and book your weekend now!

park inn

A Park Inn flyer

∞ links

www.parkinn.co.uk is Park Inn's website.

■ Background knowledge

A flyer is a piece of promotional material. Some other examples of promotional materials are:

- leaflets
- brochures
- posters
- advertisements
- websites.

Remember

Some examples of promotional techniques other than advertising are:

- merchandising – selling or giving away free, souvenirs and other branded items
- sponsorship – paying money to help another organisation in return for publicity
- direct mailing – sending promotional materials to customers in the post or electronically.

Activities

1. Describe the purpose of promotion.

2. Suggest three reasons why Photo A is likely to attract customers to Park Inn.

3. Why should Park Inn want to attract weekend leisure customers?

Extension activity

Assess the Park Inn website as a piece of promotional material. What types of customers is it likely to attract? Why?

Group activity

Collect different examples of promotional materials used by leisure and tourism organisations. What information do they provide for customers? How well do they do this? What types of customers would be attracted by them?

Coursework activity

Describe the range of promotional materials used by one leisure and tourism organisation.

Summary question

Explain how leisure and tourism organisations benefit from promoting their products/services.

Summary

Leisure and tourism organisations promote their products/services to make customers aware of them.

Promotion helps leisure and tourism organisations to succeed as businesses by helping them sell their products/services.

9.3 Attitudes and cultures

Customers can have different **attitudes** about the products/services that are provided by leisure and tourism organisations. People from various ethnic backgrounds may have different **cultures**. This can result in people either wanting different leisure and tourism products/services or wanting them provided in other ways.

Leisure and tourism organisations that recognise the variety in attitudes and cultures among their customers are more likely to meet the different needs of those customers. Meeting customers' different needs means that they feel better served. They are then more likely to return, bringing repeat business to the organisation. Satisfied customers are also more likely to recommend the organisation to other people – perhaps people with similar attitudes and cultures to themselves. In this way, the organisation's reputation can grow, helping it to attract more customers and to succeed better as a business.

Objectives

Outline how leisure and tourism organisations benefit from operating as businesses by recognising different attitudes and cultures among their customers.

Case study

Make Your Move Your Way

Make Your Move Your Way (Photo **A**) is part of b-active, a physical recreation programme organised by Derby City Council. The council acts as a leisure and tourism organisation by operating a variety of sports venues, leisure centres, swimming pools and community centres in the city of Derby.

Make Your Move Your Way aims to involve women of differing attitudes and cultures in physical recreation. Many sessions are open to women and girls only and are female staffed. Activities include:

- self-defence
- aerobics
- ladies only gym sessions
- Bollywood dancercise (dance exercise in partnership with Surtal Asian Arts)
- fitness pilates
- ladies kick-boxing
- swimming (separate sessions for women only, women and girls only and women and toddlers only)
- netball
- keep fit (introduction).

Nusrat, a volunteer Make Your Move Your Way activity leader, comments on the programme in Cartoon **B**.

A Make Your Move Your Way

I think this is a great opportunity for women in the Asian community to get more active particularly for Muslim women who need to be in a female only environment. I'm really looking forward to the women and girls' swim sessions and the introduction-to-keep-fit course. I would like to train to become an exercise instructor myself and hope that b-active might support this.

B Nusrat

Activities

1   Research and outline the meanings of:

a   Bollywood

b   pilates.

2   Outline two ways in which Derby City Council's b-active programme tries to meet the needs of customers with different attitudes and cultures.

3   Assess how well Derby City Council's b-active programme tries to meet the needs of customers with different attitudes and cultures.

Group activity

Why should leisure and tourism organisations try to meet the needs of customers with different attitudes and cultures? What issues might result?

Coursework activity

Research and evaluate how a leisure and tourism organisation other than Derby City Council is trying to meet the needs of customers with different attitudes and cultures.

Summary question

Illustrate how a leisure and tourism organisation can benefit as a business by recognising different attitudes and cultures among their customers.

Key terms

Attitudes: how people feel about something. Attitudes are based on people's views and beliefs.

Cultures: beliefs, behaviours and ways of life that typify different social groups.

links

www.derby.gov.uk is Derby City Council's landing page.

Remember

Different types of customers are:

- single people
- couples
- families with children
- groups
- people of different ages: children, teenagers, young adults, mature adults, retired people
- different ethnic and cultural groups
- people with special needs.

AQA Examiner's tip

People may have different attitudes to leisure and tourism whether or not they are from different ethnic or cultural backgrounds.

Summary

Leisure and tourism organisations can benefit as businesses by recognising different attitudes and cultures among their customers.

Leisure and tourism organisations are responsible for the health and safety of:

- customers
- staff
- the public.

Leisure and tourism organisations need to ensure that they employ qualified staff who are capable of ensuring the health and safety of their customers. They need to make sure that facilities and equipment are safe to use, food is safe to eat and proper procedures are in place in the event of an emergency such as a fire.

Leisure activities involve an element of **risk**. Indeed for some physical activities (white water canoeing, for example) risk is part of the fun. Leisure and tourism organisations try to keep risk to a minimum.

Background knowledge

Resort representatives are employees of tour operators. They are responsible for the welfare of the company's customers while they are staying in a destination. This responsibility includes health and safety.

Objectives

Outline how leisure and tourism organisations benefit from operating as businesses by dealing with health and safety.

Key terms

Risk: the chance of accident or mishap.

Holiday villages: purpose built tourist accommodation facilities that include a number of mobile homes or cabins.

Kids' Club: supervised children's activity sessions at leisure and tourism facilities such as hotels and campsites.

Case study

Eurocamp

Eurocamp is a tour operator that specialises in camping and self-catering holidays in Europe and Florida. The company's resort representatives are based in the campsites and **holiday villages** where Eurocamp's customers stay. Eurocamp's main customer type is families with children. So Eurocamp employs specialist children's representatives who are called children's couriers. Eurocamp's childen's couriers organise kids' clubs (Photo **A**) to help meet customers' needs.

Ensuring the health and safety of the children attending a **kids' club** is a very important duty for Eurocamp's children's couriers. Eurocamp's success as a business depends on attracting family customers. The reputation of the Kids Club as a safe, as well as fun activity is a very important part of the company's appeal for families with children.

As part of ensuring the health and safety of its Kids Club customers, Eurocamp provides a Children's Club Parent Guide (Diagram **B**).

A   *Eurocamp Kids Club*

Children's Club Parent's Guide (edited extract)

- There must be a completed Consent Form for each child attending any of our children's clubs Parents should complete the form and bring it to the first session.
- Places are limited for safety reasons, therefore at peak times of the season, there may be a booking system operating on a first-come-first-served basis.
- You must complete the Registration form at the start of each session. You must sign your child in to each session and clearly note your intended whereabouts during the session.
- Children aged 10 and above can travel to and from children's club on their own and sign themselves in and out accordingly, provided a parent has given their authorisation on the Consent Form..
- Children will be asked to wear a wristband during session. This allows us to easily identify the children if they are involved in activities around the campsite
- Drinking water will be provided.
- If the weather is warm, sun cream should be applied before each session and a sunhat worn.
- All staff are registered/cleared through the Criminal Records Bureau (in the same way as teachers and other who work with children).
- Staff attend a comprehensive safety training programme.

B *Children's Club Parent Guide, Eurocamp*

AQA *Examiner's tip*

It is useful for you to realise that leisure and tourism organisations are obliged to ensure health and safety by law.

⚭ links

www.eurocamp.co.uk is the Eurocamp website.

Activities

1 Why do leisure and tourism organisations deal with health and safety?

2 Outline two ways in which Eurocamp deals with the health and safety of its customers.

3 Study Diagram **B**.

a Explain why three of the measures shown help ensure health and safety.

b Suggest at least one other way in which Eurocamp could ensure customers' health and safety at the Kids Club.

Group activity

What leisure and tourism organisations/facilities have members of the group used as customers? What health and safety measures did you observe? How effective do you think these were?

Coursework activity

Collect and comment on two items of promotional materials used by one or more leisure and tourism organisation that highlight health and safety considerations.

Summary question

Explain how leisure and tourism organisations benefit as businesses by dealing well with health and safety.

Summary

Leisure and tourism organisations ensure the health and safety of their customers, staff and the wider public.

Ensuring the health and safety of customers helps leisure and tourism organisations succeed as businesses.

Leisure and tourism organisations operate as businesses. They provide their customers with leisure and tourism products/services. How well leisure and tourism organisations do this is a measure of their success as businesses.

Table **A** lists examples of types of leisure and tourism businesses that:

- are run commercially to try to make a profit
- belong to the public sector and are run to provide the public with a best value service
- are voluntary organisations concerned with providing benefits to people or the environment.

A *Some types of leisure and tourism businesses*

Commercial (private)	Public sector	Voluntary
• health and fitness clubs	• leisure centres	• youth hostels
• cinemas	• tourist information centres	• visitor attractions run by charitable trusts
• home-based leisure providers	• visitor attractions run by government organisatons (for example English Heritage)	
• many visitor attractions		
• restaurants		
• hotels		
• travel agencies		
• airlines		

Case study

English Heritage

English Heritage belongs to the public sector. Its job is to protect and promote the historical environment of England. English Heritage is a leisure and tourism organisation in that it operates over 400 abbeys, castles, **stately homes** and palaces as historic-site visitor attractions. Stonehenge (Photo **B**) is one of English Heritage's most visited attractions. Facilities provided for customers include a gift shop, and refreshments are on sale.

B *Stonehenge*

∞links

www.english-heritage.org.uk is the website of English Heritage.

Remember

Historic sites are one type of visitor attraction. Other types are:

- natural attractions
- theme parks
- major sports/entertainment venues
- built attractions.

AQA Examiner's tip

Promotion and selling are the twin essential steps to leisure and tourism business success. The point of businesses is to provide products/services to customers, and promotion and selling are the means by which that is done.

Key terms

Stately homes: large houses often on big country estates, which are the ancestral homes of landowning families. They are now heritage tourism attractions.

Commercially run leisure and tourism organisations seek to make profits. To succeed in that business aim they need to promote and sell leisure and tourism products/services to their customers. Promotion is necessary to bring the products/services to the attention of customers, and sales are needed to generate income.

While the main aims of public sector and voluntary leisure and tourism organisations are not to make financial profits, these organisations are still run as businesses. They try to make sales that cover as many of their costs as possible. To make a profit, certainly for a voluntary organisation, would be a welcome bonus. Both sets of organisations want to attract customers, and so promotion matters to them too.

Activities

1 Give named examples of leisure and tourism organisations or facilities that are:

a commercially run

b in the public sector

c voluntary.

2 Visit the English Heritage website. Describe and assess how well English Heritage uses the website to promote Stonehenge to a variety of customer types.

Coursework activity

Describe the range of promotional materials used by one leisure and tourism organisation to promote a visitor attraction other than Stonehenge.

Summary question

Explain why it is important to leisure and tourism organisations to promote and sell products/services.

Group activity

'Promotion and sales are just as important to public sector organisations as they are to other types of leisure and tourism organisations.' How true do you think this statement is? Why?

Summary

Promotion and sales are important to leisure and tourism organisations because they enable them to provide their customers with products/services.

9.6 Promotional materials used by leisure and tourism organisations

Promotional materials are used by leisure and tourism organisations to make people aware of their products/services to encourage sales. These promotional materials are:

- leaflets, brochures and flyers
- posters and other advertisements such as **bus wraps** (Photo **A**), printed advertisements in newspapers and magazines, and internet pop-ups
- websites
- TV and radio commercials
- **merchandise** and souvenirs.

Merchandise consists of objects that are sold by a leisure and tourism organisation to help promote its products/services. Examples are hats, T-shirts, mugs and glasses. Souvenirs may be given to customers free of charge. Many leisure and tourism organisations such as hotels have souvenir pens or pencils that customers can take. The organisations' contact details are printed on souvenir items therefore they become advertisements.

A Bus wrap

Case study

Cadbury World advertisement

Cadbury World is a visitor attraction in Bournville, a suburb of Birmingham. Cadbury World is a built attraction that is themed around Cadbury chocolate. Diagram **B** is an advertisement for Cadbury World.

Applying the AIDA method (Diagram **C**) to Diagram **B**, the advertisement is likely to be successful in promoting the Cadbury World visitor attraction to families with children because of:

- attention: Diagram **B** grabs customers' attention with its design of chocolate splashes (plain, milk and white) on a purple (the trademark colour of Cadbury chocolate) background.
- interest: the advertisement promises fun and a variety of activities. The use of the made-up word 'funly' implies fun for the family and helps to capture the interest of family customers.
- desire: vivid descriptions such as 'spangly interactive games' and 'create your own chocolatised yumlump' raise the desire to visit Cadbury World among the families with children.
- action: the advertisement gives telephone number and website address action points for customers.

B Cadbury World advertisement

◼ Background knowledge

The effectiveness of promotional materials in leisure and tourism depends on their design. This includes the text, images and colours that they use.

C *AIDA*

		AIDA: a method for evaluating a piece of promotional material		
A	Attention			grab customers' attention
I	Interest	How well is the piece of promotional material likely to . . .		capture customers' interest in the organisation's products/services
D	Desire			raise customers' desire to buy or use them
A	Action			show customers what action to take to buy or use them?

Key terms

Bus wraps: advertisements usually spray-painted that look as if they are wrapped around a bus (Photo A).

Merchandise: objects that are sold by a leisure and tourism organisation in order to help promote its products/services.

AQA *Examiner's tip*

Use the AIDA method (Diagram C) to evaluate promotional materials.

Activities

1 Make a chart to illustrate a variety of different types of promotional materials that is used by leisure and tourism organisations.

2 a Design a piece of promotional material for a leisure and tourism organisation of your choice.

   b Evaluate your design.

Group activity ⬤⬤⬤⬤

Assemble a range of promotional materials used by leisure and tourism organisations. What customer types are their targets? How successful are they likely to be in attracting customers of these types?

⚭ **links**

www.cadburyworld.co.uk is the Cadbury World website.

Extension activity

Collect examples of promotional materials used by a variety of leisure and tourism organisations. Make a visual presentation to illustrate the variety of types of materials used.

Summary

Leisure and tourism attractions use a variety of promotional materials to bring their products/services to the attention of customers.

The likely effectiveness of promotional materials can be assessed using the AIDA method.

Summary questions

1 Account for the range of promotional materials used by one leisure and tourism organisation.

2 Evaluate the likely success of two of these materials in attracting one customer type.

9.7 Promotional techniques used by leisure and tourism organisations

Promotional techniques are the methods that leisure and tourism organisations use to distribute promotional materials.

The aim of a leisure and tourism organisation's promotional activities is to make customers aware of the products/services that are provided. Promotional materials are designed to highlight the advantages of an organisation's products/services so that customers will find them attractive, and sales will be made. However, it does not matter how well designed promotional materials are if customers do not receive them. So leisure and tourism organisations choose promotional techniques that they think will mean that customers will receive the materials.

Promotional techniques often used are:

- advertising
- sales pitching, for example telephoning potential customers or sending them promotional emails
- product and promotional material placement, for example placing merchandise and souvenirs in a gift shop or displaying leaflets in another facility
- sales promotions, for example making special offers.

Background knowledge

Leisure and tourism organisations classify customers as:

- potential customers – those who might use their facilities or buy their products/services
- actual customers – those who already use their facilities or buy their products/services.

Objectives

Account for and evaluate promotional techniques used by leisure and tourism organisations.

Think about it

Returning customers are very important to leisure and tourism businesses. Pitching special offers to actual customers is a useful technique aimed at persuading them to return: yesterday's actual customers are tomorrow's potential customers.

AQA Examiner's tip

The promotional activities of leisure and tourism organisations include materials and techniques. While they are different in meaning it can be difficult in practice to talk about one (advertisements, for example) without the other (advertising).

Case study

National Express East Coast's 1st birthday promotion

National Express East Coast (NXEC) is a train operating company. Since 2007 it has run trains (Photo **A**) on the UK's East Coast main line between London and Leeds, Edinburgh and the north of Scotland. In 2008 NXEC celebrated the 1st birthday of its train service.

Customers of NXEC who were on its mailing list were sent an email sales pitch making them a special offer (Diagram **B**).

A NXEC train

B   *NXEC promotional email*

Activities

1   Analyse Diagram B.

a   What piece of promotional material was used?

b   What two promotional techniques were used?

c   Use AIDA to evaluate the promotional material.

d   Suggest why the two techniques you identified in b were chosen.

2   Suggest how NXEC could have used two other promotional techniques to attract customers.

Coursework activity

Account for and evaluate the range of promotional techniques used by one leisure and tourism organisation other than a train operating company.

Summary question

Assess the suitability of two different promotional techniques for one leisure and tourism organisation.

Extension activity

Compare the range of promotional techniques used by two transport operating companies other than National Express.

Group activity

Collect a range of promotional materials used by leisure and tourism organisations. Discuss appropriate techniques the organisations could use to help make sure that these materials reach their customers.

Summary

Leisure and tourism organisations use a variety of promotional techniques to help promotional materials reach customers.

A leisure and tourism organisation's market is its set of potential customers. Some types of customers may be attracted to a leisure and tourism organisation's products/services. Others may not. Market segmentation divides the market by customer type.

Some ways of segmenting the market for leisure and tourism products/services are shown in Table **B**. Other criteria that can be used are:

- ethnic and cultural background
- social class
- level of disposable income
- special need.

Identifying the **market segments** that are most likely to want its products/services is important to a leisure and tourism organisation. To make its promotional materials and techniques as effective as possible it needs to aim them at the right people. Promotions cost money. Any materials which do not reach the people who really are the organisation's potential customers are wasted. If promotional techniques aim at exactly the right market segment then the amount of money, time and effort spent on promotion is justified.

Objectives

Describe how the market for a leisure and tourism organisation's products/services can be segmented.

Key terms

Market segments: divisions of a leisure and tourism organisation's market (Table **B**).

Market research: investigating the demand for products/services.

Case study

Fourcroft Hotel, Tenby

Fourcroft Hotel (Photo **A**) is located in the seaside resort of Tenby in south-west Wales. Fourcroft is an independently operated 40-bedroom hotel and overlooks the resort's old fishing harbour. Most rooms offer a sea view. Children under 15 who share a room with adult family members can stay at the hotel free of charge. The hotel's leisure facilities include a heated outdoor swimming pool, which is open from Easter to October. The hotel's conference facilities are the Dewi Sant conference suite and, for smaller events, the Seacroft meeting room.

A *Fourcroft Hotel, Tenby*

Background knowledge

Leisure and tourism organisations use **market research** to investigate the market segments they should target.

Market research techniques that leisure and tourism organisations use include:

- questionnaires – asking people what they like
- observation – watching who makes use of different products/ services
- focus groups – using small discussion groups to find out what people like.

B *Market segments*

Criteria	Segments
Group	single people, couples, families, other groups
Age (stage in life cycle)	children, teenagers, young adults, mature adults, retired people
Purpose of visit	business, leisure, VFR

Activities

1 Compare how well Fourcroft Hotel meets the needs of leisure customers and business customers.

2 Suggest why it is important for a leisure and tourism organisation to segment its market.

Coursework activity

Evaluate the promotional materials used by two hotels in one beach (or seaside) resort other than Tenby.

Group activity

Research the promotional materials of leisure and tourism organisations other than Fourcroft Hotel. Which market segments do these materials address? Why do you think that? How likely are they to attract these customer types?

Summary question

Describe how the market of one leisure and tourism organisation other than a hotel can be divided into segments.

AQA *Examiner's tip*

Promotional materials are aimed at certain segments of the market. Studying them can help you assess which segments make up a leisure and tourism organisation's market.

links

www.fourcroft-hotel.co.uk is Fourcroft Hotel's website.

Remember

UK seaside resorts such as Tenby have declined since the 1960s following the growth of package holidays abroad. Efforts to regenerate them have included promoting them as conference destinations for business tourism.

Fact

Research techniques such as those used in market research are:

- primary when new information is collected and investigated
- secondary when information that has already been collected is investigated.

Summary

A leisure and tourism organisation's market is made up of different customer types.

These customer types are the organisation's market segments.

A leisure and tourism's **target market** is the market segment at which it pitches its promotional materials. The target market is the type of customer to whom the organisation thinks it can sell its products/services.

The target market of Eurocamp is families with children; for Fourcroft Hotel it is the same customer type plus business tourists.

The target market of a leisure and tourism organisation may be limited geographically. For example Derby City Council leisure services are intended for people who live in and around the city of Derby, and its Make Your Move Your Way programme is aimed specifically at women who live in that area.

Objectives

Describe how the market for a leisure and tourism organisation's products/services can be segmented.

Key terms

Target market: the set of customers at which a leisure and tourism organisation aims its promotional activities.

Grey market: the market segment of mature adults who are nearing retirement or who are recently retired.

Case study

The Adventure Company

The Adventure Company is a tour operator that specialises in adventure tourism. Its 2009–10 brochure cover is shown in Diagram **A**. The company organises group tours of destinations that are 'off the beaten track' so that its customers have the opportunity to experience challenging natural environments and the heritage and traditions of destinations. Many of the Adventure Company's destinations are long haul – Africa, South America, Asia and Antarctica (Diagram **B**).

Experienced and qualified group leaders guide each group so that customers can feel confident and safe in what to them may be a strange environment. Accommodation is described as 'comfortable and characterful rather than stylish and luxurious'. It includes Bedouin encampments in the Sahara Desert and local family homes, as well as small hotels and lodges.

The Adventure Company promotes its holidays as offering 'the perfect blend of adventure and comfort'. The Adventure Collection brochure is aimed at tourists who are 'reasonably active and healthy' and who want a 'blend of comfort and adventure'. Some itineraries are intended for families travelling with children, for example a desert and wildlife safari in Namibia in Africa. The brochure is published in five languages, including English – the others are Dutch, French, German and Turkish.

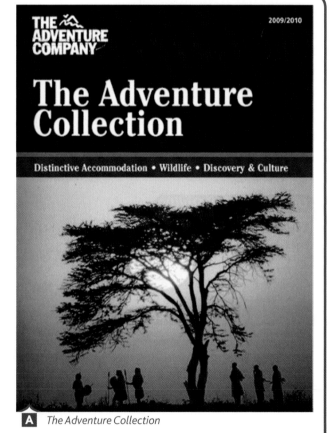

A   *The Adventure Collection*

NEW Emperor Penguin Safari

This is a rare opportunity to travel to an area of unrivalled beauty to witness a sight few others have experienced – a colony of nesting emperor penguins on ice. Reaching this location is far from easy, and the Kapitan Khlebnikov is one of the only vessels capable of penetrating the spectacular icy seascapes early in the season. The undoubted highlight will be the emperors themselves, but your journey to this icy wilderness takes you to see so much more.

B   *Emperor Penguin Safari*

Background knowledge

A recent trend in leisure and tourism has been the growth of the **grey market**. This market segment consists of late middle-aged adults who may be nearing retirement or who have recently retired. They are likely to be reasonably fit, in good health and quite well off financially since their grown children have left home. The grey market is an attractive target market for leisure and tourism organisations.

∞links

www.adventurecompany.co.uk is the Adventure Company's website.

Remember

Long-haul leisure and tourism destinations are those that are located beyond Europe and the Mediterranean basin – usually more than 6–7 hours flying time away from the UK.

AQA   Examiner's tip

Target markets are the market segments at which leisure and tourism organisations aim their promotional materials and techniques.

Group activity

What do you think are the target markets of leisure and tourism organisations in your local area? What evidence backs up your judgements?

Activities

1   What is meant by:
  a   a target market
  b   a grey market?

2   Explain why Adventure Company holidays are likely to suit members of the grey market.

3   Outline two ways in which the Adventure Collection brochure is trying to broaden the appeal of Adventure Company holidays.

4   a   Suggest the Adventure Company's target market.
  b   Justify your decision.

Coursework activity

Analyse the promotional materials produced by a leisure and tourism organisation. How likely are they to attract customers who belong to the organisation's target market?

Summary

Leisure and tourism organisations aim their promotional activities at identified target markets.

Summary question

Describe the target market of a leisure and tourism organisation other than the Adventure Company.

Leisure and tourism organisations aim their promotional materials at the market segments that are their target markets.

Some pieces of leisure and tourism promotional materials feature images of people who are often good indicators of the target market. The idea is to picture people that prompt potential customers to think 'That could be me! I wish I was there/doing that'.

Some other clues to target markets in pieces of promotional materials are the:

- language used to describe the product/service
- style of the design of the material and the imagery used
- price of what is on offer and whether special offers are being made to particular customer types.

Case study

Two mailshots

Photos **A** and **B** show the front covers of two **mailshot** leaflets that were sent by different leisure and tourism organisations. The images and the words used suggest two different target markets:

- families with young children wanting seaside fun
- young/young-at-heart couples perhaps travelling as a small group, wanting attractive scenery and peace and quiet.

A Mailshot

Fancy a Caribbean holiday with a bit of action?

Fancy a Caribbean holiday that's really relaxing?

B   *Mailshot*

Activities

1   Match one of the mailshot leaflets in Photo **A** with each of these target markets:

a   families with young children wanting seaside fun

b   young/young-at-heart couples looking for a holiday with a difference.

2   Explain how you identified each of the target markets in activity 1 from the mailshot leaflets.

Remember

Leaflets, brochures, flyers and posters are all promotional materials that seem similar but are all different. A leaflet is made from a single sheet of paper that has been folded; a brochure is a booklet made of several pages. A flyer consists of a single sheet of unfolded paper; a poster is larger and is designed for display.

Extension activity

Design a piece of promotional material for a leisure and tourism organisation that is aimed at a specific target market.

Think about it

Any piece of promotional material can be investigated using AIDA analysis:

▥ attention

▥ interest

▥ desire

▥ action.

Group activity

Discuss and identify the target markets of a variety of leisure and tourism organisations from pieces of their promotional materials.

Summary question

Analyse a range of leisure and tourism promotional materials to identify the market segments they each target.

Summary

Pieces of promotional materials can be used to identify the target markets of leisure and tourism organisations.

9.11 Health and safety matters

Leisure and tourism organisations deal with health and safety. They need to look after the health and safety of their customers, employees and members of the public who may be affected by their activities.

Reasons why leisure and tourism organisations deal with health and safety are:

■ it helps them as businesses

■ it is morally a good thing to do

■ the law says that they must.

James is the manager of a visitor attraction. In Cartoon **A** James explains how dealing with health and safety helps leisure and tourism organisations succeed as businesses.

Diagram **B** shows some of the potential **hazards** that pose a risk to visitors at a historic-site attraction such as a ruined castle.

To run a visitor attraction as a business you need customers. Customers won't visit if they think the attraction's dangerous. The last thing I need is a customer who has an accident and it's on the TV news or in the paper. That puts people right off.

Customers have accidents. They can take you to court and sue you. You don't want that. It gets in the papers and costs you money. It's much better to have health and safety properly sorted out so you avoid problems before they happen.

A *Health and safety matters*

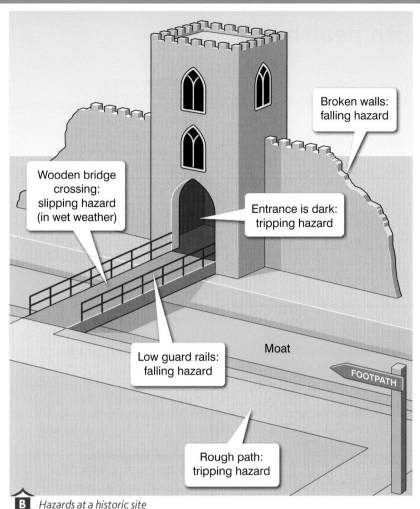

B *Hazards at a historic site*

Activities

1   a Outline three hazards to customers that are identified in
        Diagram **B**.

    b Suggest two other sources of risk in Diagram **B**.

2   Staff are employed in a café inside the castle in Diagram **B**. Describe
    the range of hazards they may face.

3   Suggest one way in which the historic attraction in Diagram **B** may
    pose a hazard to people other than to its customers.

Coursework activity

Visit a leisure and tourism facility. Assess the range of hazards there to:

a customers

b staff

c the public.

Summary question

Explain why dealing with health and safety is important to leisure and
tourism organisations.

Group activity

Talk about leisure and tourism
facilities you have visited. What
hazards were there? Do you think
the organisations concerned
should have done more to
manage the risk they posed?
What could they have done?

Summary

Leisure and tourism
organisations deal with health
and safety because it matters
to them as businesses.

Dealing with health and safety

Leisure and tourism organisations take measures to ensure the health and safety of staff and customers and members of the wider public who may be affected by their activities.

Hazards leisure and tourism organisations may have to deal with include:

- tripping, slipping and falling
- fire
- food poisoning
- hot materials, for example in a kitchen
- lifting and moving heavy objects
- dangerous substances.

Objectives

Describe and explain measures that leisure and tourism organisations have put in place to ensure the health and safety of people

Describe and compare how leisure and tourism organisations deal with a health and safety issue.

Case study

A fireworks display

Map **A** shows the layout of an organised fireworks display. The display is scheduled to take place at 7.30pm in a town's public park. In addition to the measures shown in Map **A**:

- The park will be closed to the public on the day of the display until 6pm and after the display ends at 8pm.
- Several roads near to the park will be closed between 5pm and 9pm.
- The organisers will work closely with the **emergency services** (fire, police and ambulance) to ensure health and safety.

Key terms

Emergency services: public services that help people in the event of an emergency. The three main emergency services are the fire, police and ambulance services.

Think about it

All leisure and tourism organisations take measures to ensure health and safety. Think of examples you have seen, and look out for others.

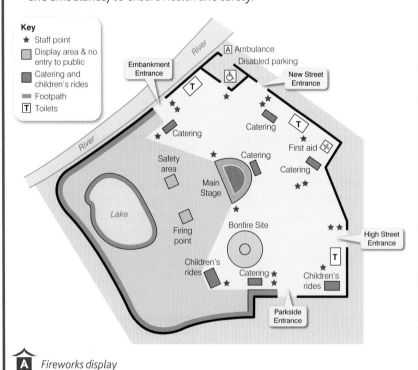

Key
- ★ Staff point
- ▢ Display area & no entry to public
- ▨ Catering and children's rides
- ▦ Footpath
- T Toilets

A Fireworks display

Fire is a health and safety issue at a fireworks display. Measures that a hotel may take to deal with the same issue include:

- training staff in evacuation procedures
- notices to tell people what to do in the event of a fire
- having clearly signed internal fire doors, emergency fire exits, fire escapes and evacuation meeting points; fire extinguishers and automatic sprays; smoke and fire alarms
- acting on the advice of the fire service.

Activities

Study Map A. Fire is one hazard to health and safety that the planned fireworks display poses.

1 Outline two hazards to health and safety other than fire that are posed by the planned fireworks display.

2 Describe and explain the range of measures that has been taken to deal with the fire hazard.

Extension activity

Visit a leisure and tourism facility. Describe and explain the range of measures that has been put in place to ensure health and safety.

Summary questions

1 Describe and explain measures that one leisure and tourism organisation has put in place to ensure the health and safety of its staff and customers.

2 Compare how two leisure and tourism organisations deal with one health and safety issue.

Group activity

How effective do you think the health and safety measures you have seen are? How would you improve them?

Summary

Leisure and tourism organisations take measures to deal with health and safety.

Different leisure and tourism organisations may deal with similar hazards in more or less different ways.

In this chapter you have learnt:

Leisure and tourism organisations benefit from operating as businesses by:

✔ using up-to-date business systems

✔ promoting their products/services

✔ recognising different attitudes and cultures among their customers

✔ dealing with health and safety issues.

More detail about two aspects of leisure and tourism businesses:

✔ marketing (promotion and sales)

✔ health and safety issues and how risks are managed.

Revision quiz

1 What are front office and back office business operations?

2 How are business activities that involve staff dealing directly with customers described?

3 What do the initials ICT stand for?

4 a How is a flyer different from a leaflet?
  b Name three other types of promotional materials.

5 Why can risk not be eliminated from leisure and tourism?

6 What is a bus wrap?

7 What does the I stand for in AIDA?

8 Outline the grey market segment.

9 Mailshots are unsolicited. What does unsolicited mean?

10 Give two hazards that are posed by paths at a visitor attraction to customers that walk on them.

AQA Examination-style questions

1 Choose one leisure and tourism organisation. Evaluate either how your organisation promotes its products/services or how it deals with one health and safety issue. *(9 marks)*

AQA Examiner's tip The instruction is evaluate. As well as describing what the organisation has done you also need to say how well it does it.

Objectives

Describe the range of employment opportunities that is available in the leisure and tourism industry

Describe the duties of two leisure and tourism jobs

Describe the personal qualities and skills expected for leisure and tourism jobs.

Introduction

There are many different types of jobs in leisure and tourism. Leisure and tourism organisations employ customer service staff at different levels of seniority. Two key levels of seniority are:

- operations level: jobs which involve delivering the organisations' products/services to customers or providing customers with information about them
- management level: jobs which involve supervising operations staff.

What is this chapter about?

Chapter 10 is about the wide range of employment opportunities that is available in leisure and tourism at operational and management level. The chapter focuses very clearly on customer-fronting roles. These are job roles that involve dealing with customers. They are the only jobs in leisure and tourism that you should learn about for your GCSE.

Starter activity

Discuss what leisure and tourism customer service jobs you know of. What do they involve doing? What sort of people do you think they most suit? Make a chart to illustrate your thoughts.

Leisure and tourism organisations vary a lot, as this list of the types of organisations that you need to learn about shows:

- leisure centres and health and fitness clubs
- theatres, cinemas, arenas, museums and art galleries
- sports venues and facilities
- home-based leisure providers: computer gaming and DVD rental shops, libraries and internet home-based leisure providers
- visitor attractions
- restaurants, cafés and takeaways
- hotels and self-catering accommodation
- travel agencies and online booking websites
- tourist information centres
- airlines, ferry, train and coach operators and car hire firms.

All these different types of leisure and tourism organisations employ people:

- in different **customer service roles**
- at different **levels of seniority**.

The result is that there is a very wide range of employment opportunities available in leisure and tourism.

Objectives

Understand that there is a wide range of leisure and tourism jobs.

Key terms

Customer service roles: jobs that involve dealing directly with customers to provide them with products/services or information about them. These roles are customer-fronting roles.

Levels of seniority: ranks or levels of importance within an organisation.

Case study

Arriva

Arriva is one of the largest transport operators in Europe and employs more than 40,000 people. In the UK, Arriva operates:

- buses to different parts of the UK, including London where Arriva also runs the Original Tour open-top bus sightseeing tours
- trains – Arriva Trains Wales and CrossCountry are both Arriva operations.

Table **B** gives examples of job opportunities provided by Arriva Trains Wales. The organisation's operations and management staff who work at railway stations (Photo **A**) and in the passenger sections of the trains have customer-fronting roles. Train drivers and head office managers do not.

A *Railway station operations staff member*

Background knowledge

Arriva is an international leisure and tourism organisation. It operates in 12 European countries, including the UK. The others are:

- the Czech Republic
- Denmark
- Germany
- Hungary
- Italy
- the Netherlands
- Poland
- Portugal
- Slovakia
- Spain
- Sweden.

∞links

www.arriva.co.uk/arriva/en/careers is the gateway page for the Arriva website careers section.

B   *Employment opportunities provided by Arriva*

Employment level	Locations	Examples of job opportunities
Operations	On trains and at railway stations	Conductors on trains sell and check tickets and provide information to customers. Station operators sell tickets and provide help and information to customers. Catering staff provide refreshments for customers on trains.
Management	At head office in Cardiff and at railway stations	Managers at Arriva Trains Wales head office in Cardiff lead departments, including: • marketing • human resources • safety • planning. Station managers supervise staff at major railway stations.

Derived from www.arriva.co.uk/arriva/en/careers

AQA *Examiner's tip*

Stick rigidly to jobs:

■ in leisure and tourism organisations of the types listed above and in the AQA GCSE Leisure and Tourism specification

■ that are customer-fronting.

Activities

1   Outline the range of employment opportunities provided by Arriva Trains Wales.

2   Research and describe one of these job roles in more detail.

3   a   Find out about the range of employment opportunities provided by Arriva's UK businesses other than Arriva Trains Wales.

  b   Make a table to summarise your findings.

Extension activity

Access the websites of a variety of leisure and tourism organisations of different types. Make a display to illustrate the breadth of employment opportunities that the organisations provide.

Coursework activity

Visit a leisure and tourism facility. Find out about and describe the range of employment opportunities that is provided by the organisation that runs the facility.

Summary question

Make a poster to illustrate the wide variety of leisure and tourism jobs.

Group activity

If you worked in leisure and tourism what type of leisure and tourism organisation would you prefer? What job roles would you like and not like and why?

Summary

Leisure and tourism organisations provide a wide range of employment opportunities.

Jobs are either at operations or at management level.

Relevant leisure and tourism jobs are customer-fronting jobs.

Some leisure and tourism organisations provide products/services largely for the local community. They are sources of employment for local people too.

Local leisure jobs and **careers** are provided by a variety of health and fitness, and catering and hospitality businesses:

- leisure centres
- health and fitness clubs
- restaurants, cafés and takeaways.

These facilities provide customer-fronting jobs at both operations and management level. For example in a restaurant:

- restaurant manager
- head waiter/waitress and waiting staff
- bar manager and bar staff.

Key terms

Careers: progression of job roles in people's working lifetimes, for example from operations to management level roles.

Case study

David Lloyd Leisure

The David Lloyd Leisure group is a leisure and tourism organisation that operates 78 health and fitness and racquet sports clubs in the UK. It employs 6,000 people, including a health and fitness team of more than 750.

Customer-fronting employment opportunities in David Lloyd Leisure clubs range from health and fitness instructors and racquet coaches to jobs in sales, club operations (in reception (Photo **A**), for example), catering and hospitality.

Table **B** lists some health and fitness clubs operated by a UK leisure and tourism organisation.

A *Customer-fronting at reception*

B *Health and fitness job vacancies*

East of England, December

Job title	Location
General manager	Ipswich
Member adviser (reception)	Luton
Lifeguard	Luton
Swimming instructors	Cambridge and Luton

Activities

1 Describe the range of customer-fronting employment opportunities provided by David Lloyd Leisure:

a at operations level

b in management.

2 Explain how catering and hospitality jobs may be available in these types of leisure facilities:

a visitor attractions

b sports and entertainment venues

c transport facilities.

Extension activity

Research the role of a leisure and tourism facility general manager. Describe:

a what a general manager does

b the sort of person leisure and tourism organisations look for as a general manager.

Coursework activity

Describe the range of employment opportunities that is available in the health and fitness, and catering and hospitality sectors of the leisure and tourism industry in your local area.

Summary question

Describe the range of employment opportunities that exists in either the health and fitness sector or the catering and hospitality sector of the leisure and tourism industry.

∞ links

www.davidlloyd.co.uk is the homepage for David Lloyd Leisure.

Think about it

Employment opportunities in catering and hospitality are found in many types of leisure and tourism facilities not just in restaurants, cafés and takeaways: for example health and fitness clubs also provide jobs in catering and hospitality.

AQA Examiner's tip

You only need to be able to describe the range of employment opportunities in these sectors of the industry:

- health and fitness
- catering and hospitality
- visitor attractions
- retail travel
- transport
- tour operators
- accommodation.

Group activity

What differences are there between a job and a career? What can people do to help themselves progress from operations to management level jobs?

Summary

Local leisure jobs are often available in the health and fitness, and catering and hospitality sectors of the leisure and tourism industry.

Employment opportunities in travel and tourism may be available locally or they may involve travelling or moving to another area.

Leisure and tourism businesses that may offer travel and tourism employment opportunities are:

* visitor attractions
* **retail travel** agents
* transport providers
* tour operators
* accommodation providers.

Objectives

Describe the range of employment opportunities that is available in the following sectors of the leisure and tourism industry:

visitor attractions

retail travel

transport

tour operators

accommodation.

Case study

Go There: jobs in retail travel

Go There is a travel industry newspaper that is also available online. The *Go There* website job section (Diagram **A**) allows users to search for current vacancies in 14 identified categories of travel jobs. Retail travel is one. Employment opportunities in retail travel listed by the *Go There* website include management and operations level jobs:

* senior travel consultant and travel consultant (full and part time), including specialist positions in cruise and business travel

* branch manager and assistant manager.

Many listed jobs are featured on behalf of recruitment agents such as Blue Strawberry. Travel industry employers use agents to advertise for and select staff on their behalf. *Go There* provides a place for such agents to list vacancies.

The *Go There* job section features a careers advice section that includes articles about employment prospects in retail travel.

◄ ► | C | + | http:// | Q-

Go There jobs

Travel Jobs from Go There Jobs

At Go There Jobs you can search our database for hundreds of travel jobs.

Regestration is free and you can upload your CV, set up email job alerts, subscribe to RSS feeds and apply for travel jobs online. Start your job search now.

JOB SEARCH

Select one or more Job categories:

☐ All	☐ Arline	☐ Business Travel
☐ Conferences and Events	☐ Cruise	☐ Foreign Exchange
☐ Home Working - Travel	☐ Online Travel	☐ Overseas Travel
☐ Retail travel	☐ Tour operator	☐ Travel Admin / accounts and ticketing
☐ Travel HR / Training	☐ Travel Management	☐ Travel Sales and Marketing
☐ Other		

A *Travel jobs section*

Activities

Study a travel and tourism job vacancies listing such as the *Travel Weekly* job section.

1 Describe the ranges of management and operations level employment opportunities you find there.

2 Choose one advertised vacancy. Find out and outline the:

a duties of the job holder

b experience, qualifications and skills expected.

Group activity

Working individually or as a pair, choose one of the following sectors of the leisure and tourism industry: visitor attractions, retail travel, transport, tour operators and accommodation. Research the range of employment opportunities that is available in your chosen sector. Pool your results with those of other members of the group and describe the range of employment opportunities that is available in the sectors of the leisure and tourism industry that are listed above.

Coursework activity

Research and evaluate the range of travel and tourism employment opportunities available for young people in your local area.

Extension activity

Do you think jobs in travel and tourism are going to increase in number? Why/why not? Which types of jobs may increase and decrease in number?

Summary question

Describe the range of employment opportunities that can be found in one sector of the travel and tourism industry.

Key terms

Retail travel: organisations that sell holidays and business travel products/services directly to customers.

AQA Examiner's tip

Many travel and tourism employment opportunities are in the UK.

Visitor attractions and transport and accommodation providers are important sources of travel and tourism employment.

Remember

Recent changes in leisure and tourism have included a reduction in the number of travel agent shops in town centres. More people have been taking advantage of the internet to make their own travel arrangements.

Travel agents have responded by setting up their own online booking services and call centres and by opening out-of-town travel supermarket outlets on retail parks.

∞ links

www.travelweekly.co.uk/jobs is the internet address of the job search pages of the *Travel Weekly* website.

Summary

Travel and tourism employment opportunities are provided by a variety of different types of leisure and tourism organisations.

10.4 Resort representatives

Resort representatives work in leisure and tourism destinations. They are employed by tour operators. Their role is to look after their company's customers':

- health, safety and security
- holiday enjoyment.

The UK's major package tour operators offer people employment opportunities as resort reps. Thomson, Thomas Cook, First Choice and Kuoni, for example, employ reps in destinations overseas and so do tour operators specialising in camping and self-catering holidays such as Eurocamp and Keycamp.

Objectives

Describe the resort representative employment opportunity.

∞ links

www.tuicareers.co.uk is the website for careers with TUI UK and Ireland.

Case study

First Choice resort representative

First Choice is part of the TUI group of leisure and tourism businesses that also includes Thomson. Overseas employment opportunities with First Choice include jobs as resort representatives (Photo **A**) in beach (or seaside) resorts around the Mediterranean, and ski/snowsports resorts in the Alps. Table **B** shows the range of summer season customer-fronting opportunities.

A First Choice resort representatives

B *Resort representative roles*

Role	Description	Previous experience/qualifications
Overseas travel adviser (rep)	Caring for the welfare of customers from arrival to departure. Providing expert resort advice. Promoting excursions and activities. Building customer loyalty.	Varied customer service experience. Second language desirable.
Children's representative	Looking after customers' children. Running a children's club and entertaining children of different ages.	Previous experience working with groups of children or a childcare qualification.
Specialist representative	Working as a resort representative for TUI's more upmarket brands (Sovereign, Citalia and Meon).	Previous resort representative experience. Aged over 21. Hold a full manual driving licence.

Derived from www.firstchoice4jobs.co.uk/fe/tpl_firstchoice01.asp

Reps in many resorts work as members of a team. They need to ensure that package holiday customers are met at their point of arrival and safely transferred to their accommodation. Hotel or campsite-based reps organise **welcome meetings**. At these they give customers information about the destination. Reps also use welcome meetings to promote and sell excursions and activities that they have organised.

AQA *Examiner's tip*

Resort representative is one overseas employment opportunity in leisure and tourism. Hotels, for example, offer others.

Promoting such **optional extra** trips is an important part of the rep's role. The commission earned significantly adds to the rep's income.

Reps need to be on-hand or contactable throughout customers' holidays to:

- help them deal with any emergencies
- provide information
- sell and take part in optional extra excursions and activities.

Reps need to ensure that customers are safely transferred to their departure airport and that they are informed of any delays.

Many reps are employed on a seasonal basis. Reps for the coming summer season are usually recruited in the preceding autumn or winter. Successful or experienced reps are sometimes offered year-round contracts because the tour operator wants to retain its good staff.

Background knowledge

First Choice and Thomson are tour operator brand names. Each business is a part of TUI UK and Ireland, which is itself a division of the TUI international travel company TUI Travel plc.

Remember

There are two sorts of integration: horizontal and vertical. The 2007 merger between tour operators First Choice and Thomson was horizontal integration.

Vertical integration happens when business activities from different stages in the chain of distribution join. First Choice operates travel agent shops, as well as acting as a tour operator.

Activities

1. a Outline the range of resort representative employment opportunities offered by a tour operator such as First Choice.
   b Suggest the kind of person that one of these opportunities would suit well.

2. a Prepare a welcome meeting in an overseas leisure and tourism destination.
   b Explain why welcome meetings are important to:
      i tour operators
      ii resort representatives.

Group activity

Would you like to work as a resort representative? What do you think are the advantages and disadvantages for a young college leaver of working as a resort representative?

Coursework activity

Describe the employment opportunities provided by a tour operator other than resort representative.

Summary question

Describe the work of a resort representative.

Summary

UK-based tour operators provide resort representative employment opportunities overseas.

Resort representatives are the face of the company in the destination. They have to be able to deal with a wide variety of customer service situations.

The duties of a leisure and tourism job are the tasks that the holder of that job must perform.

The duties of a particular job are usually given in a **job description**. Leisure and tourism organisations give these to potential applicants for a job. Job descriptions help:

▪ potential applicants to decide if the job would suit them and whether they should go ahead and apply

▪ employers to clarify to employees exactly what is required of them so that the job the organisation wants doing is the job that is done.

Key terms

Job description: a formal statement of what a job entails.

Case study

Hotel manager

A hotel manager (Photo **A**) is responsible for:

▪ the day-to-day running of the hotel and the supervision of its staff

▪ the hotel's services, including front-of-house operations such as reception, food and drink operations and housekeeping

▪ maximising the hotel's profits

▪ setting an example to staff by personally delivering excellent customer service.

Diagram **B** is part of a job description for a hotel manager. It lists the daily activities carried out in performing that role.

Manager's daily activities

• plan and organise accommodation, catering and other services of the hotel

• promote and market the hotel

• manage the hotel's finances

• keep accurate records

• set and achieve sales targets

• recruit, train and supervise staff

• plan staff work schedules

• meeting and greeting customers

• deal with customer complaints and comments

• solve problems

• ensure that events and conferences run smoothly

• supervise the maintenance of the hotel building and furnishings

• deal with contractors and suppliers

• check the hotel is secure

• inspect the hotel and the products/services it is providing

• check that regulations including licensing laws and health and safety requirements are properly followed.

B *Job description: hotel manager*

A *Hotel manager*

Sources

Leisure and tourism organisations' own websites often have careers or working-for-us sections that give information about employment opportunities, including current vacancies and job descriptions.

Background knowledge

The manager of a large hotel is likely to spend much of the day in meetings with heads of department to oversee the running of the business. However, such managers may well spend time observing staff and talking with customers to check on the delivery of customer service.

Departments in a hotel typically include:

- reception
- restaurant and catering
- conference and meetings
- housekeeping
- maintenance.

In a smaller hotel the manager is much more likely to be involved daily in the hands-on running of the place. This may include carrying out reception duties or serving meals if the need arises, for example at busy times.

Activities

1   Make a presentation to illustrate the duties of a hotel manager.

2   Choose one of the duties listed in Diagram **B**. Explain why it is important to the hotel as a business that the manager carries out the duty.

Group activity

Research a variety of leisure and tourism job descriptions. Display your results. Compare the duties of two jobs at different levels of seniority in one leisure and tourism organisation.

Coursework activity

Describe the range of employment opportunities available for young people in the hotels of one leisure and tourism destination.

Summary question

Describe the duties of two customer service jobs at different levels of seniority in leisure and tourism.

links

www.prospects.ac.uk and **www.gumtree.com** are two websites that give information about jobs and careers in hotels.

AQA   *Examiner's tip*

Leisure and tourism jobs are at different levels of seniority. Learn about jobs at two levels:

- operations
- management.

Summary

Duties are the tasks that a leisure and tourism job holder has to do.

Operations and management staff have duties they are required to perform.

10.6 Skills and qualities

Skills are abilities that people can learn. Qualities are personality traits that people have and which are part of their make-up as a person. Different leisure and tourism jobs call for different skills and personal qualities.

People can do jobs because they have the necessary skills or abilities. There are two main types of skills:

- people skills
- technical skills.

People skills are abilities needed to work with and communicate successfully with other people. These are:

- speaking clearly, politely and persuasively face-to-face and over the telephone
- listening carefully
- communicating accurately in writing.

Technical skills are skills that are specific to doing a certain job or to working in a particular leisure and tourism organisation. Technical skills may include:

- using equipment safely and efficiently
- using specific pieces of computer software
- the ability to complete numerical tasks such as calculating amounts of money
- performing set tasks and procedures as laid down by an organisation.

Case study

Travel consultant

Travel consultants advise customers about leisure and business tourism travel. Their role is to sell their employers' products/services to customers. Travel consultants work in a variety of environments:

- travel agent shops
- travel supermarkets
- call centres
- at home.

Diagram **A** is an advertisement for a travel consultant job in a call centre.

Travel Consultant

Job Hours: Full-Time

Job Position: Permanent

Job Role: Travel Web sales consultant

Travel Consultant required for call centre.

We are looking for a suitably experienced travel consultant. The successful candidate will be a hard-working person who is familiar with on-line travel. You will already have the skills to load information onto websites and to sell a wide variety of travel products, including on-line travel, dynamic packages and cruises.

We offer a very competitive salary with excellent commission.

 Advertisement for a travel consultant job in a call centre

Leisure and tourism customer-fronting jobs require personal qualities, as well as skills if they are to be done well. Organisations are keen to recruit people who have appropriate personal qualities such as confidence, friendliness, cheerfulness, calmness, patience and a good sense of humour.

When they are recruiting new staff some leisure and tourism organisations see personal qualities as more important than technical skills. Such organisations prefer to select people because they have a positive attitude towards serving customers. They train new staff in the skills that are needed to do a job in the way the organisation wants it done. This is often done through **on-the-job training**.

Background knowledge

Home-working (sometimes called teleworking) has increased in recent years. The growth of the internet has made it possible for many people to work at home. They communicate with colleagues and customers online and via fax, telephone and post. In leisure and tourism this trend has led to the growth of home-based travel consultancy work.

Activities

1 Explain the differences between:

a skills and qualities

b people skills and technical skills.

2 Study Diagram **A**. Analyse the range of skills and personal qualities that the employer is seeking in the successful applicant.

Group activity

What leisure and tourism jobs would you like to do? What skills and personal qualities do you think are needed to do these jobs?

Extension activity

Investigate the skills and qualities sought by a range of leisure and tourism organisations.

Coursework activity

Find out about a leisure and tourism job that is currently available in your local area that would suit a school or college leaver. Describe and explain the range of skills and qualities that the employer is seeking.

Summary question

Describe the personal qualities and skills that two leisure and tourism organisations expect of the holders of jobs in customer service.

Key terms

On-the-job training: learning a task while doing it.

⊚⊃ links

www.careersadvice.direct.gov.uk/ helpwithyourcareer/jobprofiles/ profiles/profile335 is a UK government careers advice webpage about travel consultancy work.

AQA Examiner's tip

Be very clear about the links between specific skills and personal qualities and people doing specific jobs well.

Travel agents' websites often have job links. Look on the site map or in the About us section to find them.

Summary

Skills are needed to perform the duties of leisure and tourism jobs.

Personal qualities enable people to do their jobs well.

Leisure and tourism organisations look for people who have an appropriate balance of skills and qualities.

Leisure and tourism organisations know that people do well in leisure and tourism jobs if they have the right skills and personal qualities. When **recruitment** managers **select** new staff they look for people who have good people skills and a positive approach to dealing with customers. Interviews are an important way in which leisure and tourism organisations assess the personal qualities of job applicants. Leisure and tourism organisations often train new young staff in the technical skills they need to do their jobs **in-house**.

Objectives

Describe the personal qualities and skills expected of the holders of customer service jobs in leisure and tourism.

Case study

What Fitness First want

Fitness First is a leisure and tourism organisation that runs health and fitness clubs across the UK. Personal qualities are very important to Fitness First when managers are selecting new staff. Cartoon **A** is an extract from an interview with Fitness First's UK recruitment manager.

Key terms

Recruitment: the process of looking for new staff.

Select: to choose which people to employ.

In-house: job training that a leisure and tourism organisation provides for its own staff.

> What do you look for at interviews?

> We look for people to be positive from the start to the end. This industry is based squarely on customer services and the personality of staff.

> What about experience and skills?

> Certain jobs need to have relevant qualifications especially in fitness jobs. Get some experience. This is easy enough to do by offering to work some hours a week, unpaid if necessary, at a local gym.
>
> Finding good-quality, qualified fitness staff can be a struggle. However, we have our own purpose built training academy in Chesterfield where we can train people in the relevant qualifications if they show the right desire and attitude.

> What is your top tip when applying for a job?

> In the interview ... SMILE! I have had a few people who claim to be 'outgoing, enthusiastic and friendly' while not smiling once!

A *Interview with a leisure recruitment manager*

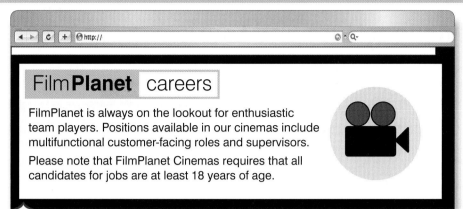

FilmPlanet is always on the lookout for enthusiastic team players. Positions available in our cinemas include multifunctional customer-facing roles and supervisors.

Please note that FilmPlanet Cinemas requires that all candidates for jobs are at least 18 years of age.

B *FilmPlanet careers*

Activities

1 Explain why interviews are an important way for leisure and tourism organisations to assess people's personal qualities.

2 Study Cartoon **A**.

a Suggest why it is important to be positive in an interview for a leisure and tourism job.

b Outline one example of in-house training that Fitness First provides for its staff.

3 Study Diagram **B**.

a Analyse the personal qualities needed to be an 'enthusiastic team player'.

b i   What is meant by multifunctional customer-facing roles?

  ii Suggest what these are likely to be in a multiplex cinema.

c Explain why FilmPlanet requires all job applicants to be at least 18 years old.

Group activity

How true is it that for doing a leisure and tourism job well, personal qualities matter more than skills?

Coursework activity

Evaluate the skills and qualities needed for leisure and tourism employment opportunities that are available for young people in your local area.

Summary question

Explain why skills and personal qualities are needed to do leisure and tourism jobs well.

Remember

Skills are abilities that can be learned, so leisure and tourism organisations can train staff to gain them.

Personal qualities are parts of a person's make-up. They cannot be taught so leisure and tourism organisations look for staff who already have the personal qualities they want when they recruit.

AQA Examiner's tip

You need to be able to describe leisure and tourism opportunities for people in their teens or 20s. Leisure and tourism organisations look for young people who have a positive attitude to serving customers.

Extension activity

Investigate the skills and qualities sought by a variety of leisure and tourism organisations other than Fitness First. Share and discuss your findings.

Summary

Leisure and tourism organisations are keen to recruit staff with a positive attitude to customer service. Therefore personal qualities are very important.

Working in leisure and tourism

Jobs in leisure and tourism involve working with people. Customers of leisure and tourism organisations may be:

- enjoying their own leisure time locally or in a leisure and tourism destination
- away from home on business.

Demand for organisations' products/services is often at times other than those when many people are at work. As a result, working in leisure and tourism often means:

- working unsocial hours
- seasonal employment
- part time or casual work.

Background knowledge

The Beeches is one of five residential conference centres run by the Chartridge Conference Company in the UK. The company takes its name from the Chartridge Conference Centre in Chesham, Buckinghamshire.

links

www.chartridge.co.uk is the homepage of the Chartridge Conference Company website.

Case study

The Beeches

The Beeches (Photo **A**) is a conference centre in Birmingham. It is located in the residential suburb of Bournville. Business tourists who are presenting or attending meetings at Beeches often stay overnight in one of the centre's own bedrooms. There is a restaurant, bar and fitness room for such customers. Beeches organises social events such as weddings – some of the guests may stay overnight (Cartoon **B**).

Many staff are full time workers whose hours are based on a 40-hour week. Employees work five days out of seven. A rota system is used to ensure that Beeches is staffed at weekends and that weekend working is shared out fairly among the staff.

A *The Beeches*

Full time employees work from Monday to Friday some weeks but during others they work for at least one weekend day.

Some of the catering and bar jobs at Beeches are part time or casual opportunities that are taken up mostly by people who live locally. Other, generally younger, staff such as restaurant waiters are live-in employees.

I present meetings for my company at Beeches quite often. I come across staff in a variety of customer-fronting roles: at reception, in IT support (I need that for my PowerPoint presentations) and serving food and drink in the coffee lounge, restaurant and bar.

B *A customer's experience*

AQA *Examiner's tip*

Business tourists travel to destinations to work at meetings or conferences. However, they also create a demand for leisure and tourism products/services outside their working hours especially during the evenings.

Activities

1 Describe how Beeches tries to meet the leisure needs of its business tourism customers.

2 Outline ways in which employment at Beeches can involve working unsocial hours.

3 Suggest why:

a part time work at Beeches may suit people who are local

b live-in work may suit younger staff members.

Extension activity

Research and analyse the nature of employment in a leisure and tourism organisation other than a conference centre.

Group activity

Would you like to work in leisure and tourism? How would you feel about working in the evenings and at weekends? How would you cope with a seasonal job?

Coursework activity

Investigate two leisure and tourism employment opportunities for young people in your local area. Compare how much they involve part time, casual and unsocial hours and seasonal working.

Summary question

Describe, using examples, how leisure and tourism employment can be:

▪ full time, part time or casual

▪ seasonal

▪ at unsocial hours.

Summary

Leisure and tourism employment can be:

full time, part time or casual

seasonal

at unsocial hours.

10

In this chapter you have learnt:

There are many different employment opportunities in leisure and tourism. Leisure and tourism customer-fronting staff are:

✔ operational – delivering organisations' products/services to customers or providing customers with information about them

✔ management – senior to operational staff, supervising their work.

Revision quiz

1 What is meant by a customer-fronting job?

2 Give two levels of seniority at which leisure and tourism staff work.

3 Where would you be likely to find a job description?

4 a What is the difference between a skill and a personal quality?
  b Give one example of each.

5 What is?:
a a duty
b in-house training
c on-the-job training.

6 Why is seasonal employment quite common in leisure and tourism?

7 What is?:
a an unsocial hour
b casual work.

AQA Examination-style questions

1 Choose a leisure and tourism organisation. Describe the duties of two customer-fronting jobs in your organisation.

2 Compare the personal qualities and skills needed to do these jobs. *(8 marks)*

Examiner's tip | Customer-fronting jobs are ones that mostly involve dealing with customers.

Glossary

A

Actual customers: people who are visiting or have visited a leisure and tourism destination or attraction.

All-inclusive hotels: hotels where customers pay for products and services by a one-off payment, in advance.

Appeal: what it is about a destination that attracts people to visit.

Après-ski: evening leisure activities provided in ski and snowsports resorts.

Areas of outstanding natural beauty (AONBs): scenic areas of countryside, legally protected but distinct from a national park. In 2008 there were 49 AONBs in the UK.

Arenas: large indoor venues.

Artery: a principal transport route such as a main railway line or motorway.

Assess: decide how well something is done or how important it is.

Attitudes: how people feel about something. Attitudes are based on people's views and beliefs.

B

Beach vendors: people who sell products/services informally to tourists on beaches.

Biodiversity: the variety of species.

Boutique hotels: small luxurious hotels with individual character. They normally charge premium prices.

Brands: trade names under which products/services are provided.

Brownies: a voluntary organisation that provides leisure activities for girls aged from 7 to 11 years.

Budget carriers: transport providers that carry people at discounted fares. Budget airlines operate more basic services than flag-carrier airlines.

Built attractions: attractions that were specifically developed or purpose-built to be visitor attractions.

Bus wraps: advertisements usually spray-painted that look as if they are wrapped around a bus.

Business class: a more comfortable and expensive class than economy.

Business operations: an organisation's activities that help it provide products/services to its customers.

Business tourism: being away from the usual home/work area for work-related reasons.

C

Carbon footprint: the amount of carbon a person or activity adds to the environment.

Carbon neutral: an equal balance between carbon added to and absorbed from the atmosphere.

Carbon-neutral resort: does not add net carbon to the atmosphere.

Careers: progression of job roles in people's working lifetimes, for example from operations to management level roles.

Charter: flights that are arranged for the use of tour operators' customers.

Closed questions: questionnaire or interview questions that may be answered briefly – yes or no, for example.

Commercial: attractions that are operated usually by a private sector organisation, to try to make a profit.

Community Centre: a building in a community that consists mainly of rooms that can be hired for leisure activities.

Companies: business organisations that are run by a group of people or by an individual.

Component: a discrete assessable element within a controlled assessment/qualification that is not itself formally reported, where the marks are recorded by the awarding body. A component/unit may contain one or more tasks.

Conservation groups: voluntary organisations who try to keep the environment as natural as possible and to protect it from negative tourism impacts.

Corporate hospitality: companies entertaining customers, for example by organising tickets and a party at a major sports event.

Countries of origin: countries where inbound tourists come from.

Cricket nets: lane-like practice facilities for cricket that are enclosed by large nets to stop the ball being hit far.

Cultures: beliefs, behaviours and ways of life that typify different social groups.

Customer-fronting: business activities that involve dealing directly with customers.

Customer service roles: jobs that involve dealing directly with customers to provide them with products/services or information about them. These roles are customer-fronting roles.

D

Discount price: a cheaper price than standard.

Disposable income: the money left over after paying for the necessities of life such as housing, energy and food. Leisure and tourism products/services are paid for from disposable income.

Dynamic packaging: customers creating their own travel package by combining trip elements usually chosen on a website.

E

Eating out: going out of the home to enjoy a meal with other people in a leisure and tourism facility such as a restaurant.

Eco-lodges: small hotels or guest houses that are run to ecotourism principles.

Economic well-being: how financially well off people are. How much money they have and whether they have secure employment are aspects of economic well-being.

Economy class: basic, cheaper, standard class.

Ecotourism: visiting a destination to enjoy its natural environment without damaging it.

Ecotourist-receiving area: a region visited by people taking part in ecotourism.

Emergency services: public services that help people in the event of an emergency. The three main emergency services are the fire, police and ambulance services.

Entertainment facilities: leisure facilities such as cinemas and theatres where customers enjoy shows.

Event: a single, specially organised leisure occasion that acts as a temporary visitor attraction. Sports matches and competitions, concerts, festivals and fêtes are examples.

Express trains: long-distance, relatively fast trains that make only limited stops.

F

Fast track: a means of allowing customers to avoid queuing by paying a premium price.

First class: most luxurious class.

Flag carrier: a traditional (as opposed to budget) airline that is regarded as its country's national airline.

Flyer: a piece of promotional material that consists of a single, unfolded sheet of paper.

Function room: a room (often quite large) in a facility such as a hotel or public house, which is available for hire for social events.

Funding: financing for a leisure and tourism facility. Sources of funding may, for example, be public (such as a council subsidy or government grant), from ticket sales or from voluntary donations.

G

Global positioning system (GPS): a means of accurately fixing a location on the earth's surface using a satellite signal. GPS devices can act as handheld electronic guides to visitor attractions in leisure and tourism destinations.

Green destination: one which appeals to visitors because of its clean, natural environment.

Grey market: the market segment of mature adults who are nearing retirement or who are recently retired.

Guest houses: small hotels with limited facilities that concentrate on providing accommodation and meals.

H

Hazards: elements of the risks that a leisure and tourism facility or activity poses to customers, staff or the public.

Heritage site: a place that helps us understand how people used to live.

Heritage tourism: visiting a destination or attraction whose appeal is linked to how people have lived.

Holiday villages: purpose-built tourist accommodation facilities that include a number of mobile homes or cabins.

Home-based leisure: spare-time activities people take part in at home.

Homestay: accommodation in someone's home.

Hoteliers: people who own and run hotels. Hotels may be run by individuals or by companies.

I

ICT systems: ways of carrying out business operations using information and communications technology.

Independent travel: tourists making their own travel and accommodation arrangements.

In-house: job training that a leisure and tourism organisation provides for its own staff.

Issue: a debate in which different people hold different views.

Itineraries: detailed journey programmes.

J

Job description: a formal statement of what a job entails.

K

Kids' Club: supervised children's activity sessions at leisure and tourism facilities such as hotels and campsites.

L

Leisure: the set of activities people enjoy in their spare time, when they are not working, sleeping or occupied with the necessities of life.

Leisure activity: a spare-time relaxation that is fun to do. Examples include reading, swimming and going to the cinema.

Leisure and tourism facilities: resources, including buildings, attractions and outdoor areas such as playing fields, that are provided by leisure and tourism organisations.

Leisure complex: a building or site where several leisure and tourism facilities are located.

Leisure market: the set of customers of leisure and tourism organisations who are local.

Leisure tourism: visiting a destination to relax, take part in leisure activities and have fun, for example going there on holiday.

Levels of seniority: ranks or levels of importance within an organisation.

Local leisure provision: leisure facilities that are provided in a place mainly for the people who live in it.

Locality: a small area such as a town, suburb or rural village.

Long-haul destinations: places that UK tourists travel to that are further from the UK than Europe or the Mediterranean basin.

M

Mailshot: a promotional technique. Pieces of promotional materials are sent unsolicited through the post (or electronically via email) to potential customers.

Marina: a harbour used for yachts and other pleasure craft.

Marine transport: water transport that crosses the sea rather than a freshwater body such as a river or lake.

Market: the set of people who may buy leisure and tourism products/services.

Market research: investigating the demand for products/services.

Market segments: divisions of a leisure and tourism organisation's market.

Market share: the fraction of the market that a leisure and tourism organisation wins for its products/services.

Merchandise: objects that are sold by a leisure and tourism organisation in order to help promote its products/services.

Migration: the permanent movement of people away from their home area.

Modes of transport: forms of transport, for example rail and air.

Motorway: the top grade of road.

Multiplex cinema: a multiscreen cinema.

N

National Park authority: a management organisation responsible for one UK national park.

National parks: large areas of attractive countryside that are legally protected for people to enjoy.

National trends: patterns of change over time that affect a whole country.

National Trust: a charity that conserves historic and scenic sites.

Negative impacts: the harm that tourism causes.

No-frills: the policy of budget airlines, which is to keep costs low by eliminating or charging for 'extras' such as in-flight catering.

O

Online travel providers: internet-based businesses that supply travel services, often acting as tour operators. Expedia, Travelocity and Opodo are examples.

On-the-job training: learning a task while doing it.

Open questions: questionnaire or interview questions designed to allow the subject to answer in some detail.

Optional extra: a product/service that is not included in the basic or package price and which customers may choose to buy.

Out of season: a time of year when a destination or facility has a quiet period. Some facilities may close out of season.

P

Partner organisation: an organisation that works with a leisure and tourism organisation to jointly provide products/ services.

Peak or high season: the busiest period of the year for a leisure and tourism destination. Tourism flow is high.

Physical recreation: a physical leisure activity that participants enjoy non-competitively.

Pistes: snow slopes in ski resorts that have been prepared for skiing and/or snowboarding.

Positive impacts: the benefits that tourism brings.

Potential customers: people who may decide to visit a leisure and tourism destination or attraction.

Premium price: a higher price than standard, paid for better quality.

Private transport: transport used by the owner and/or invited guests only: examples include private cars and cycles.

Promotion: how leisure and tourism organisations bring the products/ services they provide to the attention of their customers.

Public money: money that is collected from the population and spent on its behalf.

Public sector: attractions that are operated by a public body.

Public transport: transport that is available for anyone to use and for which fares are charged: common examples include buses and scheduled airliners.

R

Ramblers: people who walk in the countryside as a leisure activity.

Recruitment: the process of looking for new staff.

Regional tourist boards: government-funded authorities responsible for the development of tourism in a particular area.

Renewable energy sources: ways of obtaining power from sources that can be replaced.

Responsible tourism: leisure and tourism organisations or individual tourists behaving in ways that maximise the positive and minimise the negative impacts of tourism.

Restaurateurs: people who own and run restaurants. Restaurants may be run by individuals or by catering companies.

Retail travel: organisations that sell holidays and business travel products/services directly to customers.

Risk: the chance of accident or mishap.

S

Scheduled: flights for which tickets are on sale to the public and which operate to a timetable.

Select: to choose which people to employ.

Self-packaging: customers assembling their own package deal from a menu of optional components.

Short-haul destinations: places that UK tourists travel to that are in Europe or the Mediterranean basin.

Shoulder season: tourism flows are at an intermediate level in this period, either side of the high or peak season.

Social segregation: the separation of different groups of people from each other. Gender and age are two factors which can cause people to enjoy leisure separately from people from other groups.

Socialising: going out of the home to spend leisure time with other people.

Spa: a leisure facility that people visit for health or beauty reasons. In the past, and still sometimes today, this was 'to take the waters'. Modern spas offer a range of health and beauty treatments.

Special-interest holiday: one whose main focus is a particular leisure activity.

Special-interest leisure: spare-time activities people take part in as a hobby or pastime.

Sport: an organised physical leisure activity that is competitive.

Sports spectating: watching sports events.

Stadia: the plural of stadium: a large outdoor facility where sports events such as football matches are held.

Stately homes: large houses often on big country estates, which are the ancestral homes of landowning families. They are now heritage tourism attractions.

Sun, sea and sand: a description of a summer beach holiday, particularly to an overseas destination.

Sustainability: the ability to sustain or conserve the environment and people's ways of life into the future by minimising negative impacts.

Sustainable development: growth that is planned to minimise negative impacts on the environment and on people's lives.

T

Tailor-made holidays: holiday packages especially assembled to meet a customer's individual needs.

Target market: the set of customers at which a leisure and tourism organisation aims its promotional activities.

Taxi ranks: roadside locations where people can hire a taxi.

Transport interchanges: points or facilities (such as a rail terminal or airport) where people can change from one mode of transport to another.

Theme parks: large visitor attractions whose appeal to visitors is primarily based on mechanical rides.

Tourism: visiting a destination on a temporary basis, for example to stay overnight, with the intention of returning home afterwards.

Tourism Concern: a charity that campaigns against the negative impacts of tourism on local communities.

Tourism flow: the volume of tourists visiting a destination. This often varies according to season.

Tourism market: the set of customers of leisure and tourism organisations who have travelled to a destination.

Tourism's impact: the set of effects that tourism has on the environment and on people who live in destinations.

Tourist-receiving areas: regions that attract large numbers of visitors who live elsewhere.

Tourist town: a town which is visited by lots of tourists and where tourism plays a major part in the local economy.

Train operating companies (TOCs): leisure and tourism organisations that run trains in the UK. Examples include Virgin Trains, National Express East Coast and Arriva Trains Wales.

Transport for London: the public sector organisation that oversees the provision of public transport in London.

Transport principals: leisure and tourism organisations that provide transportation products/services.

Transport providers: leisure and tourism organisations that operate travel services.

Travel and tourism industry: the set of leisure and tourism organisations that provides for the needs of tourists.

Travel options: ways of travelling to a destination.

Traveline: a partnership of transport providers and local councils, which provides information about public transport in the UK.

Trunk road: a main road that is not a motorway. In the UK these are normally A roads such as the A30.

Turnover: the total income of a leisure and tourism organisation. Profit is the difference between the turnover and the cost of running the organisation.

V

Venues: leisure facilities such as a stadium or arena where events are held or shows are staged.

VFR: going away from home to stay with friends and relatives.

Village hall: a building in a village that consists mainly of a large room, which can be hired for leisure activities. It may act as a village community centre.

Visitor attractions: leisure facilities that customers visit and which are a natural, historic or built sight, a theme park or a major sports/entertainment venue.

Voluntary: attractions that are run on a not-for-profit basis, usually by a charity.

W

Welcome meetings: gatherings of customers organised by a resort representative to provide information and promote trips and activities.

World Heritage Site: a destination or attraction of great historic or cultural importance that is listed for protection by the United Nations (UN).

Glossary of terms for Controlled Assessment

Component

A discrete assessable element within a controlled assessment/qualification that is not itself formally reported, where the marks are recorded by the awarding body. A component/unit may contain one or more tasks.

Controlled Assessment

A form of internal assessment where the control levels are set for each stage of the assessment process: task setting; task taking; and task marking.

External assessment

A form of independent assessment in which question papers, assignments and tasks are set by the awarding body, taken under specified conditions (including detailed supervision and duration) and marked by the awarding body.

Mark scheme

A scheme detailing how credit is to be awarded in relation to a particular unit, component or task. A mark scheme normally characterises acceptable answers or levels of response to questions/tasks or parts of questions/tasks and identifies the amount of credit each attracts.

Task

A discrete element of external or controlled assessment that may include examinations, assignments, practical activities and projects.

Task marking

This specifies the way in which credit is awarded for candidates' outcomes. Marking involves the use of mark schemes and/or marking criteria produced by the awarding body.

Task setting

The specification of the assessment requirements. Tasks may be set by awarding bodies and/or teachers, as defined by subject-specific rules. Teacher-set tasks must be developed in line with awarding body specified requirements.

Task taking

The conditions for candidate support and supervision, and the authentication of candidates' work. Task taking may involve different parameters from those used in traditional written examinations, for example candidates may be allowed supervised access to sources such as the internet.

Unit

The smallest part of a qualification which is formally reported and can be separately certificated. A unit may comprise separately assessed components.

Index

Acknowledgements

Illustrations: Russ Daff (Beehive Illustration), David Russell Illustration, Abel Ippolito (Beehive Illustration)

The authors and publisher are grateful to the following for permission to reproduce copyright material:

Source material:

1.1 D © Kuoni; 1.3 B © www.macpherson-neil.co.uk/JustLuz/Beaches.htm; 1.6 A © TUI Travel PLC www.thomsonski.co.uk/destinations/italy/cervinia/zz1_cervinia_ski.htm, 1.6 C Ski Club of Great Britain Snowsports Analysis 2007; 2.3 Thanks to easyjet.com; 2.4 B Thanks to NEC; 2.6 B © County Durham Tourism Partnership; 3.3 © Fountains Abbey and Phrogg Design (The National Trust); 3.7 A text The Alnwick Garden Trust; 4.4 C text © Windermere Lake Cruises Ltd; 4.7 B www.easyjet.com 27/12/08; 4.9 B Thanks to www.easyjet.com 28/3/09; 5.7 Foster and Partners Architects; 6.1 B Kuoni; 6.3 C Tourism South East 2007; 6.4 D positivebeats.co.uk; 6.8 A The Travellers' Friend Limited; 6.8 B Park Inn by the Rezidor Group; 7.7 text Chelmsford Borough Council; 8.3 A, B Thanks to easyjet.com; 8.6 A Thanks to easyjet.com; 9.4 B Eurocamp; 9.7 B National Express East Coast; 10.1 B Arriva.co.uk; 10.4 B firstchoice4jobs.co.uk; 10.6 A www.leisurejobs.com

Photographs:

Cover photograph: courtesy of Getty Images

Chapter 1 panel and banner Getty Images; 1.1 B Getty Images, C Getty Images, D © Kuoni, E Getty Images; 1.2 A Fotolia, B Fotolia; 1.3 B Alamy, C Getty Images, D Getty Images; 1.4 A i–iv Fotolia; 1.5 A Getty Images, B Getty Images, C Corbis; 1.6 B Fotolia; 1.7 B Alamy; Chapter 2 panel and banner Alamy; 2.2 B Alamy; 2.3 B Corbis; 2.4 C Fotolia; 2.5 A Corbis; 2.6 A Alamy, B © County Durham Tourism Partnership; 2.7 A Corbis; Chapter 3 panel and banner iStock Photo, openers Corbis, iStock Photo, Corbis, Alton Towers; 3.1 B Alamy, C Corbis; 3.2 A iStock Photo; 3.3 B and C © Fountains Abbey and Phrogg Design (The National Trust); 3.4 A Legoland Windsor, B Alamy; 3.5 A iStock Photo; 3.6 A, B, D The Deep (EMIH Ltd); 3.7 A Alamy; Chapter 4 panel and banner Alamy; 4.1 B Getty Images, 4.2 A Alamy, B Virgin Trains; 4.3 B Alamy; 4.4 A Alamy, C Fotolia, D Alamy; 4.6 B Belfastairport.com, C Alamy; 4.7 C Alamy; 4.10 A Corbis; Chapter 5 panel and banner alamy; 5.1 A Corbis; 5.3 A, B Alamy; 5.5 B Corbis; 5.6 Alamy; 5.7 B Foster and Partners Architects; 5.7 D Corbis; 5.8 A, B Stephen Rickerby; 5.8 C Park Inn by the Rezidor Group; 5.9 A, B Alamy; 5.10 A Stephen Rickerby; Chapter 6 panel and banner Alamy; 6.1 B Kuoni; 6.2 A, B Edgbaston Indoor Cricket Centre; 6.2 C Fotolia; 6.3 A Wikipedia, B Alamy; 6.4 A, B, C Stephen Rickerby; 6.4 D positivebeats.co.uk, E Alamy; 6.5 B Alamy; 6.6 B Getty Images; 6.7 A Alamy, B Alamy; 6.8 A The Traveller's Friend Limited; 6.8 B, C Park Inn by the Rezidor Group; 6.9 B Guild of British Coach Tour Operators; 6.10 B Grand Theatre Leeds; Chapter 7 panel and banner Alamy; 7.1 A Alamy; 7.2 A, C Alamy; 7.3 A Alamy; 7.4 A Alamy, B Hotel du Vin; 7.5 A, B, C Alamy; 7.6 A Lundy House Hotel, B iStock Photo; 7.7 A i–vi Fotolia; 7.8 A © Serge Detalle Accor Hotels, B © Jack Burlot Accor Hotels; 7.9 A, B Bannatyne Group; 7.10 A Corbis, B Windsor Leisure Centre, C Royal Adelaide Hotel; Chapter 8 panel and banner The Travel Foundation; 8.1 C Alamy; 8.2 A Alamy; 8.4 A Fotolia; 8.6 A Thanks to easyjet.com; 8.7 B The Travel Foundation; 8.8 A Ireland Eco Tours; Chapter 9 panel and banner Alamy; 9.1 A Alamy, B Bannatyne Group; 9.2 A Park Inn by the Rezidor Group; 9.3 A Alamy; 9.4 A Alamy; 9.5 B iStock Photo; 9.6 A Alamy, B Cadbury World; 9.7 A Alamy, B National Express East Coast; 9.8 A Fourcroft Hotel; 9.9 A, B Surf Public Relations Limited; 9.10 A Haven Holiday Homes, B Ocean Village; Chapter 10 panel and banner David Lloyd Leisure Group; 10.1 A Arriva; 10.2 A David Lloyd Leisure Group; 10.4 A First Choice; 10.5 A Getty Images; 10.8 A The Beeches